TREASURES OF
North Carolina

by Damon Neal

a part of the Morgan & Chase Treasure Series
www.mcpbooks.com

 MORGAN & CHASE PUBLISHING INC.

Published by:
Morgan & Chase Publishing, Inc.
531 Parsons Drive, Medford, Oregon 97501
(888) 557-9328
www.treasuresof.com

Printed by:
C & C Offset Printing Co., Ltd. - China

First edition 2006

ISBN: 1-933989-01-7

THE
TREASURE
SERIES

I gratefully acknowledge the contributions
of the many people involved in the writing and production of this book.
Their tireless dedication to this endeavor has been inspirational.
—William Faubion, *Publisher*

Managing Editor:
David Smigelski

Senior Story Editor:
Mary Beth Lee

Revisions Editors:
Tamara J. Cornett and Robyn Sutherland

Proof Coordinator:
Andrea Hewitt

Contributing Writers:
Dave Fox, Charlie Darden, Lori Golden, Lisa Henry-Wire, Linda Jordan, Delaine Smith,
Nichole Landis, Anne Boydston, Chris McCrellis-Mitchell, Dusty Alexander, Emily Wilkie,
Gregory Scott, Jan Maddron, Jennifer Coles, Linda R. Reid, Maggie McClellen, Susan Vaughn

Graphic Design:
Jesse Gifford, C.S. Rowan, Christi Courian

Photo Coordinators:
Wendy Gay and Donna Lindley

Website:
Casey Faubion and Jessica Guaderrama

Special Recognition to:
Cindy Tilley Faubion, Anita Fronek, Molly Bermea, Sarah Brown, Mariska Pactwa,
Cari Qualls, Clarice Rodriguez, Mike Stallcop, Kimberley Wallan, Jolee Moody, Craig Tansley

dedicated to the memory of
Dale Earnhardt

Announcing Golden Opportunities to Travel

Receive Your FREE Gold Treasure Coins

Treasures listed inside this book can also be found on our popular and interactive website: **treasuresof.com**. For your convenience, this book's treasures are easily located by clicking the corresponding area on the map on our home page. This will lead you to a list of cities covered by this book. Within each city, treasures are listed under headings such as accommodations, attractions, etc.

Look for treasures that have a **Treasure Chest** next to their name. This means they have made a special offer, redeemable by presenting one of our gold treasure coins. **The offer may be substantial; anything from a free night's stay to a free meal or gift. Many offers can be worth $100.00 or more!**

To get your **three free gold treasure coins**, just send the receipt for the purchase of this book to:

Morgan & Chase Publishing
Gold Coin Division
PO Box 1148
Medford, OR 97501-0232

Please include your name and address and we will send the coins to you.

Table of Contents

Forward

Welcome to the Treasures of North Carolina. This book is intended as a resource that can guide you to some of the most inviting places in the great state of North Carolina. From the Atlantic Ocean to the mighty western mountains, North Carolina is a state rich in culture, history and diversity. It is a state we often associate with agriculture and great natural beauty, yet it is also a state with both feet planted firmly in the present, with bustling cities, cutting-edge technology, and some of the finest galleries, shopping and cuisine to be found anywhere in the world.

You wouldn't want to visit North Carolina without seeing the Outer Banks or trekking the gorgeous beaches on the Eastern shore. Yet how could you resist the allure of the Blue Ridge Parkway, Mt. Mitchell, or such charming, progressive towns on the western fringe as Asheville and Black Mountain. This is a state with natural features that make you want to pull out the hiking boots, fishing poles and sunscreen. Yet it's also a place of great refinement, with perhaps the finest assortment of hotels, bed-and-breakfasts, galleries, shopping destinations and restaurants in the South.

Many of the attractions covered in the Treasures of North Carolina will be familiar to the first-time traveler, such as The Biltmore Estate and the Blue Ridge Parkway. The real value of this book, however, comes from the spotlight we are able to shine on the hidden treasures, the gems that dot the North Carolina landscape like so many stars. We will introduce you to talented and dedicated people who have followed their dreams, opening businesses large and small. We will describe their products and services, of course, but we will also tell you their stories. In doing so, we hope to give you insights that will make your travels through North Carolina as memorable for you as it was for us.

—*David Smigelski*

How to Use This Book

The Treasures of North Carolina is divided into five geographic regions: the Appalachians, Southern Piedmont, Triangle Area, Northern Piedmont and Coastal Plain.

The regions are subdivided into the types of businesses and attractions you will find on your journey through the state, including accommodations, restaurants, wineries, coffeehouses, bakeries, gift shops, health and beauty outlets, flower and produce markets, museums, galleries, recreation options, fashion and more.

Regions of North Carolina

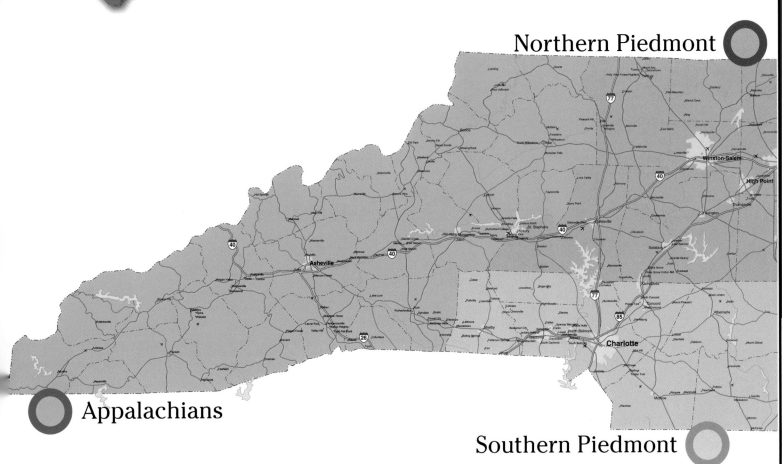

Northern Piedmont

Appalachians

Southern Piedmont

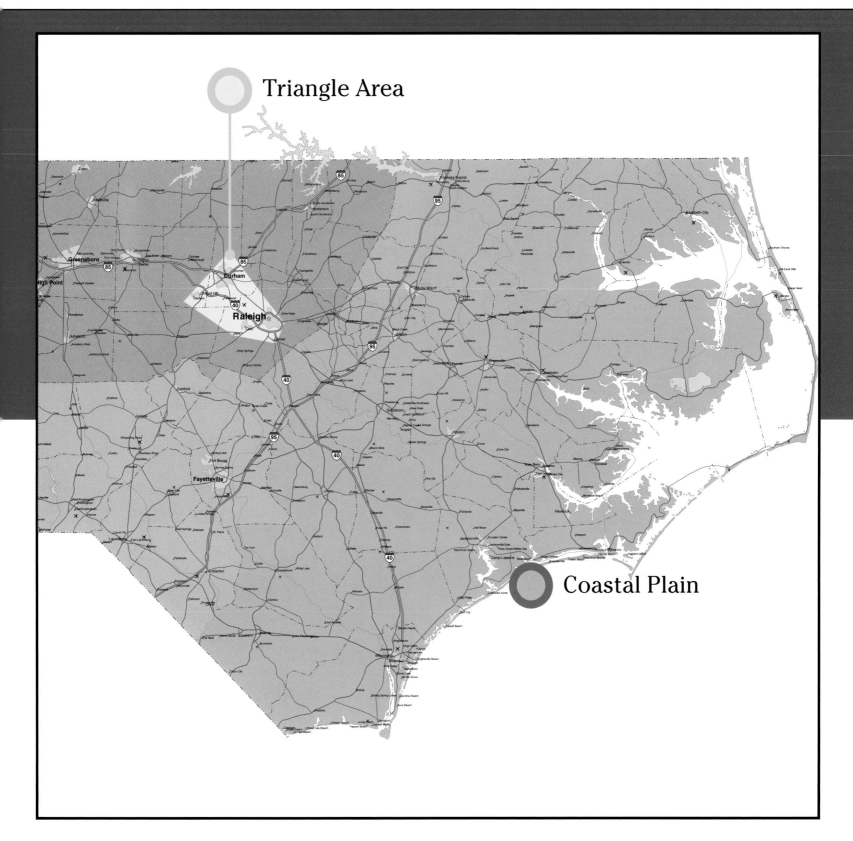

Triangle Area

Coastal Plain

Appalachians

Appalachians Accommodations

Raspberry Hill Bed & Breakfast

Nestled in the heart of the Black Mountains of Western North Carolina is the Raspberry Hill Bed & Breakfast. The inn, which opened in 2005, was named for the large raspberry patches behind the house where guests are welcome to spend time picking fresh berries when they're in season. Raspberry Hill is a beautifully restored, early 1900s homestead located on 30 pristine acres with the stately Broad River running through the property. The inn offers four private rooms, each equipped with a private entrance, full bath and a lovely porch. Owner Herb Van Roekel paid extra attention to every detail during each phase of the restoration process, which is one of the reasons this inn is so extraordinary. Raspberry Hill is filled with a wonderful selection of unusual antiques, many of which were discovered during restoration. The barn, located just a short distance from the main house, was built by Herb and his daughter Amanda, and is now home to more than 25 quilts that were all made by the original owners of Raspberry Hill. In the future the barn will serve as a woodworking studio and gift shop. The tranquil, inviting atmosphere of Raspberry Hill is an ideal setting for intimate weddings or other special occasions. Guests who choose to venture away from the idyllic setting of Raspberry Hill can take in many nearby attractions, including Lake Lure, Chimney Rock and the Bat Caves, each within 10 miles of the inn. Guests can also set out on foot and discover a charming landscape filled with green pastures and small country churches. Serenity awaits you at Raspberry Hill Bed & Breakfast.

77 Stroud Valley Road, Black Mountain NC (828) 669-7031
www.raspberryhillbandb.com

The Inn on Mill Creek

If you want to escape the noise and crowds of the big city, a relaxing weekend at The Inn on Mill Creek may be just the respite you need. The only skyscrapers around the property are the beautiful trees of the Pisgah National Forest surrounding the inn's two buildings. Seven guest rooms or suites are divided between the Main House and the Lake House, all with gorgeous views. The retreat ambience at Lake House includes rooms with maple cathedral ceilings, private baths with double Jacuzzi tubs, love seats or rockers, and a fireplace. Open the sliding-glass doors from your quarters to step out onto a lakeside deck. The private mountain lake is stocked with plenty of trout, so remember to bring your fishing gear. If you have the kids along, two suites feature a sleeping loft to give them an away-at-camp experience. The Main House has four rooms comfortably spread out over three floors. The Lake View Suite is the largest, its 600 square feet giving snapshot-worthy lake views. Wake up to a hot gourmet breakfast with the inn's own homegrown organic fruit, hot-from-the-oven baked bread and fresh squeezed juice. Then explore the Pisgah National Forest on bike or on foot, or catch up on some uninterrupted reading with the music of nature in the background. Later on, take a short drive to Black Mountain and Asheville for fun shopping and great dining. Spend some down time alone, with your loved one, or with the whole family while you stay at The Inn on Mill Creek. It's so close, yet so far away from it all.

3895 Mill Creek Road, Old Fort NC   (828) 668-1115 or (877) 735-2964
www.innonmillcreek.com

Chetola Resort at Blowing Rock

"What a glorious setting," says *Southern Living* magazine of Chetola Resort at Blowing Rock. As you drive into Chetola Resort, you circle beautiful Chetola Lake. Along the lakefront you approach the Bob Timberlake Inn and Chetola Lodge. Just a short distance beyond are Chetola condominiums that range in size from one to four bedrooms and sleep up to 10 people. The historic Bob Timberlake Inn opened in the fall of 2004. The inn is a tribute to North Carolina artist Bob Timberlake, who is internationally acclaimed for his magnificent paintings, home furnishing designs and décor. The Bob Timberlake Inn has eight estate rooms, each named after a prominent local figure or past owner of Chetola Estate. Chetola Lodge features 42 rooms and suites, most overlooking Chetola Lake and the beautiful mountains of the Blue Ridge. Chetola Resort is the only Orvis-endorsed fly fishing lodge in North Carolina, and offers fly fishing packages for all skill levels. Other on-site amenities include a huge indoor pool, fitness center with sauna and whirlpool, yoga classes and a variety of massage therapies. There's also boating, hiking, tennis and kid's camp. Nearby, enjoy snow skiing, whitewater rafting and horseback riding. There are several restaurants and a pub on site. A variety of year-round events take place at Chetola, including the North Carolina Symphony by Chetola Lake, Winterfest Polar Plunge and the annual Blue Ridge Celtic Festival at Blowing Rock. Chetola has a large selection of packages, including the Holiday Shopping Spree, Merlefest, Winterfest Getaway and Celebrate the Arts. *Southern Living* says Chetola is "one of the best stays in the Blue Ridge." It's easy to see why.

PO Box 17, N Main Street, Blowing Rock NC (828) 295-5500 or (800) 243-8652 (chetola) www.chetola.com

Crooked Oak Mountain Inn

On your next trip to Asheville, think hard about making your reservations at the Crooked Oak Mountain Inn. Since 2003, Patti and Michael "Bear" Strelec have been welcoming guests to their relaxing and picturesque bed and breakfast, located just three miles from popular downtown Asheville. Patti has more than 20 years experience in the hospitality industry and has received professional culinary training. Bear is a general contractor, as well as an accomplished chef. His carpentry skills are reflected everywhere in the beautifully remodeled inn, which was built in 1970. Crooked Oak features six beautifully appointed rooms that are cozy and comfortable for any member of the family. Each room has a private bath, luxurious linens, terry cloth robes, fresh flowers, irons, hair dryers, wireless Internet access and Thymes custom amenities. Patti and Bear treat guests of the inn to a full gourmet breakfast each morning and a scrumptious brunch on Sunday, as well as complimentary afternoon beverages and hors d'oeuvres. Dinner is available upon request. Enjoy the beautiful sunsets from the stone patio. Read your morning paper out on the front porch or in front of one of the stone fireplaces. Patti and Bear are delighted to do what they can to make your stay at Crooked Oak Mountain Inn a memorable and relaxing one. They are happy to arrange dinner reservations or provide detailed directions to area trails and attractions such as the Biltmore Estate. They will help you schedule yoga lessons or private in-room massages. They will pack a lunch for your day trip or do any number of the little things to make your stay very special. Make new friends and memories at Crooked Oak Mountain Inn, where you can relax, renew and enjoy the splendor of the mountains.

217 Patton Mountain Road, Asheville NC   (828) 252-9219 or (877) 252-9219   www.crookedoakmountaininn.com

Grafton Lodge

National Geographic has designated Lake Lure in North Carolina as one of the top 10 most beautiful man-made lakes in the world. With 27 miles of coastline and clean fresh water, this fabulous lake provides stunning views and a plethora of water sport opportunities. The town of Lake Lure offers several exciting attractions, fine dining and great shopping. The Grafton Lodge, owned and operated by Susan and Martyn Watts, is located just off the lake and provides visitors with fantastic accommodations, lake access, and gourmet breakfasts without the typical lakefront pricing. This charming and gracious lodge consists of five in-lodge rooms, three with private balconies, along with three beautifully designed rustic cabins. Each of the rooms features television with HBO and twin-shower bathrooms. The three cabins offer Jacuzzi tubs, fireplaces and a full kitchen. In the morning, guests can dine on a complimentary breakfast of daily hot specials, muffins or toast, and eggs, along with choice of beverage. The Grafton Lodge has its own private boathouse, with a sunning deck, along 100 feet of coastline located just two miles from the inn. From here, you can swim or rent a canoe. Additionally, the innkeepers are avid golf fans and are happy to introduce you to any of the area's numerous courses. The Watts are happy to further assist you by making reservations or providing detailed directions to your day's destination. The Grafton Lodge is proud to offer full disability access facilities. Smoking is allowed outside only. Enjoy the peace and hospitality provided by Susan and Martyn Watts while staying at the Grafton Lodge.

122 Harris Road, Lake Lure NC   (828) 625-5567   www.graftonlodge.com

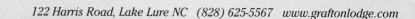

Lake Toxaway Country Club and Greystone Inn

Lake Toxaway has been a popular retreat since the turn of the century, when it played host to such notable personalities as Henry Ford, John D. Rockefeller and Thomas Edison, who were drawn here for the same reasons people are still drawn today: the incredible beauty and majesty of the area. The resort destination features stellar accommodations, a world-class country club and exquisite dining. The Lake Toxaway Country Club offers an 18-hole, par 71 golf course, a golf learning center designed by Tom Fazio, six tennis courts, a pool, fitness center and numerous other amenities. Just a hop, skip and jump away is the exquisite AAA four-diamond Greystone Inn. Guests of the Inn have 33 masterfully designed rooms to choose from. Gourmet dining, afternoon tea, relaxing spa treatments, champagne cruises, hiking and skiing are just a few of the indulgences awaiting you. Sports enthusiasts staying at the Inn may also use the Country Club's golf, tennis,

fitness and pool facilities. The breathtaking vistas, combined with all the amenities at Lake Toxaway Country Club and Greystone Inn, provide everything you need for the getaway of your dreams.

Lake Toxaway Country Club
(828) 966-4020
www.laketoxaway.com
The Greystone Inn
(800) 824-5766
www.greystoneinn.com

Meadowbrook Inn

Uniqueness, tradition, location and customer service make Meadowbrook Inn a treasured vacation and meeting site. This 63-room hotel is five minutes from the Blue Ridge Parkway and is situated in western North Carolina's charming town of Blowing Rock. The hotel offers access to outdoor activities, shopping, sightseeing, dining or the chance to just shut out the stress of life. The lobby welcomes guests with seasonal decorations, cozy seating and a fireplace. The Meadowbrook features an indoor pool and fitness center, plus the Ciao Bello! Italian restaurant, which provides frequent entertainment and a casual lounge. Wild mallards that frequent the inn's ponds can be fed with complimentary duck food from the front desk. Some of the ducks will eat out of your hands. The well trained and friendly staff provides guests with individualized service. Whether it's an individual vacation or a tour group, a romantic getaway or a corporate meeting, good customer service is always present. Attending to detail and making guests feel both welcome and special are keystones of this successful hotel. Winner of the Blowing Rock Chamber of Commerce Business of the Year Award, and the Management, Service and Cuisine award from Military Officers Association of America, this inn won't disappoint. Meadowbrook Inn's guest rooms are large, and each is decorated individually. An array of suites offer such amenities as four-poster beds, whirlpool tubs for two, and fireplaces. Two suites even feature indoor private pools. Room service, in-room massage, and complimentary breakfast, plus a penchant for satisfying individual guest requests, make this an exemplary hotel. For great customer service, ambience and true hospitality, visit Meadowbrook Inn.

711 Main Street, Blowing Rock NC   (828) 295-4300 or (800) 456-5456   www.meadowbrook-inn.com

Monte Vista Hotel

Travel across the threshold of time with a visit to the stately Monte Vista Hotel, the oldest hotel and event center in Black Mountain. This traditional 1930s-style Southern inn has welcomed travelers since 1919. They strive to preserve the elegance of earlier times, while adding the amenities needed for a memorable stay, such as cable television and Internet access. From the minute you enter the spacious lobby with its comfortable sofas, piano and inviting fireplace, you'll be surrounded by the simple charms of a bygone era. Individually decorated guest rooms are available in several sizes and styles, from large family suites to units perfect for that romantic getaway. The full-service restaurant and catering service offer a variety of fare, from homestyle Southern favorites to elegant multi-course dinners. Guests can enjoy a drink after a day of hiking or sightseeing in the downstairs lounge, which features a pool table, darts and live music. The lovely, plant-laden porches offer wicker rockers and swings, while the grounds, home to birds and squirrels, offer space for picnics and games of catch. A renovated outdoor pool and landscaped courtyard with a stone fountain invite visitors to enjoy the beautiful mountain weather, making the exterior spaces of the hotel as genteel as the interior. The nearby Farmhouse building was completed in 1926 and is for family reunions and wedding parties. The Monte Vista Hotel continues to be an ideal destination for vacations, weddings, holiday gatherings and corporate retreats. Make your reservation today for a trip back in time at the Monte Vista Hotel.

308 W State Street, Black Mountain NC
(828) 669-2119 or (888) 804-8438
www.montevistahotel.com

Inn Around the Corner

Black Mountain, known as the front porch of western North Carolina, is a jewel. Visiting this quaint yet vibrant town is like taking a step back in time. From the inspiring galleries and fabulous dining to the music venues and myriad recreational activities, Black Mountain offers something for everyone. If you want to be within walking distance of all that Black Mountain has to offer, then consider staying at the Inn Around the Corner. Choose from one of five spacious guest rooms or pamper yourself in one of two suites. Each lovely room has a private bath and has been beautifully decorated with a distinct style. Grandma's Room, for instance, has soft colors, quilts on the beds and hand-stitched samplers on the walls. The Hugging Oak Hideaway suite features a soaring ceiling, massive twig furniture, a fireplace, Jacuzzi tub and private deck. Guests are served a sumptuous breakfast and Southern hospitality resonates throughout. Relax on one of the porches and view the splendor of the surrounding mountains. The inn is open year round and offers special getaway packages December through April. Discover the arts and crafts of the area. Take advantage of the breathtaking scenery and outdoor activities in every season. Owners Roger and Nancy Schnepp will work hard to make your visit a relaxing and memorable one. Call to make reservations today, and discover what's waiting for you in beautiful Black Mountain at the Inn Around the Corner.

109 Church Street, Black Mountain NC
(828) 669-6005 or (800) 393-6005
www.innaroundthecorner.com

Orchard Inn

On a 12-acre crest of the Warrior Range in the Blue Ridge Mountains sits the perfect getaway. Built by the Brotherhood of Railway Clerks in 1926, the Orchard Inn is family owned and operated by Bob and Kathy Thompson, their son, chef Robert Thompson, and daughter-in-law Charley. The inn, with its panoramic views and five-course candlelight dinners, has been named by *Bed and Breakfast Journal* as one of the Top 15 bed and breakfasts in North America, and is listed on the National Register of Historic Places. Guests from all over the world return here year after year to relax in peace and quiet at this mountaintop escape.

Visitors to the airy, sun-porch dining room are treated to chef Robert's tantalizing skills, an exquisite wine list and spectacular views. The Orchard Inn has nine warmly decorated guest rooms, featuring period pieces and antiques, and five cottage suites equipped with fireplaces, whirlpool baths and private decks. Each room and cottage has its own distinct character. Take a walk outside on the Orchard Inn nature trail. Immerse yourself in the striking beauty of the rhododendron and hardwood forest, or stroll into the village of Saluda, where the entire downtown area has been designated as a National Historic Site. Reserve a room at the Orchard Inn and let the world fall away in this picturesque mountain getaway.

100 Orchard Inn, Saluda NC   (828) 749-5471 or (800) 581-3800   www.orchardinn.com

Mountainaire Inn & Log Cabins

The Village of Blowing Rock, located off the Blue Ridge Parkway, has long been a comforting retreat for those seeking rest and relaxation in the High Country. Mountainaire Inn & Log Cabins, located by Memorial Park, is the perfect place to spend a romantic weekend or just escape the hectic pace of life. The rustic, pine-paneled cabins at the Mountainaire feature wood-burning fireplaces and Jacuzzis. Cabins include kitchens with microwaves and relaxing front or back porches that are perfect for lounging and enjoying the beautiful grounds. All rooms and cabins include telephones with free local calling, cable television, ceiling fans, air conditioning and heat. Mountainaire Inn is proud to be a smoke-free establishment and does not allow pets. The inn is a brief walk from the historic downtown and is located close to many area attractions, including Grandfather Mountain, Moses Cone State Park, five ski slopes and Appalachian State University. Mountainaire's original 11 rooms were built in 1954 with the cabins added in the early 1990s. Visitors to Mountainaire Inn & Log Cabins will feel as though they have gone back in time while strolling along the lovely graveled pathways lined with beautiful trees and botanicals. The gentle gurgling of the property's mountain stream soothes your soul and lifts your spirit. Jim and Deborah McDowell, the new owners of the Mountainaire, invite you to see for yourself why folks return year after year.

827 N Main Street, Blowing Rock NC
(828) 295-7991 www.mountainaireinn.com

Bear Creek RV Park & Campground

Bear Creek RV Park & Campground offers seclusion amidst the beautiful scenery of the surrounding mountains and the grounds of the historic Biltmore Estate. Bea and Harry Coates are the camp hosts and will make your visit both enjoyable and relaxing. Asheville's finest recreational vehicle park and campground features 90 paved and level hookups with cable television, patios and complimentary wireless Internet service. The secluded tent sites are outstanding, with amenities such as water and electricity. A heated swimming pool is an added bonus to an already pleasurable visit. The beautiful clubhouse offers a fireplace and kitchen to accommodate wedding receptions, reunions and other large groups. For the youngsters, there is a game room and playground. Many attractions are available within a short drive of the park, including the Biltmore Estate, Chimney Rock, Linville Caverns and the North Carolina Arboretum. You can spend your time outdoors riding horses, whitewater rafting, mining for gems, or playing at three of the greatest golf courses in the state of North Carolina. The park is open year round and all clubs are welcome. All three bathhouses and both laundry facilities are exceptionally clean. After settling in to this comfortable place you might find you don't want to end your vacation. Here, you can enjoy the beautiful sunsets that were featured on Pat Boone's *Wish You Were Here* television show. After you have stayed at the Bear Creek RV Park & Campground, you will find yourself counting the days until you can come back again.

*81 S Bear Creek Road,
Asheville NC
(828) 253-0798 or (888) 833-0798
www.ashevillebearcreek.com*

Madison's Inn and Restaurant

Nestled in the Blue Ridge Mountains, set back off the beaten path, Madison's Inn and Restaurant of Black Mountain is a delightfully romantic bed and breakfast. The inn consists of 10 rooms and three suites, each decorated in a different theme. The Dogwood Suite includes a wall mural featuring a paradise garden influenced by the dogwood tree that can be seen from the window. The Cedar Retreat, reminiscent of sanctuaries of yore, was named for the local poet, Cedar Ava Denali. Though the comfortable rooms may tempt you to stay indoors, follow the stream outside that trickles alongside a stone walkway and you will find the restaurant. Southern hospitality meets European elegance in this enchanting eatery. Dinner is served in the main dining room, the more secluded Library, or on a serene terrace. The menu offers a wide variety and an extensive and worldly wine list. The restaurant offers Sunday brunch, is an ideal place for events, and even has a brown bag license, which allows customers to bring their own liquor. Reservations are suggested. A Southern-style country breakfast in the main dining room is open to the public. The inn is roughly 20 miles east of Asheville, where you can walk the Urban Trail, visit the Biltmore House, or catch a show. Outdoor activities abound in the area, from mountain biking to whitewater rafting to the scenic Blue Ridge Parkway. Mount Mitchell, the highest peak in the eastern United States, is a short drive away. Pets are welcome. Whether for a weekend getaway or a longer trip, Madison's Inn is the perfect place to escape from the bustle of everyday life.

10 Florida Avenue, Black Mountain NC
(828) 669-4785
www.madisonsblackmountain.com

Mountaineer Inn

Chris Moutos, proprietor of the Mountaineer Inn, arrived in Georgia from Greece in 1951. He originally settled in Augusta before relocating to Asheville, a decision that came about when he accidentally took the wrong bus on a trip to Greenville. He fell in love with the area and the climate and decided that Asheville was the place to put down roots. He opened both the Cosmos and the Acropolis restaurants. In 1964, he purchased The Mountaineer Inn, originally built in 1939. The Mountaineer Inn has been used as the backdrop for popular television shows and movies, such as *Lassie, Bull Durham* and the Sundance award-winning *All The Real Girls*. Chris received the Small Businessman of the Year Award in 1994 from the Asheville Chamber of Commerce, and was selected for the Ronald Reagan Man of the Year Award. The Mountaineer Inn has 77 comfortable rooms that are modest, clean and ideal for the adventurous traveler. Several area restaurants and attractions are conveniently located near the inn. Moutos and The Mountaineer Inn have been featured in major publications, such as *National Geographic* and *Life*. The inn provides wireless Internet service and a large pool, as well as numerous modern amenities that don't clash with the vintage 1930s feel of this roadside favorite. Nostalgia, comfort and excellent service await you at this family-operated motel. Come experience an historic and popular traveler's landmark at The Mountaineer Inn.

155 Tunnel Road, Asheville NC (828) 254-5331 or (800) 255-4080 www.mtinnasheville.homestead.com

Abbington Green Bed & Breakfast Inn

Abbington Green Bed & Breakfast Inn is a magnificent Colonial Rival home that was designed by Biltmore Estate's supervising architect in 1908 and built for a prominent local businessman. Valerie Larrea purchased the house in 1993 and renovated the 6,300-square-foot space in just four and a half months. Abbington Green carries an English theme, with fireplaces, antique furnishings and fine rugs. A love seat, cushioned chairs and rockers make the front porch a comfortable and inviting place to relax. An antique sleigh next to the front door is always filled with fresh flowers and decorations. At Abbington Green Bed & Breakfast Inn, candlelight breakfast is served every morning in the dining room, which is decorated with many fine, antique mahogany pieces. There are three suites in the Carriage House and five guest rooms in the Main House. Each has been decorated with an upscale style that characterized the best of Britain for centuries. All the suites and the king-size guest rooms have working fireplaces, some of which bear the original mantels with quarter-sawn oak surrounds decorated with original tiles. All guest rooms have private baths, and the suites feature thick towels, rugs and bath mats. A series of authentic English garden rooms, each with it's own theme, dot the premises. The award-winning British gardens feature hundreds of perennials and roses. Enjoy tranquility at Abbington Green Bed & Breakfast Inn.

46 & 48 Cumberland Circle, Asheville NC (828) 251-2454 or (800) 251-2454 www.abbingtongreen.com

The Village Inns of Blowing Rock

The Village Inns of Blowing Rock offer stylish mountain luxury at three distinctive inns that are as unique as the village of Blowing Rock. The three properties, conveniently located around town, are the Hillwinds Inn, the Ridgeway Inn and the Village Inn. They offer smoke-free accommodations, complimentary continental breakfasts and daily afternoon wine and cheese receptions. Pet friendly rooms are available. Amenities include deluxe guestrooms, suites and cottages, some with fireplaces, full kitchens, Jacuzzis and 30-inch, flat-screen televisions. The Hillwinds Inn is located on Sunset Drive, just a short walk to Main Street shopping, restaurants and art galleries. Hillwinds features a rocking chair porch, an ideal place to gather for morning coffee or an afternoon get-together with friends. During the winter months, guests can enjoy the afternoon wine and cheese reception around the fireplace in the library. Located just off Main Street on Yonahlossee Road, the Ridgeway Inn was one of the first inns built in Blowing Rock. Its exterior features golden cedar shakes and is surrounded by gardens overflowing with mountain flowers and shrubs. The spacious guestrooms offer décor that celebrates the gardens and the scenic views surrounding the inn. The Village Inn is located on Valley Boulevard and features a beautifully landscaped pond and a picnic area on the banks of the New River. This inn's Nickajack Lodge captures the charm of the Blue Ridge Mountains with its exposed beams, stone fireplace and 50-inch, flat-screen television. The guestrooms, suites and cottages feature an elegant mountain décor and private decks, some with hot tubs. To book your vacation, call The Village Inns of Blowing Rock.

(800) 821-4908
www.thevillageinnsofblowingrock.com

The Chalet Club

Lake Lure is widely recognized as being one of the most beautiful man-made lakes in the world and is an established vacation destination for families, honeymooners and prominent society figureheads. In 1925, it became home to Dr. James Murry Washburn. Little did he know that his initial purchase of a lot from the Chimney Rock Mountains land development company was destined to become a resort that would still be going strong after 70 years. The Chalet Club has been continually owned and operated by the Washburn family since 1934. When James and his wife succumbed to the "lure of Lake Lure," they left their Chicago home and his medical practice to become innkeepers. Today this popular resort offers five rooms and seven cottages that will accommodate up to 40 vacationers. The Chalet Club houses an exceptional restaurant with a formal yet inviting atmosphere. It is open to the public, as well as guests. Conveniently located near many area attractions, The Chalet Club is the ideal place to stay while enjoying all that the region has to offer. The club offers hiking trails, tennis courts and boating on the lake. The current innkeepers, Bob and Anne Washburn, are delighted to welcome guests both old and new, many of whom either have or will become like family. Come and meet the Washburns, explore the beautiful area, and rejuvenate mind, body and soul with a stay at The Chalet Club.

532 Washburn Road, Lake Lure NC
(800) 336-3309
www.chaletclub.com

Bella Luna Inn

Some vacations aren't really vacations at all. You are running so fast from one place to another, trying to see all you can in a short period of time, that go home needing a vaction from your vacation. For a truly mellowing experience, rest your mind and body at Bella Luna Inn. This 1920 Cape Cod, arts-and-crafts style home offers large rooms with private baths, and suites with whirlpool baths and sitting areas to help you relax and rejuvenate your senses. You can read a book or take it easy under the sun on their private porch. Don't worry about getting breakfast. Bella Luna Inn provides a gourmet feast every morning and complimentary beverages throughout the day. For those who just can't sit still, historic Black Mountain is only half a mile away, and the city of Asheville offers arts, antiques and other outdoor activities. There are also many great restaurants to sample when you decide to dine away from the inn. Bella Luna Inn can be rented out for any special event. Owners Cynthia and Brad Bradsher will gladly help ease your mind by assisting with everything from decorations to catering. For a quiet place to put up your feet, take off your coat and stay awhile, call Bella Luna Inn.

99 Terry Estate Drive
(828) 664-9714 or (800) 249-6979
www.bellalunainn.com

Yonahlossee Resort and Club

On the grounds of the former Camp Yonahlossee, a popular girls camp established in 1922, lies Yonahlossee Resort and Club. Owner, developer and manager John Rice purchased the property in 1985 and began the transformation from camp to world-class resort. Standing at 4,000 feet in the heart of the Blue Ridge Mountains and encompassing more than 300 pristine acres, Yonahlossee Resort is known for its terrific tennis facilities, beautiful homes, and proximity to adjoining National Park Service lands. The resort offers guests eight elegantly appointed rooms along with a hospitality room, conference facilities and a state-of-the-art fitness center. Guests can choose from one of 12 studio cottages, located in quiet, wooded settings just a short walk from the main inn. Each cottage comes with a fireplace, whirlpool, kitchenette and private deck. The inn combines the services of a hotel with the intimacy of a lodge. Guests receive the highest level of personal attention while enjoying first-class accommodations. If you're vacationing with extended family or friends, the Yonahlossee can provide condominiums, town houses and luxurious private homes ranging in size from two to five bedrooms. The majestic setting and exemplary staff make the resort an ideal setting for weddings, reunions, corporate retreats and other gatherings. The resort is home to the Gamekeeper Restaurant, offering regional Southern cuisine and exotic wild game dishes. Nearby area attractions include galleries, boutiques and a plethora of recreational activities. Enjoy the lifestyle you've been looking for at the Yonahlossee Resort and Club.

226 Oakley Green, Boone NC
(828) 963-6400 or (800) 962-1986
www.yonahlossee.com

Appalachians Attractions

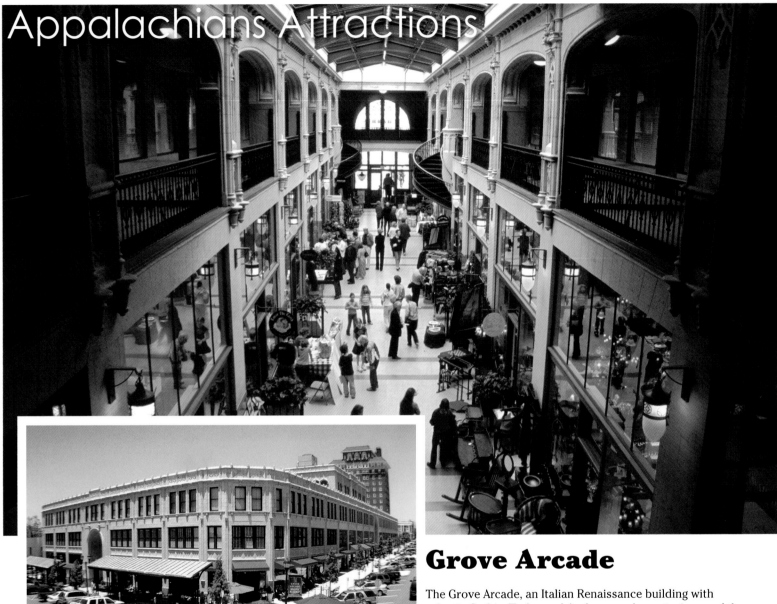

Grove Arcade

The Grove Arcade, an Italian Renaissance building with eclectic Gothic, Tudor and Arabesque elements, is one of the architectural jewels of Asheville. The elaborately embellished building, guarded by gargoyles and flying lions, occupies a full city block. Built by E.W. Grove, the visionary creator of the Grove Park Inn, the Arcade opened in 1929 and thrived until World War II as one of the country's leading indoor markets. During the war, the building was occupied and modified by the federal government and eventually housed the National Climatic Data Center. In 1985, city leaders developed a plan to return the Arcade to its original use and in 2002 the historically renovated structure was returned to its former grandeur to house locally owned galleries, shops, restaurants and specialty food purveyors. The second floor is occupied by offices and the third through fifth floors contain luxury apartments. The Grove Arcade is located in the heart of the Battery Hill neighborhood in downtown Asheville. The building is open daily and often hosts regional music performances, craft demonstrations and other public programs.

One Page Avenue, Asheville NC (828) 252-7799 www.grovearcade.com

Biltmore House

Biltmore House, completed in 1895 by George W. Vanderbilt, is a 250-room French Renaissance-style chateau, and the centerpiece of the Biltmore Estate. A National Historic Landmark and the largest private home in the country, it receives approximately one million guests annually. Architect Richard Morris Hunt designed the home, and Frederick Law Olmsted designed the gardens, fields and forests on the 8,000-acre property. Vanderbilt's grandson, William A.V. Cecil, still owns the estate. Guests at Biltmore House can explore Vanderbilt's original collection of priceless antiques and art objects, including works by Renoir, Sargent and Whistler. Another attraction is the Biltmore Estate Winery, America's most-visited winery. Self-guided tours are followed by a complimentary tasting of the estate's own wines. The newest addition is the historic horse barn with its farmyard and kitchen garden. Blacksmiths, woodworkers, traditional Appalachian musicians, dancing and special events can be observed and enjoyed year round. The property also offers the 213-room, Mobil four-star, AAA four-diamond Inn on Biltmore Estate, with luxurious accommodations and outstanding views of the surrounding Blue Ridge Mountains. Exciting outdoor activities, such as horseback riding, biking, rafting, fly-fishing and the Land Rover Experience Driving School complete the mix, so that Vanderbilt's historic property offers something for everyone.

One N Park Square, Asheville NC
(877) 324-5866
www.biltmore.com

Used with permission of The Biltmore Company, Asheville, North Carolina.

Mariam and Robert Hayes Performing Arts Center

Nestled within the Blue Ridge Mountains, an $8 million performing arts center is taking shape. The Mariam and Robert Hayes Performing Arts Center aims to produce and present a challenging and diverse spectrum of live performance that speaks to the imagination of the community. Opened in August of 2006, it is the new home of The Blowing Rock Stage Company. Since 1986, the Company has presented 100 productions for more than 260,000 audience members, including Neil Simon's *Lost in Yonkers* and North Carolina's own Robert Inman's *Crossroads*. The 26,156-square-foot, three-story Mariam and Robert Hayes Performing Arts Center features two theatres, affording The Blowing Rock Stage Company the ability to perform up to three different productions in two days. The center was named in honor of Mariam Cannon Hayes and her late husband because of their great love of children, philanthropy and vision. The center also specializes in children's education and programming. The Mariam and Robert Hayes Performing Arts Center is a new jewel that will reach out to arts lovers from far and wide.

152 Sunset Drive, Blowing Rock NC   (828) 295-0112   www.brcac.org

French Broad Rafting Expeditions

If you're looking for a whitewater adventure for the whole family, then head to French Broad Rafting Expeditions in Marshall. Located just 24 miles outside of Asheville, this family-owned and operated outfitter has everything needed to enjoy the river trip of a lifetime. Michael and Mitch Hampton, along with their wives, Jennifer and Korey, have been treating guests to the scenic beauty of one of the oldest known rivers since 1990. Brothers Michael and Mitch have more than 24 years of combined whitewater rafting experience, having been introduced to the rivers of East Tennessee as youngsters by their grandfather. The company has been approved by the U.S. Forest Service and belongs to several related organizations, including the North Carolina Paddlesport Association. French Broad Rafting Expeditions offers morning and afternoon trips that are geared to different experience levels. Each trip includes safety equipment, lunch or snack, and a qualified guide in each boat. The French Broad, which runs 210 miles, cuts through Asheville and then heads north to Tennessee on its way to the great Mississippi. This makes the French Broad River one of the few north flowing rivers in the United States. Explore the stunning views and fabulous waters of the French Broad River with an excursion from French Broad Rafting Expeditions.

7525 Unit 2, US Highway 25/70, Marshall NC
(800) 570-RAFT (7238)   www.frenchbroadrafting.com

Appalachian Ski Mtn.

Appalachian Ski Mtn. is a first-class family resort for fun. Owned by Grady and Reba Moretz and family, this resort has been creating memories for 44 years. It is the premier winter resort in the Blue Ridge region. Nine slopes, five lifts and state-of-the-art snow-making and grooming equipment keep you skiing all day, all night and all season long. The resort offers an outdoor, fully lighted ice skating arena, situated so that it overlooks the slopes, lodge and Blue Ridge Mountains. Special events include Ski with Santa on Christmas Eve, torchlight skiing and fireworks on New Year's Eve. In March, you can join in the annual meltdown games, one last crazy weekend of fun before the snow melts. Ski and Stay packages are customized to your specific getaway needs. Alpen Acres Motel is the closest lodging to the slopes and is very economical. The privately owned motel has 18 rooms and a two-person chalet for a more romantic stay. Slopeside lodging consists of four houses, one just a two minute walk to the slopes, two with direct access to the slopes, and one overlooking the slopes. There are many other options for lodging while visiting the resort, and any one can be incorporated into your planned stay. Appalachian Ski Mtn. offers great prices on ski and snowboard rentals. Group rates on rentals and lift tickets are available. No matter what your skill level, or whether you prefer snowboarding to skiing, you are welcome at Appalachian Ski Mtn.

940 Ski Mountain Road, Blowing Rock NC
(800) 322-2373
www.appskimtn.com

Appalachians
Candies, Ice Cream, Bakeries & Coffee

Chelseas and The Village Tea Room

Chelseas is two jewels in one. Since 1989, Cindy Piercy and her daughter, Jennifer, have been charming customers at Chelseas with their distinctly elegant and engaging Country French & English Store and The Village Tea Room. Located in the historic Biltmore Village, Chelseas occupies two Old World-style craftsman's houses. Chef Jennifer creates daily gourmet delicacies, soups and quiches, while pastry chefs Ashley and Jeremy prepare tantalizing desserts, such as the famous fresh lemon curd cake and authentic English trifle. Their specialty is the English cream tea, with freshly made scones served with double Devonshire cream and strawberry jam imported from England. To partake of these delicacies is to delight in the senses. The food is delicious and the service is impeccable, which is why Chelseas has gained a reputation among tea lovers as a truly great tea room. After enjoying the irresistible desserts and teas, guests will be captivated when they enter the gourmet food hall stocked with preserves, chocolates and specialty items from Europe. The adjoining cottage features unusual gift items, such as Gien china from France, Jay Strongwater jewelry, and

Annick Goutal perfumes. You're cordially invited to behold the wonder that is Chelseas.

6 Boston Way, Asheville NC
(828) 274-4400
www.chelseastea.com

Roan Mountain Highlands Photo by Marty Hulsebos HighCountryImages.com

Appalachians Galleries

The Bob Timberlake Gallery

Charles Kuralt once said, "Bob Timberlake's paintings have reminded me of the homey beauty of ordinary things, of the careless perfection of nature, of the richness of human talk and song, and the value of friendship and neighborliness." Bob Timberlake, a self-taught artist, left the family business 35 years ago to pursue the art he loved. The Bob Timberlake Gallery in Lexington invites visitors to step into the artist's life and immerse themselves in his world. The opening of the Lexington Gallery in June 1997 represented the culmination of the artist's dream. It serves as a visitors' center and museum, offering an impressive collection of Timberlake's original paintings and limited-edition reproductions, plus Timberlake-branded home furnishings, accessories and apparel. The second Bob Timberlake Gallery opened in 2001 in Blowing Rock. Nestled in the majestic Blue Ridge Mountains, its design and garden remain true to the Timberlake character. The Bob Timberlake galleries are truly works of art you will not want to miss.

1714 E Center Street Extension, Lexington NC   (800) 244-0095
946 Main Street, Blowing Rock NC   (828) 295-4855
www.bobtimberlake.com

Appalachians Gifts

Black Mountain Iron Works

Since the dawn of civilization, the iron forge has been a part of nearly every village and town that could support one. It was where the community came to shoe their horses, hone their weapons and buy their nails. This ancient skill has largely fallen from the public eye with the growth of factories and new advancements in metalwork. Luckily Black Mountain Iron Works in Black Mountain can still provide you with beautiful wrought iron pieces that will endure the tests of time. Owners Tekla and Dan Howachyn specialize in hand-forged, wrought iron, from intricate gates and fences to simply stunning doors. Black Mountain Iron Works can literally forge your fantasy into reality. The sounds of hammering, the smell of metal and the sights of the unexpected and the unusual are all found at Black Mountain Iron Works, where you can tour the grounds and enjoy the peace of a trickling fountain. As you wander through the yard, you will be delighted with the incredible sculptures and metal art that is elegantly arranged. From clever banisters to fire screens and tools, Black Mountain Iron Works can fashion most anything you can imagine. Stop by Black Mountain Iron Works and peruse their distinctive selection of fixtures and other home items, or commission a piece that will be exclusively yours.

120 Broadway, Black Mountain NC
(828) 669-1001 or (888) 689-9021
www.blackmountainiron.com

The Gardener's Cottage

Inspiration flows naturally from a beautiful garden. As seen in *Southern Accents* and *Southern Living*, the Gardener's Cottage is an experience full of enchantment. Since 1997, Owners Libby Endry and Laura Belsinger have featured an incomparable mix of antiques, gifts and hand-picked items to enhance the home and garden. Located in Biltmore Village, just outside the entrance to the famous Biltmore Estate, the Gardener's Cottage resides in a charming historic building along a quaint tree-lined street with a brick sidewalk. The shop was originally founded by flower designers Bee Sieburg and Molly Courcelle, who were both deeply inspired by the surrounding mountains. Libby and Laura have kept the tradition with fresh flowers and botanicals, while adding a few touches of their own. You'll find creative, handmade centerpieces, French and English antiques, ornaments, one-of-a-kind gifts, watercolors, hand-painted furniture and antiques. Not only is Biltmore Village one of the Carolinas' most unique touring and shopping environments, but because of its history, its range of retailers and its fine restaurants, historic Biltmore Village has an international reputation, as well. Experience for yourself why The Gardener's Cottage has stood out for so long.

34 All Souls Crescent, Asheville NC
(828) 277-2020

Susan Marie Designs

Stunning design with incredible brilliance and enduring quality only begins to describe the fine jewelry available at Susan Marie Designs. Owner Susan Marie Phipps personally selects gemstones of maximum beauty and clarity, which she pairs with her graceful and elegant designs to create one perfectly crafted piece of jewelry at a time. Susan is very accomplished in the art of jewelry making. After discovering her talent in high school, she furthered her knowledge by taking metalsmithing classes. She has been a professional goldsmith for more than 25 years, and is a GIA graduate gemologist. Using her expertise, she selects only the most vibrant diamonds, Tahitian pearls, sapphires and a broad spectrum of other gemstones for her designs. She has received several national and international awards, including the De Beers Diamonds Today award. Susan Marie Designs began in 1993 and is known for its one-of-a-kind pendants, rings, necklaces, earrings and other jewelry items of the highest quality. Charlie, the studio cat, and Susan invite you to see her exquisite collection of timeless gold and precious stone jewelry. Delight in her passion and enthusiasm for excellence as she works with you to design your dream.

One All Souls Crescent, Asheville NC
(828) 277-1272
www.susanmphippsdesigns.com

Howard's Antiques and Vintage Emporium

Step back in time and immerse yourself in history with a stop at Howard's Antiques and Vintage Emporium. Howard's Antiques fills two floors with a wide variety of classic and rare items. The top floor features vintage apparel and unique accessory pieces, including jewelry, hats and coats. The ground floor is home to a huge array of the unusual and nostalgic, including lovely furniture, traditional books and games, as well as a tantalizing assortment of collectibles. Howard's Antiques carries the distinctive pieces to make your home décor complete, gifts for those special someones, or even a perfect addition to a private art or antique collection. Owner Diana French invites you to discover your treasure at Howard's Antiques, where the charm of the past will certainly be a treat that won't soon be forgotten.

121 Cherry Street, Black Mountain NC
(828) 669-6494

The Blue Ridge Parkway

Appalachians
Home Décor, Flowers, Gardens & Markets

Foam & Fabrics Outlet

If you get starry-eyed watching shows like *Trading Spaces* or *How Do I Look*, the Foam & Fabrics Outlet is for you. Many projects require, among other things, a little shopping for the right look. At Foam & Fabric Outlet in Fletcher, you can find all sorts of fabrics to make over anything from that old-but-comfortable-burnt-orange-colored chair (with a blanket hiding it, of course) to a quilting project. Or maybe you need some luxury fabric for a special occasion, such as a prom or wedding. Owner Allen Gurley takes pride in making sure that his customers have the best selection of fabrics to choose from at both store locations, in Fletcher since 1977 and at Carolina Fabric Outlet in Swannanoa since 1986. The Fletcher store alone has more than 28,000 square feet of space filled with fabrics in every size, shape, design, pattern and color imaginable. The shop also carries quilting and craft supplies. The choices are endless, and the friendly help of the caring and engaging staff is a breath of fresh air to the weary makeover artist. Stop by Foam & Fabric Outlet, and you're sure to find exactly what you need for that new project. The local tour bus stops by regularly. You should too.

3049 Hendersonville Highway, Fletcher NC
(828) 684-0801

301 Patton Cove Road, Swannanoa NC
(828) 686-3336

Earth Fare

With the proliferation of fast foods, genetic engineering and chemical additives in our food supply, we have devolved into a culture of processed foods that are far removed from the earth. Earth Fare, the ingenious concept of Roger Derrough, is North Carolina's answer to healthful food. After Roger grew ill from eating conventional foods, he delved into the world of organics and natural nutrition. In 1975, he opened his first natural foods store in Asheville. Originally called Dinner for the Earth, this whole foods outlet continued to expand and relocated many times. In 1993, the name changed to Earth Fare. In 1995, Earth Fare won the award for Best New Store of the Year from *Health Foods Business* magazine. In 1997, a second store opened, and today Earth Fare has seven North Carolina locations. In 2000, Earth Fare was named *Whole Foods* magazine's Retailer of the Year, just one of numerous accolades from community and national publications. Earth Fare is dedicated to its mission of serving the community by providing quality foods and products in a healthful environment. The company is dedicated to the overall health, development and well being of both its employees and customers. The markets carry a wide range of whole foods that are free of additives. You'll find an extensive array of organic vegetables, macrobiotic staples, whole grains, bulk foods, supplements, body care products and more items in more categories than we can list here. Their employees are knowledgeable and completely up-to-date on the ever-evolving state of natural products. Earth Fare also features an in-store cafe that serves tasty dishes made from store products that will leave your body feeling nourished. Earth Fare is a whole foods supermarket that rivals any market in the country. Look for locations in Charlotte, Raleigh, Chapel Hill, Boone and Greensboro.

66 Westgate Parkway, Asheville NC
(828) 281-4800
www.earthfare.com

Appalachians Restaurants

Black Mountain Bistro

Nestled in the heart of beautiful and scenic Black Mountain is a place called Black Mountain Bistro, where true Southern cuisine is the special of the day. Locally owned and operated, Black Mountain Bistro serves up appetizing, freshly made offerings daily, including seafood, steak and succulent hickory-smoked baby back ribs. Signature items such as fried green tomatoes and crab cakes provide a taste of authentic down-home Southern cooking. The seasonal outdoor seating will surround you with the picturesque splendor of the area, including views of the Black Mountain Range. Owner Amy Lyda would be happy to cater your next party or special event. Black Mountain Bistro is available for group gatherings depending on availability. Quality food at reasonable prices and a quaint dining atmosphere are in store for you at Black Mountain Bistro. Amy invites you to see how Black Mountain Bistro symbolizes the best of what western North Carolina has to offer.

203 E State Street, Black Mountain, NC
(828) 669-5041

Morning Glory Café

Black Mountain is one of those charming Southern towns where all the locals know each other and visitors are welcomed with true charm and hospitality. Black Mountain is also home of the Morning Glory Café, owned by sisters Colleen Raulerson and Calleen Freeburg. The menu at this little family restaurant boasts something for everyone, from vegetarians to died-in-the-wool meat lovers. The café offers reasonably priced breakfasts and lunches seven days a week. Serving a variety of favorite comfort foods, the Morning Glory uses only the finest ingredients. For breakfast patrons will find hearty offerings, such as stone ground grits, stuffed French toast, real sausage gravy, fluffy buttermilk pancakes and the Mountain Man Breakfast that few could finish in one sitting. The lunch menu features homemade soups, hearty sandwiches, market-fresh salads and Dad's Famous Fish Tacos, so delicious you can't believe it until you try them. After lunch, treat yourself to a scrumptious piece of warm cobbler or a slice of home baked pie or cake. Inside the café, the cheerful dandelion yellow walls highlight some of Black Mountain's finest local artists, creating a lovely backdrop for oils, watercolors, mixed media and photography plus other arts and crafts displayed for sale. Start your day off on the sunny side of the street with a tasty meal from the Morning Glory Café.

400 E State Street, Suite 1-A, Black Mountain NC
(828) 669-6212 (828) 669-2119 or (888) 804-8438 www.montevistahotel.com

Rezaz Mediterranean Cuisine

Located in Asheville's historic Biltmore Village, Rezaz Mediterranean Cuisine, owned by Reza and Eva Setayesh, offers diners an eclectic array of Spanish, Italian, Greek and North African fare. Since its opening in 2003, Rezaz has been branded a favorite of both locals and visitors, and has been recognized in a variety of publications, including the *Boston Globe* and *Southern Living*. The relaxing, yet upscale, interior at Rezaz showcases beautiful hardwood floors, high ceilings, hanging light fixtures and brightly painted walls. Rezaz seasonal menus feature local ingredients, fresh seafood and meats, and exotic spices that are tastefully blended to create one exciting recipe after another. Favorites include the Wood Grilled Ceasar salad, Veal Osso Bucco, Arborio Crusted Sea Scallops, Seared Duck Medallions and Goat Cheese Ravioli. Attached to the main dining room is Rezaz newest conception, the Enoteca. Rezaz Enoteca is an Italian wine bar and cafe that is open for breakfast, lunch and dinner. Offerings include grilled panini sandwiches, imported meats and cheeses, petite entrees, housemade desserts and gelato, and fresh baked breads. For an unforgetable dining experience, excellent menu selections, an attentive waitstaff, and a full bar, be sure to visit Reza and Eva at their highly acclaimed extablishments.

28 Hendersonville Road, Asheville NC
(828) 277-1510
www.rezaz.com

Corner Kitchen

Tucked into a quiet corner of Biltmore Village, in one of Richard Sharpe Smith's original cottages, is one of Asheville's most surprising restaurants. Chef Joe Scully brings years of culinary experience to bear in his special North Carolina take on Pan-American cuisine, while host Kevin Westmoreland makes you feel as welcome as an old friend for breakfast, lunch or dinner. Recognized as having one of the best breakfasts in the South by *Southern Living* magazine, the Corner Kitchen's Sunday brunch and dinner menus have received regional acclaim. With rooms that deliver a romantic dinner for two, or a great meal for up to 40, the Corner Kitchen welcomes you and your friends or business associates. Dine year round on the side porch, where tables cluster around the big, beautiful bar, or in one of the cozy fireplace rooms. When the weather is right, you can relax on the patio, where you can enjoy your meal with the soothing sound of a unique fountain, designed and built by local artisans. Next time you're looking for a meal that's enticing and a mood that's relaxing, drop into the Corner Kitchen.

3 Boston Way, Asheville NC   (828) 274-2439   www.thecornerkitchen.com

Paris Bakery and Tea Room

The French are renowned for their talented bakers. With more than 20 years of baking experience, Pierre-Ange Lestieux is no exception. Pierre-Ange and Martha Lestieux own Paris Bakery and Tea Room in Asheville. Pierre's first bakery was in Limoges, France. The Paris Bakery and Tea Room is reputed for light, flaky pastries, Sacher tortes and incomparable quiches. Inventions of whimsy such as the mouse mousse are amusing and delicious. The chocolate mouse is filled with an airy mousse, and charmingly decorated with delicate icing whiskers and red eyes. The croissants do double duty as a breakfast treat and lunch sandwich. The bakery offers the popular French beignets with café au lait on hand to accompany the tasty treat. This authentic French bakery rises above the rest. For a spectacular cake, call and describe your dream dessert to Pierre. He will bake and decorate your cake to order. Paris Bakery and Tea Room participates in various charities, generously contributing to hospitals, associations and schools in the community.

301 Merrimon Avenue, Asheville NC
(828) 252-2315, (828) 669-2119 or (888) 804-8438   www.montevistahotel.com

Urban Burrito

In May of 2002, Chad Bright and Jeff Tacy made history in Asheville by opening the first fast Mexican grill the town had ever seen, winning a popular vote for Best Burrito in western North Carolina two years running. Crisp salads with a choice of toppings whet your appetite for the big selection of fat burritos. The meat choices include cilantro lime chicken or steak, jerk chicken or tofu and tilapia. A meatless entry is offered in each category on the menu. In addition to soft drinks and bottled water, the over-21 crowd can choose from a number of domestic, import and micro brews. Any size party will appreciate the no-hassle, affordable catering options. All catering packages come with the same high quality of fresh food offered in the restaurant. Group orders for more than 25 people receive free local delivery. Chad and Jeff are steadfast believers in self-employment, offering franchise investments to entrepreneurs interested in opening their own Urban Burrito. Whether you want to eat a good meal, feed your party or start your own business, Urban Burrito has you covered.

640 Merrimon Avenue, Suite 203, Asheville NC   (828) 251-1921
1865 Hendersonville Road, Asheville NC   (828) 277-2002
129 Bleachery Boulevard, Asheville NC   (828) 298-9802   www.urbanburrito.com

Barley's

Located in a renovated 1920s appliance and furniture store, Barley's Taproom & Pizzeria is a step back in time. Doug Beatty was a carpenter when he purchased this 8,000-square-foot property, located in the heart of the arts and entertainment district of Asheville. With the assistance of Jimmy Rentz, Doug renovated the space into two floors of redecorated genius, including building the bar and all the tables. Patrich Huss is the general manager who started as a pizza cook. The main floor houses the restaurant and stage. The smell of sourdough pizza greets you at the door. New York-style pizza and subs, lasagna and burgers are served with fresh, locally grown produce and meats. Three or four nights a week, the stage is home to live music, including bluegrass, country, jazz and Americana sounds. There's never a cover charge at Barley's. The bar has 24 taps featuring the South's best selection of American craft-brewed beers. The open room creates a family atmosphere that is comfortable and inviting. The upstairs features four nine-foot pool tables, available by the hour, and five dart lanes, available for private use or tournament play. The upstairs bar features an 19 more taps. With 55 beers on tap and excellent food to go with it, it's no wonder Barley's has been recognized as Best Taproom in the South by *Southern Draft Beer News* and picked as Top Tap in the South by *Celebrator Beer* magazine.

42 Biltmore Avenue, Asheville NC   (828) 255-0504   www.barleystaproom.com

Berliner Kindl German Restaurant

If you're in search of the authentic taste of Germany, then it's time to head to Berliner Kindl German Restaurant in Black Mountain. Located on the main street in Black Mountain, just off Interstate 40 at exit 64, this popular eatery is a full service restaurant that specializes in traditional German cuisine. You will find such classic favorites as bratwurst dinners, schnitzel dinners, jagerschnitzel, and kassler rippchen, along with many other dishes. The warm and inviting atmosphere is reminiscent of Old World Bavaria. The cozy bar offers an extensive selection of German beers as an accompaniment to Berliner Kindl's delicious and satisfying German fare. The friendly service will make you want to return again and again. A deli, in a separate retail area within the restaurant, features more than 200 different cookies, cakes, spices, vinegars and other specialties from Germany that you can take home to enjoy. There is also a cosmetic and toiletries area featuring some favorites from Germany. Reservations are accepted, but they are not necessary. With its savory meals and wonderful atmosphere, you are in for a treat at Berliner Kindl German Restaurant.

121 Broadway, Black Mountain NC
(828) 669-5255

Peking Garden

Nothing satisfies a hunger craving quite like delicious Chinese food. For 15 years, Peking Garden has been known, quite lovingly, as the old faithful of downtown Asheville. The restaurant serves the finest Chinese cuisine in Szechwan, Hunan and Cantonese styles. Since 2003, Thomas Zhou has taken great care to provide authentic and healthful Chinese food to his valued customers. Using only the freshest ingredients, Peking Garden offers an excellent lunch buffet, lunch and nightly specials, as well as a selection of vegetarian dishes, all without MSG. Tom, Annie and the great staff will welcome you with friendly attention as you prepare to sample Chef Bobby's cuisine. Executive Chef Bobby trained in Nanjian, China and perfected his skills at premier hotels before coming to Asheville. Peking Garden specializes in seafood and vegetables. The presentation of the superb a la carte dinner classics rivals their equally superb flavor. You'll find a broad selection of wines to complement your meal. For a house favorite, order Chef Bobby's fresh steamed Hunan-style sea bass topped with the house's special ginger and garlic sauce. You can dine in or take out, and catering is available. Regardless of which entrée you select from the menu, you are sure to learn just why Peking Garden is held in such high regard by the locals.

208 Charlotte Street, Asheville NC   (828) 236-3839

Knight's On Main

When Knight's on Main opened on November 1, 1995, it served nearly 300 people breakfast, and business has been booming ever since. This popular restaurant is located near the charming center of downtown Blowing Rock, and it's not uncommon to see regular patrons lined up out the door waiting for a table. Once you bite into one of Knight's famous, fluffy omelets or tender baby back ribs, you will see why Knight's is the place locals love to eat. Owners Tim and Jessica Knight pride themselves on the hard work and constant dedication that have gone into making their restaurant a success. The friendly staff continuously provides excellent service with a smile. This family-oriented restaurant is nonsmoking and caters primarily to the local community. However, the cheerful, relaxed atmosphere and kind patrons make this a great place to eat. Even if you're on your own, you never feel like you're eating alone. The menu at Knight's on Main offers something for every member of the family. The extensive breakfast menu features 10 different omelets, tasty biscuit dishes, breakfast sandwiches, pancakes and French toast. At lunch choose from such items as the chopped pork barbeque or the veggie plate. Dinner menus change daily and feature entrées that utilize seasonally fresh ingredients. Desserts also vary daily and include such decadent delights as blackberry cobbler and chocolate cream pie. Whenever mealtime rolls around, it's time to visit Knight's on Main.

870 Main Street, Blowing Rock NC   (828) 295-3869
www.blueridgemedia.com/knightsonmain

My Father's Pizza

My Father's Pizza is one of Black Mountain's premier family eateries. It offers guests a wonderful selection of freshly made and perfectly prepared entrées that will please even the most discerning palate. Owned and operated by Larry and Donna Robinson and family, My Father's Pizza opened with the goal of providing customers with great food at an affordable price and has met that goal admirably. The restaurant's fabulous garlic bread is baked on the premises each day, and is a flavorful accompaniment to the tempting antipasto or the artichoke, Caesar, Greek or pasta salads. My Father's Pizza offers an extravagant array of made-to-order pizzas with a wonderful selection of both traditional American and Mediterranean toppings, such as prosciutto, rib eye, Italian roasted chicken, pine nuts and feta cheese. My Father's Pizza also offers freshly baked Stromboli, as well as a marvelous selection of fresh pasta dishes. Relax and enjoy the best Italian cuisine that Black Mountain has to offer with a visit to My Father's Pizza.

110 Cherry Street, Black Mountain NC   (828) 669-4944

Veranda Café

In beautiful Black Mountain, the Veranda Café offers guests a refreshing change from the same old thing. Owner Jeff Smith opened the doors to his lively café in March of 2005 and offers a fabulous menu filled with tasty, made-from-scratch entrees that are as filling as they are flavorful. His diverse and eclectic menu offers a wide range of both traditional and contemporary dishes, including their variety of homemade soups, such as the rich and creamy Hungarian Mushroom, and some mouth-watering sandwiches, including turkey with cranberry chutney or chicken salad. Other popular items include chef Paulette's crawfish enchiladas and a must-try tamale pie. The Veranda offers patrons a wide selection of popular and flavorful beers and wines that are ideal accompaniments to the cuisine. You will want to be sure to save room for the Café's decadent desserts, such as buttermilk or coconut cream pies, tender carrot cake, sugar-free chocolate cake, spice coffee cake or the fresh and feisty cherry-peach pie. The Café offers a choice of quiet inside dining or al fresco, where all of Black Mountain can serve as your dinner show. Veranda Café can also provide you with on- or off-site catering, and features a lovely selection of collectible gifts. Come and enjoy the light and lovely atmosphere, friendly people and fantastic food at Veranda Café on Cherry Street.

119 Cherry Street, Black Mountain NC
(828) 669-8864

The Greenery Restaurant

A memorable evening of casual dining is sure to be had in Asheville's well known Greenery Restaurant. For two decades, owners Melanie and Bill Cooke, with their daughter Aimie as hostess, have provided an imaginative and well executed dining experience in a comfortable atmosphere. Locals know the Greenery is where to go for continental cuisine and those famous Maryland crab cakes everyone talks about. Dinner is popular with the local patrons and with visiting celebrities. The restaurant boasts an impressive wine list featuring more than 200 selections and a copper bar area invites guests with an intimate ambience for cocktails and conversation. In 2005, the Greenery received the Award of Excellence by *Wine Spectator* magazine for the 15th consecutive year. Bill studied the chef's art in Baden Baden, Germany. His passion for fine dining is evidenced by his skillful presentation and choice combinations. Freshness is top priority and the storeroom is stocked with local suppliers' produce and wares. An award-winning food and wine destination, the Greenery Restaurant is a great place to experience classical dining and comfortable elegance with beautifully presented fare.

148 Tunnel Road, Asheville NC
(828) 253-2809
www.greeneryrestaurant.com

Autumn Sunrise Photo by Marty Hulsebos HighCountryImages.com

Northern Piedmont

Northern Piedmont Accommodations

Rosemary House Bed & Breakfast

In 1912, Logan Womble built the historic house in Pittsboro that became the Rosemary House Bed & Breakfast. Karen and Mac Pullen named the house for the herb rosemary, often associated with friendship and remembrance. Rosemary House underwent eight months of extensive renovations to upgrade the five-room bed and breakfast while preserving its gracious charm. The result is a selection of spacious guest rooms, complete with individual air-conditioning, private baths, ceiling fans, telephones, optional cable television and beautiful antique furnishings. The well stocked library features a cozy fireplace, and the wrap-around front porch has a selection of swings and rocking chairs. A vine-covered patio in the back, surrounded by herbs and perennials, makes a nice retreat. Guests receive a full vegetarian breakfast. The rooms each have their own distinctive character. The popular, secluded Haven features hand-painted murals, a large bow-foot iron bed, fireplace, whirlpool for two and separate shower. Retreat is located in an upstairs corner with a fireplace and large four-poster rice bed. Meadow is a two-room suite in soft pastel colors with a brass bed, twin sleeper and claw-foot tub with a shower. Sunny Willow is blue and white, and Holly is sage and red toile with a Windsor bed. Rosemary House enjoys proximity to galleries, antique stores, art studios, shops and restaurants. To help remember your stay, each guest receive a packet of rosemary as they leave Rosemary Bed & Breakfast.

76 W Street, Pittsboro NC   (919) 542-4369 or (888) 643-2017
www.rosemary-bb.com

Bed & Breakfast at Laurel Ridge

At the edge of a dense hardwood forest overlooking the Rocky River in central North Carolina lies a charming bed and breakfast that offers total relaxation. Welcome to the Bed & Breakfast at Laurel Ridge, where owners David Simmons and his wife, Lisa Reynolds, have created an intimate and ruggedly beautiful paradise. Built in 1983, the inn's timber-frame architecture, filled with exposed beams and rich hardwood floors, blends with perfect harmony into the surrounding landscape. The lush perennial gardens at Laurel Ridge, recognized as a Backyard Wildlife Habitat by the National Wildlife Federation, provide the backdrop for a lazy stroll or perfect country wedding. The inn offers four accommodations. Enjoy the Rose Suite with a whirlpool bath and a private balcony overlooking the forest or the cozy elegance of the Jewel and Pine Rooms. The Carolina Cottage, nestled into the woods next to the main inn, offers additional privacy and fabulous views. Regionally renowned chef Dave will greet you in the morning with such culinary delights as pumpkin-basil pancakes with chicken apple sausages, poached eggs on herb roasted potatoes, and sautéed baby spinach with hollandaise sauce. Expect a guest-spoiling array of breads, muffins and sweets to start your day. A rejuvenating massage for mind, body and spirit can be a perfect addition to your stay at Laurel Ridge. Chatham County, the home of Laurel Ridge, boasts a large arts community, which allows for ample shopping and exploration. Lose yourself in leafy vineyards, vibrant art galleries and a plethora of recreational and historical sites.

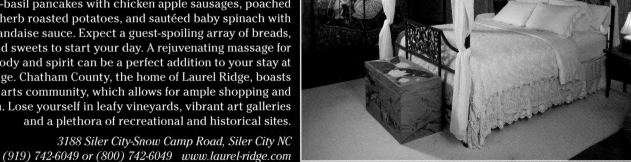

3188 Siler City-Snow Camp Road, Siler City NC
(919) 742-6049 or (800) 742-6049   www.laurel-ridge.com

Northern Piedmont Attractions

North Carolina Zoo

Civic leaders in Raleigh launched the idea for a state zoo in the late 1960s. An exhibition professional football game in 1967, sponsored by the Raleigh Jaycees, raised $18,000 for a feasibility study, and planning began in the early 1970s. North Carolina Zoo first opened to the public in August 1974, with temporary exhibits and facilities that were phased out as the permanent exhibits were completed. The North Carolina Zoo is the nation's largest walk-through natural habitat zoo. The zoo is internationally recognized as one of the largest natural habitat zoos in the world. It is the country's first state zoo and the first zoo planned from the start for natural habitats. The natural habitat philosophy was coming to the forefront in the 1970s when the zoo's planning began. This philosophy calls for exhibits that, as closely as possible, replicate the animals' wild environments and give visitors the impression they too are in the wild with the animals. Its African and North American exhibit regions span more than 500 acres with more than five miles of walkways. Another 900 acres are available for future development. The zoo currently exhibits more than 1,100 animals, representing more than 250 different species. The zoo's main focus is to encourage an understanding of and commitment to the conservation of the world's wildlife and wild places through recognition of the interdependence of people and nature. North Carolina Zoo is creating a sense of enjoyment, wonder and discovery at the park and in its outreach programs.

4401 Zoo Parkway, Asheboro NC
(336) 879-7204 or (800) 488-0444
www.nczoo.org

Rock Barn Golf & Spa

Tucked away in the foothills of the majestic Blue Ridge Mountains is Rock Barn Golf & Spa, a wonderland of sprawling valleys, gently rolling hills and picturesque waterways. The world-class course, designed by Robert Trent Jones Jr., was voted Fourth Best New Upscale Public Course in the Nation by *Golf Digest* and Best New Course in the State by *North Carolina* magazine. Rock Barn Golf offers two award-winning, 18-hole courses filled with 419 hybrid Bermuda grass fairways, bent grass greens and paved cart paths. Each year the course hosts a parade of golf legends during the Greater Hickory Classic at Rock Barn, a PGA TOUR Champions Tour Event. Here, they find a challenging and masterful display of course design that requires golfers to put forth all of their power, strategy and skill to win the championship. The Hickory Classic isn't the only tournament played each year. Annually, Rock Barn plays host to many company-sponsored and members-only tournaments. Most notably, they work with community businesses to provide charitable contributions through tournament sponsor packages. Rock Barn Golf & Spa offers an on-site pro shop that carries a full line of equipment and accessories. Golfers who feel the need to sharpen their skills may schedule time with an on-site golf pro to help improve their game through private lessons. Guests who wish to take a break from the green can enjoy casual or fine dining in one of many eating establishments. Other resort amenities include an accredited day spa, tennis courts, swimming, fitness center and equestrian center. Come play the day away at Rock Barn Golf & Spa.

3791 Clubhouse Drive, Conover NC
(828) 459-9279 or (888) RCK-BARN
www.rockbarn.com

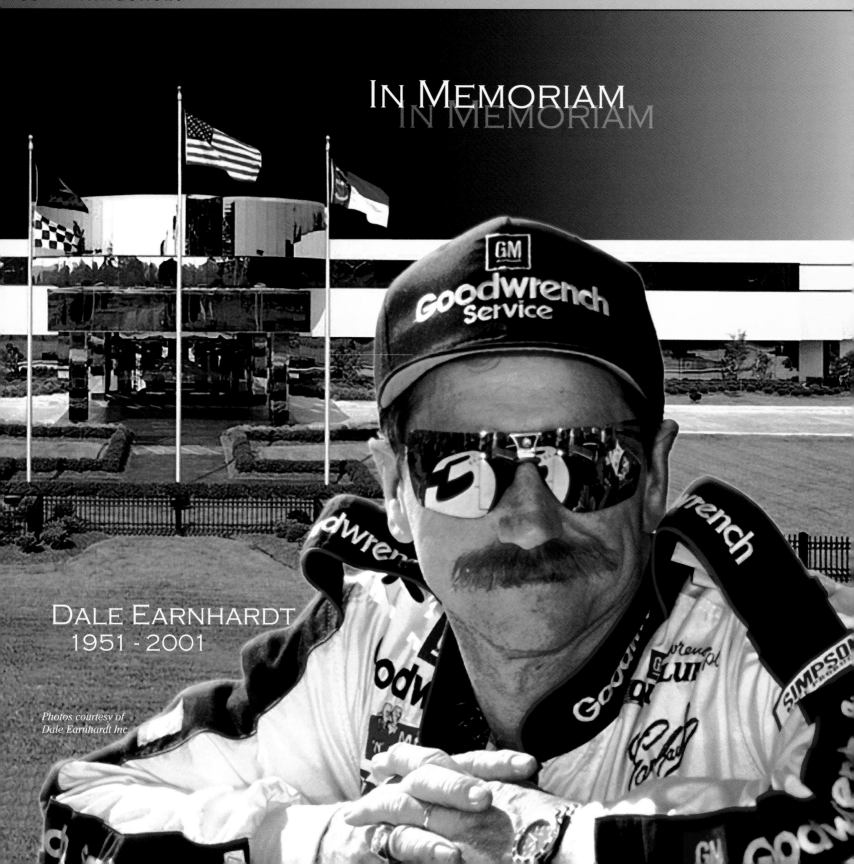

IN MEMORIAM
IN MEMORIAM

DALE EARNHARDT
1951 - 2001

*Photos courtesy of
Dale Earnhardt Inc.*

Dale Jarrett Racing Adventure

Legendary Ned Jarrett, winner of two NASCAR national championships in mostly Ford Galaxies, started the first racing generation. Originally a dirt track, Hickory Speedway saw the beginning of the Jarrett legend. Ned retired as defending champion in 1966 at the age of 34. He then went into the radio and television side of the motor racing circuit for CBS and ESPN, as a reporter, commentator and analyst. Sons Dale and Glenn continued the tradition in the 1970s and became the second generation of champions in the Jarrett family. Dale was the Nextel Cup champion in 1999 while Glenn followed in his father's footsteps in broadcasting. Dale's son, Jason, is virtually a veteran of the third generation to drive in NASCAR's Busch series, Nextel and other races. Darrell Jaret Racing Adventures was started in 1998 and is backed by the Jarrett brothers, their father, Ned, son, Jason, and Green Bay Packers quarterback Brett Favre. The Dale Jarrett Racing Adventure provides the opportunity to drive actual NASCAR Nextel Cup race cars. This publicly traded company books various dates during the year at NASCAR tracks where customers can purchase laps ranging from a three-lap ride to an 80-lap drive. Students can achieve speeds of up to 165 mph at the Super Speedways and are allowed to pass and draft with other students. An instructional session is provided to acquaint the student with the racecar, safety precautions and the proper groove of the track. Get behind the wheel with Dale Jarrett Racing Adventure when you're in Newton.

120A N Main Avenue, Newton NC
(828) 466-8837 or (888) GO-RACE-1 (467-2231)
www.racingadventure.com www.jasonjarrett.com

Queen's Landing

Queen's Landing is a family entertainment center on Lake Norman that has so much to do you can't do it all in one trip. The Landing, located 30 minutes from Charlotte, features a floating dock bar, restaurants, boat rides, miniature golf and other fun. You can eat at Jack's Lakeside Grill. You can get lunch or take a buffet cruise on the Catawba Queen, a replica of a Mississippi River boat. You can cruise the lake aboard the Lady of the Lake, a 90-foot luxury yacht. They have bumper boats for the kids, romantic cruises for adults, and a dueling piano bar named Jokers. Both the Catawba Queen and Lady of the Lake are available for private events, as is the Queen's Club Room, which overlooks the lake. Queen's Landing has something for everyone.

1459 River Highway, Mooresville NC
(704) 663-2628
www.queenslanding.com

Northern Piedmont Galleries

French Connections

French antiques and African art may sound like a strange mix for a shop in a small North Carolina town, but consider the owners. Jacques and Wendy Dufour have collectively spent more than two decades in France, three in Africa, and three in North Carolina. Now five years old, French Connections brings together the people and places of their past by offering antiques from Normandy, modern artwork from Senegal and crafts from more than 20 African countries. Beautiful fabrics make the shop a quilter or sewer's paradise, with hand-painted panels and batiks, French toiles and Provence prints. African baskets from many regions offer patterns, styles and shapes for every occasion. The vibrant art collection represents some of Africa's finest. French Connections is the sole U.S. outlet for many of the artists and craftspeople represented. The Dufours buy directly from individual artist and crafts cooperatives and work with suppliers to improve their products for the U.S. market, with an emphasis on sustainability. Their knowledge and enthusiasm for the people and countries behind the items in their store creates an international experience within the walls of the circa 1900 house. French Connections is a shop you won't want to miss.

178 Hillsboro Street, Pittsboro NC   (919) 545-9296 www.french-nc.com

Lyn Morrow Pottery— Gallery and Studio

The Lyn Morrow Pottery is both an active studio and outstanding gallery located south of Chapel Hill, just outside of the town of Pittsboro. Lyn has been recognized as an accomplished artist for both her classic forms and extensive palette of glazes. Lyn uses the pottery wheels in her studio to push the limit of porcelain, throwing 50-pound bowls with 32-inch diameters. Lyn has a delicate touch when she creates lizards chasing each other up lamps or around the lip of sinks. Whether it is small candle bowls or grand exhibition bowls, all of Morrow's work reflects both the craftsmanship and design developed when Lyn studied abroad and in North Carolina. Lyn's award-winning pottery has been featured in museums, galleries and corporate collections throughout North and South America, Europe and Japan. The Lyn Morrow gallery always features Lyn's work, as well as the work of 50 or more of North Carolina's finest potters whose styles range from traditional to contemporary. The focus of the gallery is clay, but you can also find glass, basketry, metalwork, jewelry and paper. There are utilitarian pieces ready to complete any kitchen or complement any table. Look for the distinctive turquoise and cobalt blue building with large and colorful metal flowers on the lawn for a distinctive experience at Lyn Morrow Pottery.

3449 US 15-501, Pittsboro NC
(919) 545-9078
www.lynmorrowpottery.com

above photos by Catherine Whitten, Geek & Graphix

Northern Piedmont Gifts

New Horizons Trading Company

The art community has arrived in an old town halfway between the mountains and the sea called Pittsboro. On the first Sunday of each month, downtown merchants sponsor First Sundays, a showing of art, music, crafts and sidewalk sales. The fresh influx is changing the flavor of Pittsboro. New Horizons Trading Company reflects the comfortable feeling that is part of the new town spirit. Owner Catherine Mills promotes an intuitive comfort with the merchandise she carries in her store. Natural fiber clothing in dressy or casual styles finds a home at New Horizons. Look for styles by Russ Beren, Flax and Cut-Loose, as well as Euro-comfort shoes by Dansko and Naot. The store offers a selection of eclectic gifts, jewelry and cards that seem to have been handpicked for the customers. Local artisans' work is featured on a rotating basis and is shown amongst the other specialty items that New Horizons carries, including soy candles, gift books, fashion accessories and novelty items. Future plans for the store include CDs with a focus on local and world music. New Horizons is supportive of the community and encourages you to see what's happening in Pittsboro for yourself. While you are there, stop in and try on some of their gracefully unpretentious styles. The novel ease and quality you find at New Horizons Trading Company will make you feel you have rediscovered a friend.

52 Hillsboro Street, Pittsboro NC
(919) 542-7366
http://newhorizonstrading.com

Northern Piedmont Health & Beauty

SpaDels

Lake Norman is sometimes called the inland sea, with its 520 miles of shoreline and 50 square miles of surface area. SpaDels overlooks one of Lake Norman's coves, establishing a peaceful haven for the spa's clientele. It is historical fact that all spas take their name from the Belgian village of Spa, located in the Ardennes Forest, renowned for its healing waters. Spas were some of the first known natural health centers. SpaDels continues the tradition. This intriguing spa was conceptualized and constructed by the mingled brainpower of three friends: Dale Helms, and Jan and Morris Wilson. Dale provided his unique hair design vision, while Morris brought his natural health and beauty expertise. Jan furnished the business development skills necessary to bring the dream to life. SpaDels retains a large staff of professional stylists, massage therapists, estheticians and manicurists. Its signature Diamond O2 Treatment painlessly rewinds time with a crystal-free microdermabrasion technique combined with an oxygen recovery facial. The specialty facials, body and nail care treatments, plus the hair salon are just a few of the possibilities available at this spa. SpaDels also offers a steam room and rain shower, exfoliating treatments, cellulite and body slimming programs and several types of massage. Services such as these rejuvenate the clientele, and that is the real business of SpaDels. The Spa staff both pampers and educates its customers about health and wellbeing. The spa hosts a client appreciation party each spring. You are invited to visit SpaDels early for a formal invitation.

562 Williamson Road, Mooresville NC
(704) 799-9331
www.spadels.com

The Spa at Rock Barn

Just a few miles east of Hickory, nirvana awaits those who are willing to embrace it. The Spa at Rock Barn, located in Conover, offers clients a full spectrum of spa treatments and delights designed to relax, renew and refresh. This distinguished spa recently received the title Accredited Day Spa, an honor bestowed upon them by The Day Spa Association. The Association has implemented accreditation guidelines to award those day spas that meet specific standards. This award is a seal of approval given by the only organization currently monitoring the fast-growing day spa industry. Guests of The Spa at Rock Barn will be able to achieve their own state of bliss in any one of four mineral pools, two saunas, two steam rooms or the therapeutic waterfall pool. Licensed therapists are on staff to provide you with relief from everyday stresses, aches and pains. Choose from Swedish massage, reflexology or a calming and nurturing mother-to-be massage, to name a few. The spa also offers several hair, skin and body care treatments, perfect for men or women. These include fabulous facials, like the detox or aromatherapy facial, body masques or one of many manicure/pedicure packages. You'll find casual and fine dining establishments to match your mood, two lounges and the Blue Ridge Grand Ballroom, available for private parties and special occasions. The Spa at Rock Barn invites you to refresh your spirit at this state-of-the-art facility.

3791 Clubhouse Drive, Conover NC
(828) 459-9150 or (888) RCK-BARN
www.rockbarn.com

Northern Piedmont
Home Décor, Flowers, Gardens & Markets

Flynt's Florist

Flynt's Florist is a family-owned and operated business that has been serving Pittsboro for nearly 50 years. The family moved to Pittsboro to open the shop and has been the preferred florist in town and outlying areas ever since. The Flynt family has always prided itself on offering exemplary customer service and true Southern hospitality. Flynt's is a full service flower shop and offers local delivery to Fearrington Village, the northern end of the county and Pittsboro; it can also send your order by FTD and Teleflora. This shop is small but filled with nicely displayed flowers and plants that fill the air with the sweet, crisp smell of spring. Flynt's carries a seasonally appropriate selection of silk flora and charming gifts. The friendly and knowledgeable staff makes choosing the right flowers and designs easy. Flynt's specializes in crafting and organizing floral arrangements for all occasions. Stunning ensembles can be made for engagement and wedding parties, anniversaries or other special occasions. Flynt's also creates lovely, tasteful arrangements for funerals. Flynt's Florist is a proud member of The Society of American Florists.

53 Hillsboro Street, Pittsboro NC   (800) 257-9067   www.flyntsflorist.com

Flynthill Farm

Legend has it that Belted Galloway cows are descended from the cows brought to England by the Vikings long ago. These large, striking dark beasts with white belted markings have pleasant personalities and are partial to the cold, congregating in the creek bed or shady woods during hot days. Neil and Pansy Flynt keep a herd of the Galloways on their 50-acre Flynthill Farm, occasionally selling some of this rare breed as pets or to breeders. The cows aid in the natural manufacture of valuable compost. The Flynts started out in the florist business, but this family farm now specializes in the gardening industry. The retail garden center is stocked for home and commercial landscaping, with shrubs, trees and perennials. The Flynts provide a full landscaping and nursery service as well as expert advice about planting. The gift store houses one-of-a-kind gifts. After being decked out in holiday poinsettias and Christmas wreaths, the shop closes in January and February for winter. Flynt's Florist is still around, now operated by the third generation, Dana Flynt Smoak. Whether you come to see the cows or to fulfill your landscaping needs, the family at Flynthill Farm welcomes your visit.

2411 U. S. Highway 64 W, Pittsboro NC
(919) 542-5308

The Grapevine Gourmet Market

Faux stone walls with creeping vines. Grape clusters sparkling in the sunlight streaming through the windows. Bistro tables, wall fountains and flowers in the courtyard. One would think they have ambled into an Italian villa, but instead they have found The Grapevine Gourmet Market, which has made a name for itself as the Mooresville destination for fine wines, imported ales and lagers, and gift baskets. Angela Gregory, owner of The Grapevine Gourmet Market, has been in the wine and food business for more than 15 years. She discovered that great food is the way to people's hearts and, of course, a great bottle of wine. Locals know to call Angela when they need advice on what kind of wine to serve with dinner. Angela has created a gourmet emporium where she can showcase her wine discoveries or "little gems" from smaller boutique wineries and vineyards that one doesn't generally find in the larger stores. Customers can sit outside in the courtyard and sample wines by the glass. Angela hosts a wine tasting every Thursday night. If wine is not your beverage of choice, she has more than 100 imported beers to be enjoyed, with a fine selection of artisan cheeses and other delicacies. Angela has also created a line of custom-made gift baskets, from holidays to corporate baskets, for any occasion that can be delivered or shipped. Visit The Grapevine Gourmet Market to experience one of the best secrets to be found in North Carolina–it's a wine lover's dream.

129 Williamson Road, Mooresville NC
(704) 664-wine (9463)

Patterson Farm

The Patterson family has been growing produce since 1919. James A. Patterson grew 30 acres of cotton and about three acres of tomatoes. Boll weevils destroyed all the cotton that first year, so he decided to grow 30 acres of tomatoes the next year. James' sons, Carl and Frank, farmed together until 1979, when they decided to divide the farm. In 1982, Carl's son Randall returned from college and implemented a new procedure called Plastic Culture, which involves growing on raised beds. Today, Randall Patterson is the president of Patterson Farm, Inc. and oversees the field operations. Doug Patterson, another of Carl's sons, is the vice president; his wife Michelle is the Treasurer; and Randall's wife Nora is the Secretary. The focus of this family-owned and operated business is to provide customers with the highest quality produce, plants and service at a competitive price. They are one of the largest tomato growers in North Carolina, with 350 acres dedicated to tomatoes. They also have 30 acres of pumpkins, 25 acres of strawberries and 10,000 poinsettias each year. School tours are welcome and receive educational awareness on how a working farm operates. Patterson Farm holds many great events throughout the year, such as hay rides, spring and fall tours, a John Deere tricycle track and pumpkin painting. The Farm Market on the property offers the farm's seasonal produce, as well as jams, jellies, salsa, dressings, gift items, baskets and hand dipped ice cream. Bring your family, friends and neighbors to Patterson Farm. And don't forget to bring the camera.

3060 Millbridge Road, China Grove NC
Farm: (704) 857-5242
Market: (704) 797-0013 Tours: (704) 636 4005
www.pattersonfarminc.com

Stonehenge Landscape and Stone Yard

For centuries, man has been using stone to build the foundations of their civilizations. From the Great Wall of China to a tinker's cottage in Wales, stone roads, walls and homes are symbols of safety, strength and craftsmanship. Stonehenge Landscape and Stone Yard in Mooresville carries an extensive collection of natural stone, hand-carved stone and synthetic stone along with antique chimney pots, iron vents and other treasures that have been reclaimed from centuries-old buildings such as the Saint Louis Opera House. Additionally, they carry ornamental medallions, fireplace accessories and other architectural delights. Stonehenge Landscape and Stone Yard has been serving the community since 1999 and provides delivery anywhere in the continental United States. The company has built a reputation in the industry for providing consistent, exemplary customer service, as well as a knowledgeable and personable staff. Their inventory consists of over 10 acres of assorted, top-quality stone that is ideal for any project, including walls, building stone, flagstone, river rock, boulders, mantels and coping. The first thing visitors

notice upon arrival is the stunning craftsmanship that has gone into designing the beautiful main building. Various stones were utilized during building and are displayed throughout the structure. On the property, a grand wall and walkway composed of numerous squares made from the different materials allows customers to easily visualize how a certain stone would suit their project. Whether you are a contractor, builder or homeowner, turn to Stonehenge Landscaping and Stone Yard for all your natural and synthetic stone needs.

715 Oakridge Farm Road, Highway 150, Mooresville NC
(704) 799-0750
www.stonehengestone.com

Boyles Distinctive Furniture

At Boyles Distinctive Furniture, "more by design" is more than simply a tag line. It's a promise that Boyles Distinctive Furniture makes to its customers. More selection, value, inspiration and service are found at Boyles' 12 locations in North Carolina. Larry Hendricks, the owner of Boyles, grew up in a furniture family. He purchased Boyles' Original Country Shop in 1974 and has grown the business to include eight showrooms, three clearance outlets and an interior design center. People come from all over the country to take advantage of Boyles' discounted prices and talented design assistance, selection and service. Boyles staff is well suited to guide a customer through the process of space planning, color coordination, furniture selection, accessorization and, above all else, to save time and money. Boyle's showrooms are brimming with famous name brands and one-of-a-kind designs that have been found by company buyers who search the world over. The buyers are committed to offering more of the freshest styles, many of which are exclusive to Boyles. The company never sells at suggested retail prices. Prices are always at least 30 percent to 50 percent below retail. In addition, when a factory has a special sale, Boyles passes along the extra discounts to its customers. Customer satisfaction is the number one priority during and after the sale. From the person who assists a customer in the showroom to the expert who dons the white gloves and rolls out the red carpet when delivering furniture to a home, Boyles associates strive to deliver the highest level of service. Boyles Distinctive Furniture was started with a commitment to providing exceptional service, America's favorite furniture styles and terrific prices. It's a commitment that customers continue to enjoy today.

1123 4th Street SW, Conover NC
(828) 345-5400 or (888) 316-3351
www.boyles.com

Pisgah National Forest

Northern Piedmont Museums

North Carolina Transportation Museum

The North Carolina Transportation Museum is located on the site that was once one of Southern Railway's main repair facilities for steam locomotives. Southern Railway was formed in 1894 when Samuel Spencer, the first President, began looking for a place for repair shops halfway between Washington, D.C. and Atlanta, Georgia. He purchased 144 acres from Senator John Henderson and built the first shops at Spencer in 1896. The museum, which is popular with train aficionados, preserves and translates many aspects of transportation history. Visitors can take a 25-minute on-site train ride in antique passenger cars pulled by antique steam and diesel locomotives. The 37-bay Bob Julian Roundhouse houses a collection of antique locomotives and rail cars, exhibits on rail history and a restoration shop, where an army of volunteers works to restore cars for the museum. The Bumper-to-Bumper exhibit area houses a collection of antique automobiles that represent the era during which each vehicle was manufactured. The Wagons, Wheels and Wings exhibit contains a general transportation collection. Antique artifacts include a covered wagon and a dugout canoe. The Back Shop is a mammoth structure that is in the middle of restoration. Once completed it will hold a comprehensive history of inland transportation in North Carolina. Come to the North Carolina Transportation Museum and discover a history that is timeless and vital to today's transportation industry.

411 S Salisbury Avenue, Spencer NC
(704) 636-2889 or
(877) NCTM-FUN (7-628-6386)
www.nctrans.org

Northern Piedmont Restaurants

Kelsey's@Occoneechee Steakhouse

The popular Kelsey's Café is now located inside the Occoneechee Steakhouse, which has combined to become Kelsey's@Occoneechee Steakhouse. This Hillsborough hot spot features varied kinds of entertainment and dinner specials, and can provide catering for any occasion. At Kelsey's, you can enjoy such succulent dishes as flame-broiled steaks prepared to order and served on a sizzling skillet, baked potato or fresh steamed veggies, and a crisp green salad. Other menu favorites include the tender prime rib, London broil, rib eye, New York strip steak and the Beef-K-Bob, made with Kelsey's special recipe. The restaurant also serves select seafood and pasta, T-bones and bacon-wrapped filet of beef or chicken. Customers love the freshly baked bread that accompanies meals. Friday and Saturday nights, the restaurant offers bountiful dinner buffets filled with wonderful dishes, making weekends the perfect time for a gathering of family and friends. Still other popular weekend specials include the Saturday and Sunday breakfast buffets and the Sunday lunch buffet. Kelsey's@Occoneechee a wonderful spectrum of mouthwatering desserts, including Kelsey's famous and award-winning peanut butter pie. You're invited to visit Kelsey's@Occoneechee Streakhouse, where great food and great people come together.

378 S Churton Street, Hillsborough NC
(919) 732-1155 or (919) 732-6939
www.realpagessites.com/kelseyscatering/index.html

Pavilion Restaurant

In the Greek culture, food is shared with friends in a joyful and unhurried manner. The Pavilion Restaurant in Greensboro takes the best of Greek culture and the best of American diversity to create a popular hot spot. Greek food is a blend of Oriental and European flavors, often using lots of meat and tomato, as well as fish and cheese. Pavilion serves rich Italian and Greek specialties along with a respectable wine list. In a friendly atmosphere of southern hospitality, they serve an eye-popping flaming shish-kabob beef tenderloin, Greek-style salmon filet and a Greek broiled chicken. Lamb, seafood and steak are all on the menu, as well as sandwiches, pizza and pastas. Desserts such as chocolate mousse pie and cheesecake melt in your mouth like the sweetest honey. Remember, catering for your special event is just a phone call away. Step into the Pavilion Restaurant for a little taste of Greek camaraderie.

2010 W Vandalia Road, Greensboro NC
(336) 852-1272   www.pavilionrestaurant.com

Liberty Oak Restaurant & Bar

The revitalized downtown area of Greensboro is a good example of how a city can give its original center a new lease on life. Liberty Oak Restaurant pioneered the movement back to the downtown by relocating its 20-year established business to the heart of this nostalgic neighborhood. Liberty Oak has been a pioneer in one other way, as well. It is widely recognized as one of the first restaurants in Greensboro to offer innovative, freshly prepared cuisine at a reasonable price in an informal setting. Local food critic John Batchelor refers to Liberty Oak as, "The restaurant that started it all for Greensboro." The beloved eatery was even named by *Southern Living* magazine as one of the "204 Food Finds" in the South in the "uptown foods" category. Owner-chef Walter Fancourt

has created a broad, four-star rated menu that features contemporary American cuisine. The wine list is extensive, offering 18 wines by the glass. Other attractions include an intimate full-service bar, as well as patio dining. Liberty Oak's beautiful and historic interior reflects the artful flavor of the neighborhood. The dining area is two stories with wood floors, tin-plate ceilings and sky-lights. Artwork by local artists and the chef himself add warmth and humor to the energetic, uptown atmosphere. Visit the website to preview menus and times of operation. Reservations are recommended.

100-D W Washington Street, Greensboro NC
(336) 273-7057
www.libertyoakrestaurant.com

Leblon Churrascaria

The all-you-can-eat concept has been remade over and over, yet no concept prepares you for the experience you will find at Leblon Churrascaria in Greensboro. Named for the Brazilian technique of seasoning and grilling meats on skewers over an open flame, this one-of-a-kind eatery will thrill you as much as fill you. Meals start off with as many trips to the salad bar as you want. This isn't an ordinary salad bar either. Besides the standard fresh romaine and broccoli, you'll find such interesting additions as veal carpaccio, eggplant baked with fresh herbs and cheese, hearts of palm and moqueca de salmeo (fresh salmon in a tomato broth with cilantro, red and green peppers). When you're done eating your vegetables, it's time to let Leblon's gauchos cater to your every meat-loving need. One by one, they'll stop by your table with skewers of different, delicious meats, ready to slice off whatever you want to sample. Sausage, lamb, pork chops, chicken, tenderloin, ribs, the list will seem endless and be endless until you say no more. To satisfy your thirst, try the traditional Brazilian caipirinha, an invigorating combination of sugar cane liquor, lime and sugar. If you still have room for dessert, choose from pies, cheesecake, mousse, tiramisu or crème caramel. There's no need to hop on a plane for Brazil when you can get a taste of carnival right in Greensboro at Leblon Churrascaria.

4512 W Market Street, Greensboro NC
(336) 294-2605
www.leblonsteakhouse.com

Solaris, Tapas Restaurant and Bar

Enjoy the wonderful Spanish tradition of dining on tapas at Solaris in Greensboro. Tapas are small, tasty dishes that can be used as appetizers or combined to make a meal. Solaris offers more than 30 tapas and an excellent wine list that includes choice Spanish wines, a vast array of bottled beers and seven beers on tap. Solaris further offers patrons a choice of signature martinis. The laid-back, welcoming atmosphere at Solaris is the perfect backdrop to the delicious tapas and makes Solaris an excellent venue for celebrations. Solaris has earned a reputation for being a fun and lively nightspot and regularly features live entertainment, including international music, vocalists and local bands, along with DJ nights and short, theatrical performances. Owners Christian and Courtney Reynolds pride themselves on their attentive staff and their use of only the freshest ingredients. The owners also feel strongly about supporting the arts, and to that end, they work in conjunction with Lyndon Street Artworks to feature monthly exhibits from local artists.

125 Summit Avenue, Greensboro NC   (336) 378-0198   www.gettapas.com

Bianca's

You don't have to have a passport to get great Italian food in the Triad. Go to Bianca's where authentic Italian cuisine is the specialty. This popular eatery, owned by Chef Lisa Carmella White and Salvatore Vito Matthews, opened in 1993 and offers a one-of-a-kind European dining experience. Located on the corner of South Chapman and Spring Garden Streets, Bianca's offers patrons a refreshing menu filled with perfectly prepared, traditional favorites, such as veal marsala, shrimp scampi and chicken parmigiana, as well as manicotti and meat or vegetable lasagnas. House specialties include the grilled fish Veronique and Italian stuffed pork chops, so good that Bon Appetit magazine requested the recipe. Appetizers and specials change weekly as does the wine list that is constantly updated to offer a selection of vintages that best complement the menu. While planning your meal, be sure to save room for Bianca's sumptuous desserts, such as the chocolate Amaretto mousse cake, cinnamon zabaglione and their simply decadent raspberry sponge cake. Savor true Italian cuisine while surrounded by a warm and welcoming atmosphere at Bianca's.

1901 Spring Garden Street, Greensboro NC
(336) 273-8114

Undercurrent

The award-winning Undercurrent is a simple yet elegant gourmet's delight. Not only do they serve an eclectic blend of tasty contemporary cuisine with European flair, but they pair the right wine with various foods and offer them as a package. This takes all the guess work out of the equation, resulting in a palate-pleasing meal every time, while allowing a variety of wines to be tasted and enjoyed. The pairings come in three- or four-course meals. Each course is accompanied by a different wine chosen to complement the flavors of the food. The price is extremely reasonable, and it is well worth experimenting with different combinations. Entrees include such specialties as salmon filet with phyllo crust, served with sun-dried tomato risotto, basil mayonnaise and asparagus; or a grilled duck breast with black thai rice, apricot glaze, macadamia nuts and pea shoots. Undercurrent is one of the premier restaurants in the Piedmont Triad, winning numerous *Wine Spectator* awards and the approval of critics. It is an ever-evolving entity whose goal will always be to increase the satisfaction of guests. Anyone who appreciates exceptional food paired with excellent wine would be well advised to try Undercurrent.

600 S Elm Street, Greensboro NC (336) 370-1266 www.undercurrentrestaurant.com

223 South Elm

Before you head out to see the latest Triad Stage production or catch a recital at Carolina Stage, stop by 223 South Elm. Located in the historic Southside neighborhood of Greensboro, this friendly bistro features a cathedral ceiling and light woodwork for a very open atmosphere. Grab a drink at the bar or dine upstairs with a balcony view of the first-floor dining area. Lunch and dinner emphasize Southern-style fare with an upscale twist. The lunch menu ranges from the more standard daily specials, such as Thursday's barbecue chicken wings with slaw and blue cheese dressing, to unique creations like roasted chicken breast with cumin, cilantro, oatmeal, and habanero barbecue sauce. Dinner entrées are just as varied, such as boiled quail eggs or apricot pink peppercorn tarragon marmalade expertly matched with certified Angus rib eye, rack of lamb, tuna and venison for flavor enhancing balance. To quench your thirst, choose from 19 different martinis and more than 614 bottles of wine. Weekly live jazz adds to the ambience. Visit 223 South Elm next time you're on the south side.

223 S Elm Street, Greensboro NC
(336) 272-3331   www.223southelm.com

Flying Fish

Flying Fish is a neighborhood bistro where folks can stop in for a quick bite or gather with friends over a leisurely meal. The extensive and diverse menu was designed to make enjoying yourself easy, and offers everything from soup to nuts. Here you can sample individually plated appetizers while you sip a glass of wine and unwind from your day, or you can share a platter and a bottle with the gang while catching up on the week's events. Ultimately, Owner Phil Campbell's goal is for his patrons to have a good time and enjoy the friendly, fun atmosphere. Flying Fish isn't Campbell's' first foray into the restaurant world; he also owns the popular Flying Burrito in Chapel Hill. This latest addition to the Flying family is located in the old James Pharmacy on Churton Street, and provides the same fabulous service as its sister site. Fresh fish is delivered thrice weekly from the coast and then transformed on-site into marvelous tuna tacos, grilled salmon and spinach enchiladas. The catfish burritos that are simply to die for. Flying Burrito offers a terrific vegetarian menu filled with fabulous entrées that will quickly become favorites. Bring your buddies or grab the family and head to the Flying Fish where great food and great fun come together.

111 N Churton Street, Hillsborough NC
(919) 245-0040

Bert's Seafood Grille

The most trusting barometer of a restaurant's quality is good old-fashioned word of mouth. If you read what the food critics say about Bert's Seafood Grille in Greensboro, it would be a good start. But when you consider that for 18 years Bert's has been handed the Golden Fork Award for Best Seafood in an area magazine's reader survey, you realize you can't go wrong at this eatery. Owners Mary and Drew Lacken have figured out the formula for success in Greensboro. Opened in 1988 as a more upscale alternative to the usual Southern-style fried fish, Bert's menu includes delicious variations on blue fish, mahi mahi, shark and sea bass. There are heart-healthy recipes, vegetarian cuisine and, for meat lovers, lamb, pork, chicken and game. While most restaurants brag about their fresh ingredients, the Lackens back it up with an herb and vegetable garden right outside where chili peppers, tomatoes and other spices get their start. Even the dessert menu is an intriguing mesh of non-traditional confections, such as white chocolate banana bread pudding, chocolate Kahlua mousse and wild huckleberry pie. It's no wonder Bert's has captured local acclaim for so many years. It's your turn to get reeled in at Bert's Seafood Grille.

4608 W Market Street, Greensboro NC
(336) 854-2314
www.bertsseafood.com

Bistro Sofia

Named after owner and chef Beth Kizhnerman's grandmother, Bistro Sofia is a French bistro like no other in the Greensboro area. Satisfied patrons can thank Kizhnerman for her studiousness. After graduating from the New England Culinary Institute, she interned at Season's in Boston and L'Auberge Bretonne in Britanny, France. She paid attention to detail, something that is apparent throughout the Bistro Sofia experience. Walk into the two-story brick building and choose between an indoor dining room decorated with framed menus from around the world that date back to the 1800s, or an outdoor patio in the brick courtyard out back. The Bistro features a menu of French cuisine with Asian and Eastern European flavors that earned Bistro Sofia a Golden Fork award for Best French Restaurant and Best Bistro three years in a row. A *prix fixe* menu lets you enjoy three courses for one great price. Choose from four main dishes: Moroccan fried organic chicken breast, steak frites, baked phyllo-wrapped trout fillets or spinach, rainbow kale and herbed ricotta tart. All dishes feature fresh herbs and vegetables from the on-site garden, as Kizhnerman is a big proponent of organic, sustainable farming. Two upstairs private dining rooms, one with a fireplace, can accommodate parties of 20, and off-site catering is available, as well. For an Eiffel Tower of incredible flavors, visit Bistro Sofia.

*616 Dolley Madison Road,
Greensboro NC
(336) 855-1313
www.bistrosofia.com*

Wooden Nickel Public House

Matt Fox and Matt Meek are the force behind Wooden Nickel Public House in Hillsborough. Matt is a graduate of the University of Cincinnati with a degree in economics. He spent several years with the Decanthes group, specializing in historic restoration and eventually decided to make historic Hillsborough his home. Matt Fox has worked in kitchens from Ohio to Florida and had accrued seven years of kitchen management experience before teaming with Matt. The Wooden Nickel Public House is the kind of small pub experience that brings a community together, with opportunities for rubbing elbows with neighbors over a cold draft beer and home-cooked food. Fresh peanuts fuel the appetite, while on a cold day, steamy acorn squash soup provides an aromatic and tasty way to warm up. Live music is featured frequently, but when the band is away, a jukebox keeps things lively. On Friday evenings, people will gather to play games such as checkers. This is a family pub where everyone is welcome. Whether you live nearby or hundreds of miles away, stop by and join the fun at the Wooden Nickel.

105 N Churton Street, Hillsborough NC (919) 643-2223 www.woodennickelpub.com

The General Store Café

In 1979, when two prominent women of Pittsboro opened a small natural foods store in the Hall-London house, they didn't realize they were starting a legacy that would become one of the most popular gathering spots in the Triangle. More than 25 years and several owners later, that little store has morphed into The General Store Café, a combination restaurant, cultural center and community gathering spot that has garnered headlines. Al Roker of the *Today Show* came to see what the buzz is about. *Bon Appétit* applauded the café's burritos. *Southern Living* wrote it up. Basically, the General Store Café is a fantastic gathering spot that thrives because people love it. The café walls display the works of a different Chatham artist monthly. Live music spills out several nights a week. Fundraisers for local charities are scheduled here with regularity, including the Burrito Bash, which takes place on the first Monday of each month to benefit different grassroots organizations. Lost in all of this is the fact that the General Store Café, which is no longer a health foods store, serves breakfast, lunch and dinner six days a week, plus Sunday brunch. Next time you're in Pittsboro, check it out. It's a trip.

39 W Street, Pittsboro NC
(919) 542-2432
www.generalstorecafe.com

Tupelo's

To fully appreciate what Tupelo's offers, consider the name. Tupelo honey is produced from the Tupelo gum tree which grows throughout the southeastern United States. Owners Matthew and Tracy Carroll chose the name from this sweet honey they have flown in for some of their dishes. They chose Hillsborough as the site of Tupelo's in 2000, because they felt it had a quaint, small-town feel with a large sense of community. The entire menu has a Southeastern flair. Open for lunch and dinner, Tupelo's specializes in Creole-accented Southern fare such as New Orleans gumbo, jambalaya, fried green tomatoes and red beans and rice. Hot sandwiches include blackened catfish with Tabasco aioli and Cajun turkey club with tasso ham. If you really want something exquisite try an oyster po'boy. For dinner, specialties such as Bayou voodoo shrimp, carpetbagger New York strip steak and crawfish ravioli are a few of the many palate-pleasers available. Finish the night off with Bananas Foster or a favorite of the French Quarter, crème brulée. Come by on a Tuesday evening and take advantage of their 50 percent off bottles of wine. Where to go when you're looking for a sweet meal at a reasonable price? That's a big easy, go to Tupelo's in Hillsborough.

101 N Churton Street,
Hillsborough NC
(919) 643-7722

Gagliardo's Grill

Troy Gagliardo grew up in a family that loved to cook. When he decided to pursue his own passion for cooking, Gagliardo's Grill was born. The grill is a neighborhood place with the warm, brick-lined walls and cozy feeling of a Tuscan-style restaurant in Italy. Nearly all the dishes, from meat and vegetables to pizza and pineapple dessert, are grilled over open hickory flames. There isn't a microwave or fryer in the building. When Troy saw a chef on television make an apple pie on a grill he thought to himself, "Why can't I make a pizza on the grill?" The result, after 11 years of experimentation, was a duct-tape bound book of secret recipes that Troy and his partner Clark Brewer jokingly call the bible. Gagliardo's offers a nice selection of wines, including four from a small Gagliardo vineyard in Northern Italy. The next time you're in historic Mooresville be sure to stop by Gagliardo's Grill, where the food meets the flame.

427 E Statesville Avenue, Mooresville NC   (704) 662-0344   www.gagliardosgrill.com

Blue Fin's Bistro

Born and raised in Raleigh, David Berent attended the University of North Carolina at Wilmington in 1998. During his college years, he worked in and managed several area restaurants. He gained experience in most every position of the restaurant business, including management, which he maintained for two years prior to his graduation in 2002. With a degree in communication studies and extensive restaurant knowledge, David decided it was time to bring his talents back home. In 2004, plans to build Blue Fin's Bistro began unfolding. David researched Raleigh and surrounding areas until he found a home for his dream. His search ended when he found just the right location inside Heritage Wake Forest. Blue Fin's Bistro opened its doors in March of 2005. Its warm mango-colored walls are decorated with local artwork, giving the restaurant a distinctly comfortable chic. The dining room offers plenty of space to seat large parties while offering cozy nooks for more private dinners. Living up to its name, the restaurant offers a variety of seafood dishes, including David's incredible New England clam chowder, bacon-wrapped scallops, and shrimp scampi linguini in lobster cream sauce. David takes pride in every dish that leaves the kitchen and incorporates his Italian heritage into many nightly specials. David's dream was to bring the coast home and create a place where every guest felt like family. He has succeeded. Come see for yourself at Blue Fin's Bistro.

3652 Rogers Road, Wake Forest NC
(919) 562-1118
www.bluefinsbistro.com

The Prickly Pear

In the 1400s, a group of Jesuit priests made five sets of portable rafters in Venum, Portugal. Used to construct missions, the rafters could be removed after the building was completed. One set made its way through Mexico, New Mexico, Camp Lejeune and, finally, to a church in Mooresville. The 500-year-old rafters, with bronze bracing, are still in the church, but the church is now The Prickly Pear, owned by an eclectic group of culinary visionaries. The Prickly Pear features modern Mexican cuisine with a European influence and was named 2004 Best Mexican Restaurant by *Creative Loafing.* Fresh blue marlin, wild salmon and seafood plates are served with a beurre blanc sauce and fresh papaya or mango. The restaurant offers a rainbow of specialty cocktails and margaritas along with Hibiscus flower iced tea or lemonade, espresso, cappuccino, specialty waters and sodas. You'll find tableside preparation of guacamole, tamales steamed in banana leaves, organic chicken breasts tenderly stuffed with cheeses and fresh vegetables, and spinach in a roasted poblano-avocado sauce. Live music includes classical and jazz guitar along with a Mexican oboist. This notable venue can accommodate semi-private cocktail or dinner parties of 10 to 25 people. Catering is available for up to 150 people. Going out for Mexican fare will be a delicious new experience at The Prickly Pear.

761 N Main Street, Mooresville NC   (704) 799-0875   www.pricklypear.net

The Grape Vine of Graham

The Grape Vine of Graham is a delightful coffeeshop serving American fare in the tasty Southern style. You can stop by for breakfast, lunch or dinner. For breakfast, try the eggs, an omelette or the pancakes. Of course, be sure to have some genuine old-fashioned grits on the side. For lunch, the hamburgers are top-notch. Southern fried chicken is great for either lunch or dinner, and be sure to try the pies. The Grape Vine is a friendly place where everyone will soon know your name. Graham itself the county seat of Alamance County, a historic textile center and home of the Alamance Plaids, the first commercially produced plaids manufactured in the Southern United States. The Grape Vine is a popular site for group meetings. The private room can accommodate from 30 to 50 guests. Your hostess is owner Gale Varinoski, who invites you to be at home at the Grape Vine of Graham.

614 W Harden Street, Graham WI   (336) 228-1755

Shucker's Oyster Bar

Are you in the mood for a beach party, but don't want to get sand in your shoes? Then put up the suntan oil and surfboards and head to Shucker's Oyster Bar. Shucker's has been serving the Wake Forest, Raleigh and Greater Triangle area for more than 20 years. *Spectator* magazine calls it "a pearl of a find," and we think you'll agree. Shucker's Oyster Bar is the only Triangle area restaurant to serve fresh steamed oysters shucked for you tableside. The friendly and up-beat staff uses a combined 150 years of experience to both serve and prepare the best seafood around. Stimulate your appetite with a few beginning appetizers. Once you're done clearing away the beginning goodies, dive right into one of Shucker's great entrées or all-you-can-eat crab legs. Can't decide? Try one of the combinations, such as Shucker's Sloop, a hearty fisherman's delight of mixed sausage, grilled shrimp, onions, peppers, potatoes and Cajun spices. Little ones can join in the fun with their own beach menu filled with kid-friendly choices like chicken strips, hot dogs, and fish and chips. If possible, save room for the Oyster Bar's signature Key lime pie, a zippy and refreshing end to a fantastic feast. Bottom line: Shucker's Oyster Bar offers the best seafood in the Triangle—without all the sand.

10625 Capital Boulevard, Wake Forest NC   (919) 556-7704   www.shuckersoysterbar.com

S & T's Soda Shoppe

Walking into S & T's Soda Shoppe is like stepping into the past. Right away you will be touched by the details that bring to mind an early 1900s soda shoppe. Owner Gene Oldham took great care to restore a building that was originally built to be a drug store and soda fountain, right down to adding a tin ceiling and a marble countertop with bar stools. The mahogany furniture was brought in from an old drug store in Mebane and each piece was carefully restored to its original beauty, giving S & T's an atmosphere that is hard to find anywhere today. S & T's is a place where young and old alike gather to enjoy an old-fashioned chocolate malt or tasty sandwich. It is often frequented by local sports teams and their fans who are celebrating a game well played. Known to many as Pittsboro's Hidden Treasure, S & T's Soda Shoppe is named after Gene's two sons Steve and T.J. Visit S & T's Soda Shoppe to experience Gene and Vicky's dream. Come enjoy a shake and a smile while you reminisce about the past and make memories for the future.

85 Hillsboro Street,
Pittsboro NC
(919) 545-0007

B. Christopher's Restaurant

The tradition of dinner is the very essence of the B. Christopher's experience. At B. Christopher's, you will have time to enjoy the sensational aromas wafting from the kitchens and the easy conversations that flow between friends and family. Here, you'll find time to soak in the genteel ambience that surrounds you. Relax and savor every bite with the accompaniment of wine poured into a long stemmed glass. Entrées that are not only delicious, but also a beautiful celebration of the food itself, await you. B. Christopher's encourages its patrons to deeply experience each laugh, each friendly toast, each bite and each moment. B. Christopher's offers a menu filled with perfectly prepared dishes that are created to be savored. Popular entrées from the menu include the spicy seared rib eye, Creole shrimp pasta and the marvelous stuffed pork chop, which is filled with apricot chutney and cream cheese, then slowly baked to a tender perfection and topped with onion crisps. This elegant eatery also features a wonderful selection of wines and other fine libations to complement your meal. B. Christopher's invites you, your family and your friends to a refreshing and delightful dining experience that celebrates good food, good company and delightful conversation.

2461 S Church Street, Burlington NC
(336) 222-1177
www.bchrisophers.com

Northern Piedmont Lifestyle Destinations

Cambridge Hills

The town of Pittsboro has a long tradition of independence and pride in its fortitude. In keeping with that spirit, Cambridge Hills offers independent living in a caring community atmosphere. This compassionate neighborhood features 31 cozy apartments. The staff provides transportation, meals, activities and outings. Game playing and bingo are just some of the social opportunities available to members of the community. The staff runs errands for residents once a week, and appointments can be made for in-house pedicures and/or manicures. The apartments are within walking distance to the library, banks, churches and restaurants. There is very low staff turnover, creating a setting that is warm, familiar, safe and comfortable. Cleaning days are assigned at the resident's discretion. For a nominal monthly fee added into the rent, pets under 20 pounds are allowed to live in the homes. The menu is filled with traditional Southern food, and local residents bring freshly picked garden vegetables regularly. There is a casual, home-style spirit to the surroundings with family and friends often dropping by for lunch. Cambridge Hills is more than a facility, it is a home. Come and feel the difference at Cambridge Hills Independent. You will want to stay.

25 Rectory Street, Pittsboro NC
(919) 545-0149

Daniel Stowe Botanical Gardens

Statue Downtown Concord

Cypress of Charlotte

"STORY TIME"
BY GARY PRICE
A GIFT TO THE COMMUNITY
FROM THE
MARGARET McCONNELL HOLT ART FUND
AND THE
CONCORD-CABARRUS FRIENDS OF THE LIBRARY
2001

Southern Piedmont

Downtown Charlotte

Southern Piedmont Accommodations

The VanLandingham Estate Inn and The Morehead Inn

The VanLandingham Estate Inn and The Morehead Inn are the types of places most people envision when they think of the elegant old South. These sophisticated inns, operated by the same owner, offer a unique combination of hospitality, grace, subtle ambience and fine foods. Listed on the National Register of Historic Places, the VanLandingham Estate features nine guest rooms, breathtaking antiques, timeless architecture and five acres of gardens. The Morehead Inn, just minutes from uptown Charlotte, sits in one of the city's most picturesque neighborhoods. Built in 1917, the Morehead Inn offers spacious public areas, luxurious private rooms and a lovely four-bedroom carriage house.

The VanLandingham Estate Inn & Conference Center: *2010 The Plaza, Charlotte NC (704) 334-8909 or (888) 524-2020 www.vanlandinghamestate.com*
The Morehead Inn: *1122 E Morehead Street, Charlotte NC (704) 376-3357 or (888) MOREHEAD (667-3432) www.moreheadinn.com*

Duke Mansion

One of the most luxurious bed and breakfasts in the Carolinas is located in a historic mansion in the heart of Charlotte. Built in 1915 and now on the National Register of Historic Places, Duke Mansion was once home to the legendary Duke family of North Carolina. It provides true Southern splendor, combining the charm of the Old South with 21st century innovations. Offering 20 elegantly decorated rooms and lavish seasonal menus for breakfast, brunch and more, Duke Mansion will make you feel like the honored guests who once visited the Duke family here. You will enjoy amenities ranging from goose down pillows to five-course dinners. Entering through the grand hall and crossing the original marble floors, you may think you've stepped into the past, but as a guest of Duke Mansion you'll be able to take advantage of cutting-edge technology, such as personal voicemail on your room's telephone and a dedicated data port for laptop access. Duke Mansion also offers meeting room space overseen by professional event planners. The mansion can accommodate as many as 200 guests for events. With its verdant gardens, romantic past and formal elegance, the mansion is a special favorite for wedding receptions, and newlyweds often reserve the mansion's most luxurious room, the Dowd Suite, for their honeymoon.

400 Hermitage, Charlotte NC
(704) 714-4448
www.dukemansion.com

Club K-9 of Charlotte

Charlotte has always attracted innovation and vision. Club K-9 dog kennel is a beautiful manifestation of that spirit. This is no ordinary dog kennel. Located in a converted warehouse in Charlotte's trendy NoDa neighborhood, the spacious play area and well appointed suites provide a carefree vacation for the pets of owners who are staying over for big game weekends. Owner J.P. Brewer and her staff interview the visitors to see if they can play well with the other guests at Club K-9. Custom-made lounge chairs, mood music and soft lighting work to relax the furry guests. Overnight service includes elevated beds, a belly rub and night time snacks. The term kennel seems out of place here. The design is more like that of a luxury day-care center. Brewer has a background in physical therapy. As a loving dog owner, she has personally experienced the concern that ensues when someone else is watching your dog. Club K-9 keeps pets busy and happily occupied during their stay with plenty of exercise, as well as opportunities for socialization. For pets recovering from surgery or with social issues, a VIP (very individualized playtime) program with a staff member ensures that these pets receive the optimal attention and physical exertion appropriate to their conditions. Club K-9, which recently opened a second location in Pineville, also provides dog obedience training, veterinary services, bathing and grooming. Show your companion how much you care with a vacation at Club K-9 of Charlotte.

2001 N Davidson Street, Charlotte NC
(704) 376-0801
www.clubk-9charlotte.com

Allen Tate Company

H. Allen Tate Jr. founded the Allen Tate Company in 1957 as a one-office firm in Charlotte. Since that time, Allen Tate Company has grown to become one of the leading real estate companies in the Carolinas. With 37 offices from Burlington to Lancaster, South Carolina, and more than 1,400 real estate professionals and 400 employees, the Allen Tate Company offers the advantage of hometown service with international capabilities and the latest in technology. The company's full-time sales professionals work to fulfill one objective: customer service. This mission has helped Allen Tate Company become the largest real estate firm in the region and one of the top, private real estate firms in the country. The Allen Tate organization has grown into a family of companies that includes Allen Tate Mortgage Services, Allen Tate Insurance, Builder Services Inc., Home Services and Master Title Services. Allen Tate Company offers one-stop shopping and a plethora of choices, giving consumers a complete approach to real estate.

6700 Fairview Road, Charlotte NC
(704) 365-6910 or (800) 210-0321
www.allentate.com

The Manor House

If you are in the process of planning your fantasy wedding, The Manor House can make all of your dreams for a perfect and distinctive wedding and reception come true. Since 1999, owners Kevin and Della Conner Helms have been coordinating romantic and classic weddings for happy couples around the nation. The Manor House is a stunning Southern plantation-style home featuring double front porches and that sits high on a tree-shrouded hill in historic Waxhaw, just minutes from Charlotte. On the beautifully designed two-and-a-half acres, you will discover a courtyard fountain, pergola, arbor, spring house and lovely gardens. The Manor House provides a 3,000-square-foot, climate-controlled and fully-lined tent, complete with black and white tiled floor, chandeliers, French doors and a 12-foot by 40-foot raised stage. Della and her exemplary staff can help you plan and design every aspect of your wedding and reception. Among the services provided are catering, wedding cakes, photographers, videographers, florals, directing, clergy, musicians, bands, disc jockeys, horse and carriage, formal wear, invitations, plus bed-and-breakfast accommodations. For a tour of this incredible home and its beautiful grounds, please contact The Manor House for an appointment. After determining your individual needs and desires, you will be provided with a personalized proposal addressing all aspects of your dream wedding and reception at The Manor House.

9124 Providence Road South, Waxhaw NC
(704) 843-7514
www.manorhousewaxhaw.com

The Dunhill Hotel

In the heart of uptown Charlotte, the historic Dunhill Hotel harkens back to the days of lavish rail travel and grand hotels. The distinctive architecture and opulent appointments lend historic texture to Charlotte's burgeoning artistic and cultural district. It is a true boutique hotel popular with artists, writers and musicians, including Paul McCartney, who stayed here while on tour. Every amenity is available, including privileges at the Crown Athletic Club, Charlotte's finest fitness center. Opened as the Mayfair Manor in 1929, the Dunhill is Charlotte's first member of Historic Hotels of America. The elegant guestrooms boast 18th-century European furnishings, hand-sewn draperies and four-poster beds. The penthouse, with its fireplace, oriental rugs and two balconies, offers breathtaking views of the city. In the lavish lobby, you will be warmly welcomed. The expert and personable staff, in the tradition of extraordinary service, will provide for your every comfort. The Monticello Restaurant offers fine dining in a sophisticated atmosphere of European elegance and has been named the Best Hotel Restaurant for two consecutive years. For your special someone, the firelit Wine Cellar Room affords an intimate setting for private dining. Within walking distance of many of the city's most popular attractions, the Dunhill is an experience to be savored.

237 N Tryon Street, Charlotte NC   (704) 332-4141   www.dunhillhotel.com

Morgan Hotel and Suites

Morgan Hotel and Suites in Charlotte is an art deco, upscale and contemporary boutique hotel with a fine reputation and European flair. The outstanding decor is both enchanting and entertaining. There are 133 rooms, including 56 designer two-room suites, and 77 executive guest rooms. With high-quality furnishings, bedding and in-room amenities, the Morgan is a very comfortable place to stay. The owners strive to meet the needs of business, leisure and extended-stay travelers who who are looking for extraordinary comfort at a competitive price. The Morgan Hotel and Suites is a place that breathes character. Stay here once and you'll know what we mean.

315 E Woodlawn Road, Charlotte NC
(704) 522-0852
www.morganhotelandsuites.com

Southern Piedmont Attractions

Perry's at Southpark

Perry's At Southpark is in its 30th year of business, and business is as good as ever. Perry's has seen changes in the industry and has met the challenges and changes by adhering to traditional business practices and the philosophy that if you give a customer quality and lasting value for their money, they will return again and again. A trip to Perry's at Southpark attests to Mr. Ernest Perry's preference for tradition over trend. Massive, elegantly carved 100-year-old, 12-foot-tall oak and mahogany jewelry cases line the perimeter of the store. The cases were manufactured by Wade Manufacturing of Charlotte and reportedly delivered to Van Sleen Jewelry Store in Gastonia by mule team. When Van Sleen went out of business, Mr. Perry bought the cases to complement his store's vast inventory of fine, antique and estate jewelry. Among the oldest pieces to grace the store's cases was a diamond, pearl and emerald necklace which had been owned by a Russian Czar. The piece was acquired at an estate auction. Though Mr. Perry no longer conducts estate auctions, he conducts frequent charity auctions to raise money for the city's needy. Perry's at Southpark greeted the new millennium with a much needed expansion to accommodate. The massive wooden cases still line the walls of the store; the store's inventory is as eclectic and exotic as ever; but while his neighbors in the mall have moved around, Perry's at Southpark is right where it was 20 years ago. Recently completed mall renovations have made the store more accessible than ever. Perry's at SouthPark buys and sells jewelry every day at all price ranges. "But I've found that jewelry rises to its greatest value when it has been given as a gift and has collected lots of memories. That's when it's worth the most," says Mr. Perry.

4400 Sharon Road, Charlotte NC
(704) 364-1391
www.perrysjewelry.com

The English Carriage Company

The English Carriage Company offers historic, imposing and majestic limousine service from the by-gone days of carriages. Their splendid, hand-built vintage and classic cars are expertly maintained by a dedicated staff and presented to you in outstanding condition. Their cars have all the space, comfort and luxurious refinements one would expect from Rolls Royce and Bentley master craftsmen. They boast sumptuous interiors of luxurious Connolly hide leather seating, highly polished burr walnut wood trims, Wilton carpets and covered foot rests. The owner, Dan De La Portilla, succeeded at offering the finest limosine service in the Carolinas. Check out his company's website to view the impressive vehicles that are waiting to carry you away. The company's immaculately attired, fully uniformed chauffers will drive you in a graceful and relaxing manner that befits your special occasion. In attendance throughout, they will offer you assistance both when entering and leaving the car, and provide the very highest standards of professionalism and personal service. For your special occasion, whether it is a wedding, anniversary, birthday, prom, banquet or night on the town, ride in a dazzling Rolls Royce, Bentley or Jaguar from The English Carriage Company.

445 Walnut Avenue, Charlotte NC
(704) 488-7800
www.englishcarriage.com

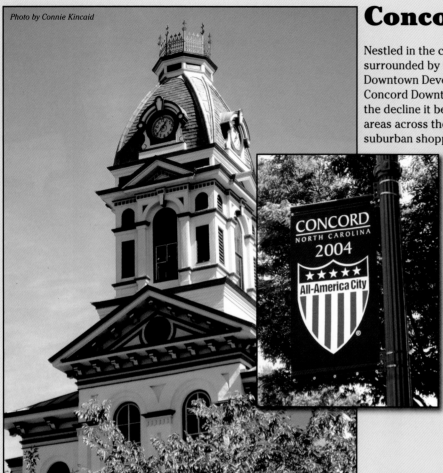

Photo by Connie Kincaid

Concord Downtown

Nestled in the center of Concord is a quaint historic downtown district surrounded by turn-of-the-century mansions. Overseen by the Concord Downtown Development Corporation, a not-for-profit group formed in 1989, Concord Downtown has brought the city's central business district back from the decline it began to suffer in the 1970s when, like so many other downtown areas across the nation, it began to lose businesses as shoppers gravitated to suburban shopping malls. Concord Downtown isn't just surviving, it's thriving. Shoppers tired of impersonal chain stores flock to such downtown businesses as ice cream shops, restaurants, coffee shops and taverns. Concord's rich history also draws many visitors to sites such as the 1876 Cabarrus County Courthouse, once threatened by demolition, and Memorial Garden, the three-acre cemetery of the 200-year-old First Presbyterian Church, once an eyesore and now restored to its former beauty thanks to the generosity of Sally Phifer Williamson and her son Marshal. The development corporation continues to implement plans for revitalizing Concord. Art galleries, antique shops, apparel and jewelry stores draw more visitors and demonstrate once again that declining downtowns are a trend that can be reversed with hard work and a sense of community commitment.

30 Cabarrus Avenue W, Concord NC
(704) 784-4208
www.concorddowntown.com

Zuma Fun Center

Grab the gang from the office or pack up your kids' soccer team and head to Zuma Fun Center in Pineville. An ideal place to celebrate a big win or stimulate some corporate camaraderie, the keyword here is fun. Kids of all ages can forget their cares and concentrate on the important things in life, such as laughing and smiling. This recreational powerhouse offers a wealth of enjoyable and engaging activities such as batting cages, bumper boats, mini-golf and Go-Karts, along with a soft play area and selection of kiddie rides for little visitors. Zuma Fun Center also has a fabulous arcade filled with favorites old and new, from the latest video games to air hockey and skee ball. Many of the games in the arcade award tickets that can later be traded at the redemption center for great prizes. Zuma Fun Center is an advocate of education, offering a reward program for school-age children where youngsters are encouraged to bring in their latest report cards and earn game tokens for their As and Bs. The Center is the perfect place to host your next team event, birthday party, reunion or company picnic. Corporate rates are available for businesses that wish to attend the park during normal hours, or the entire park can be rented for exclusive use. Zuma Fun Center has meal times and provides a family-friendly menu featuring pizza, wings and other popular snacks. Come out and play at Zuma Fun Center.

10400 Cadillac Street, Pineville NC
(704) 552-7888

SilverFox Limos

Since they were first seen rolling down the road during the roaring '20s, limousines have been an established symbol of wealth and status. Today, many of the upper echelon still use these beautifully crafted, luxury automobiles in their everyday lives. Fortunately, thanks to SilverFox Limos, you don't have to be a millionaire to ride around in style. Owner James Weymann came to North Carolina from Guatemala with his family at the age of two. After his high school graduation, he began a career in the printing business while working for a limousine service on the weekends and evenings. His love for the business grew and SilverFox Limos was the result of that love. Due to his care and innovations, the business has developed a reputation for excellence from even the most demanding of clients. In 2004, Richard Davis joined the crew as James' business partner. SilverFox strives to provide each guest with a comfortable and relaxing ride. SilverFox is the official limousine service for the Charlotte Bobcats, Clear Channel Radio Charlotte, Verizon Wireless amphitheater and St. Mary's Chapel, along with several other prominent businesses and local celebrities. They also served as the official transportation service for the Miss United States and Miss United States Teen Competitions in 2005. SilverFox has several fabulous limousines, new Towncars, mini-buses and vans, and can provide luxury transportation to any special event in Charlotte and the surrounding counties. Make getting there more than half the fun with SilverFox Limos.

4328 Deepwood Drive, Charlotte NC
(704) 622-9944
www.silverfoxlimos.com

Burgin Academy of Scottish Dance Arts

Today's contemporary Scottish dancing took root during the mid-16th century and went on to grow and flourish well into the 1800s. Intricate reels, rounds, pavans and bransles, accompanied by bagpipes, fiddles or a full dance band, delight and invigorate both the dancers and the spectators. These traditional Scottish dances are still performed and taught around the world and are popular with people of all ages. If you are interested in learning this fabulous art, move your feet over to the Burgin Academy of Scottish Dance Arts in Charlotte. This wonderful dance academy is owned and operated by Anne Burgin Andrews and her daughter Elaine Burgin. Anne and Elaine have created quite a buzz of enthusiasm and have put Scottish highland dancing on the map in North Carolina. Their primary goals are to maintain a high standard of excellence and to help their students perform at their best so they can compete anywhere in the world. Anne is well recognized for her teaching accomplishments and has been awarded both the Saint Andrews College Laurinburg Award and the Flora MacDonald Award. Additionally, Anne is a Scottish official board adjudicator and a life member of the British Association of Teachers of Dance. Elaine has won the regional championships 10 times and has several times been runner-up at the United Stated Interregional Highland Dance Championships. Anne, Elaine and the Burgin Academy have been providing expert training in the art of Scottish Dance since 1957. They are looking forward to sharing their knowledge, skills and enthusiasm with you at the Burgin Academy of Scottish Dance Arts.

201 Hillside Avenue, Charlotte NC
(704) 332-2761

Streaming Morning Light Photo by Marty Hulsebos HighCountryImages.com

Charlotte Bobcats and Charlotte Sting

The Charlotte Bobcats are the National Basketball Association's 30th franchise. The team opened its inaugural season on November 4, 2004 with a sellout crowd at the Charlotte Coliseum. In the 2004 NBA draft, the Bobcats selected Emeka Okafor after he led the University of Connecticut to the NCAA championship. Okafor won the Rookie of the Year award after leading all rookies in scoring and rebounding. Charlotte is proud of both the Bobcats and its Women's National Basketball Association team, the Charlotte Sting. Founded in 1996, the Sting has been a strong franchise from the beginning, making it to the playoffs in six of nine years since its formation. Former Charlotte NBA star Muggsy Bogues leads the Sting as head coach. Both teams are owned by Robert L. Johnson, founder of Black Entertainment Television and one of America's most successful entrepreneurs. Chosen as the most influential minority in sports by *Sports Illustrated*, Johnson is the first African-American to become the majority owner of a professional sports organization. Johnson announced in June 2006 that Michael Jordan, perhaps the greatest player of all time, has become part owner of the Bobcats. Both teams play in the Charlotte Bobcats Arena in uptown Charlotte.

www.bobcatsbasketball.com
www.charlottesting.com

Charlotte Bobcats Arena

Groundbreaking for the Charlotte Bobcats Arena began in July 2003, signaling the beginning of a new era for Charlotte sports fans. Completed in the fall of 2005, the arena spans nine acres in the heart of uptown Charlotte and can hold as many people as a 37-story building. This is the home of the NBA's Charlotte Bobcats, the WNBA's Charlotte Sting, and the Charlotte Checkers of the East Coast Hockey League. Basketball and hockey are only part of the story at this arena, which hosts at least 125 events each year. It has ideal acoustics for musical performances, and the grandstands and floors can be easily reconfigured for family shows or monster truck shows. The venue combines terrific views, seats with extra legroom and a wide variety of restaurants and social areas for pre-game and post-game gatherings. The sightlines for the building were created with the spectator in mind, putting fans right on top of the action. The arena features interactive areas for adults and children and five restaurants to tempt your taste

Smith Mountain Lake

Paramount Carowinds

Excitement awaits kids, young and old, at Paramount's Carowinds, a 108-acre theme and water park straddling the state line between North Carolina and South Carolina. The park, one of the most popular in the Southeast, offers Hollywood-style entertainment, including a variety of shows, concerts, special events and Boomerang Bay, a 16-acre, Australian-themed water park. Some of the park's more thrilling attractions include BORG Assimilator, the first roller coaster in the world to carry a Star Trek theme, where guests fly facedown at 50 miles per hour in a superhero-like position, and Top Gun: The Jet Coaster, an inverted steel coaster sending fighter pilots on a high-flying, 62-mile per hour adventure. The park's kids' area, Nickelodeon Central, features a 15-acre playground with 20 attractions, including the Phantom Flyers, where guests glide and swoop through the air with superhero Danny Phantom. Annual holiday attractions include Nights of Fire, a Fourth of July fireworks celebration; Scarowinds, the largest and spookiest Halloween event in the Carolinas; and WinterFest, a winter wonderland featuring more than one million lights. Paramount's Carowinds is owned and operated by Paramount Parks, a unit of CBS Broadcasting Inc. In operation since 1973, Paramount's Carowinds is a place that will make your visit one to remember for a long, long time.

14523 Carowinds Boulevard, Charlotte NC
North Carolina: (704) 588-2600 South Carolina: (803) 548-5300
Toll Free: (800) 888-4386
www.carowinds.com

George Pappas' Park Lanes and Liberty Lanes

George Pappas, known as "The General," was a professional bowler from 1969 to 1992, during which time he won 10 tournaments, including the Tournament of Champions in 1979. He served as chairman of the National Professional Tournament Committee for 10 years and is a force to be reckoned with on the PBA Senior Tours with two PBA Senior Titles, including the PBA Senior Open in Johnson City, Tennessee in April 2005. When George was a child, his father owned a restaurant above a bowling alley. Twenty years ago, George acquired his own bowling center, Park Lanes in Charlotte. It did so well that he acquired Liberty Lanes in Gastonia, as well. The buildings bear the style of classic 1950s bowling alleys on the outside, but inside they feature high-tech equipment and the latest bowling innovations. At Park Lanes and Liberty Lanes, there is respect for tradition as well as innovation. In the bowling alley restaurants, there's a special recipe for the homemade, individually dipped onion rings that hasn't changed in 45 years. They sell like hot cakes, so why tamper with success?

Park Lanes: *700 Montford Drive, Charlotte NC* *(704) 523-7633*
Liberty Lanes: *2501 S York Road, Gastonia NC* *(704) 868-2695*

Sullivan Dance Center

Sullivan Dance Center in Charlotte was the area's first private dance studio when it opened in 1952. Today, Sullivan Dance Center continues to train amazing performers in a myriad of dance techniques, including ballroom and tap. Originally founded by Bob Sullivan, this dynamic dance center is operated by daughter Melanie Sullivan-Coyle with the help of her husband, Mike, and the support of her son, Manuel, who is currently dancing his way across Broadway stages. Sullivan Dance Center offers numerous and varied classes for adults and children, as well as sponsoring several public events annually. Sullivan Dance Center is the home of the Charlotte-based, non-profit dance company the Queen City Jazz Company, which has been touted as a force to be reckoned with in the world of dance. Melanie serves as the artistic director for this fabulous company. Melanie is a four-time finalist in the Leo's Choreography Competitive Event, which is sponsored by Gus Giordano's Jazz Dance World Congress. Melanie continues to teach at the school and has had several students who have won coveted scholarships to such prominent institutions as the School of American Ballet, Carnegie Mellon and the Tremaine Dance Center. Melanie also has several students who have preformed professionally in such shows as *Cabaret* and *Sweet Charity*. Let the dancer in you take flight with Melanie Sullivan-Coyle and the Sullivan Dance Center.

9506 Old Monroe Road, Charlotte NC   (704) 708-4474

Charlotte Symphony Orchestra

The Charlotte Symphony Orchestra, known as the CSO, is the largest and most active professional performing arts assemblage in the central Carolinas. The CSO offers more than 115 performances from September through the first week in July. Additionally, they perform free Summer Pops concerts in their summer home at Symphony Park, which has become a Charlotte tradition. Each season, CSO performs for more than 250,000 people, presenting a breathtaking array of classics and pops, along with participating in neighborhood concert programs all across the region. The orchestra also offers summer Lollipops Family programs, which are events that take one of CSO's popular programs out of the theater and into the spotlight at Symphony Park. The Charlotte Symphony Orchestra was founded in 1932 and has performed with world-renowned guests such as the first lady of song, Ella Fitzgerald, Ray Charles, Itzhak Perlman, James Taylor and master cellist Yo-Yo Ma. In addition to its many other efforts, CSO supports the Oratorio Singers of Charlotte, which is the largest choral organization in the Carolinas, it sponsors two youth orchestras, and serves as resident orchestra for both the North Carolina Dance Theatre and Opera Carolina. They further serve the community by performing for more than 400 educational and out-reach organizations, including Healing Hand, which takes music into area hospitals, nursing homes and retirement communities. Celebrate the symphony and 75 years of powerful musical tradition with the Charlotte Symphony Orchestra.

110-201 S College Street, Charlotte NC
(704) 972-2003
www.charlottesymphony.com

Metrolina Expo Trade Center

The Metrolina Expo Trade Center is one of Charlotte's largest and most versatile event facilities. For more than 30 years, Metrolina Expo (formerly the Mecklenburg Fairgrounds) has been housing some of the most exciting and popular tradeshows, concerts and events in the city. Each of the buildings on the grounds is climate controlled. On-site concessions and catering can be provided. Options for indoor exhibit space include three large exhibition halls and a 40-by-200-foot open mall area. Additionally, the grounds feature extensive outdoor display space and parking for 20,000 vehicles. Popular events at Metrolina Expo Trade Center include the monthly Charlotte Antique and Collectible Show, the largest show of its kind on the East Coast. The Expo Center hosts various car and motorcycle shows, computer shows, equipment auctions, spa and gazebo shows and more. Metrolina Expo is also ideal for corporate functions. It is the home of North Carolina Christmas Classic Arts, Crafts and Gift Show, held each Thanksgiving weekend. Owners Linda W. and Pete Pistone, along with their incredible staff, strive to make every event a special one. They are always happy to make suggestions and help organize your event so it is perfect down to the last detail. Trust your next big show, concert, fundraiser or special event to the experts at Metrolina Expo Trade Center.

7100 N Statesville Road, Charlotte NC   (704) 596-4650
www.metrolinaexpotradeshow.com

Highland Creek Golf Club

Master your swing at the Highland Creek Golf Club on the Carolina Trail. This 18-hole championship course, designed by Clifton, Ezell and Clifton, has been rated both the best and the toughest public golf course in the Charlotte area. It was designed with extra care to preserve the natural beauty of the surrounding land. Highland Creek winds through towering trees and meandering creeks. The course stretches 6,800 yards from the back tees, and features Bent grass greens, Bermuda fairways, five lakes and water features on several holes. The challenging layout provides an enjoyable adventure amidst some of the most picturesque holes in Charlotte. Experience why Highland Creek Golf Club is Charlotte's crown jewel of golf.

7001 Highland Creek Parkway, Charlotte NC
(704) 875-9000
www.highlandcreekgolfclub.com

Waterford Golf Club

Practice makes perfect at the Waterford Golf Club on The Carolina Trail. The spectacular Waterford course was designed by three-time U.S. Open Champion Hale Irwin. With towering hardwoods and proximity to the Catawba River, Waterford Golf Club is an escape to nature that you and your guests will cherish. Just 25 minutes from uptown Charlotte, Waterford provides a tranquil journey molded by Mother Nature. Artfully constructed with rolling terrain, it is a true shot-maker's course. The practice complex includes a driving range, large putting green, short-game practice area and practice bunker. This classically designed course has received rave reviews from local and national media. Visit Waterford Golf Club and all the Carolina Trail golf courses for an experience that offers both challenge and beauty.

1900 Clubhouse Road, Rock Hill SC   (803) 324-0300 or (888) 203-9222
www.thelinksatwaterford.com

The Tradition Golf Club

When traveling to Charlotte, check out The Tradition Golf Club on The Carolina Trail. This scenic golf course was cut out of dense hardwoods and towering pines and is located on the beautiful, rolling terrain of north Mecklenburg County. Because of the course's winding, tree-lined fairways, strategic shot making is the key to scoring. Opened for play in 1996, The Tradition Golf Club is a masterpiece of understated elegance, orchestrated by golf course architect John Cassell II. His layout manifests a harmonic blend of natural beauty and championship golf. The result is a majestic, tree-lined layout that delights the senses and thoroughly challenges all facets of a player's game. The course includes a 5,400-square-foot clubhouse, comfortable mixed grill for enjoyment after your round, a fully stocked pro shop, and a night-lighted driving range. Visit The Tradition and all of the Carolina Trail golf courses for an experience that offers challenge and beauty.

3800 Prosperity Church Road, Charlotte NC
(704) 503-7529
www.thetraditiongolfclub.com

The Divide Golf Club

Get into the swing of things at The Divide Golf Club on the Carolina Trail. Opened in 1995, The Divide features a traditionally designed 18-hole golf course drawn by John Cassell, II. Spacious Bermuda fairways and large undulating greens offer golfers of any skill level an entertaining challenge. The attentive and friendly staff will treat you like a member of an exclusive club. The Divide Golf Club offers banquet and dining facilities, a driving range and a well supplied pro shop. The course is surrounded by woods and is located within the Mint-Hill, Matthews area just south of Charlotte. Rain or shine, The Divide Golf Club on the Carolina Trail is a must stop on your Carolina golf tour.

6803 Stevens Mill Road, Matthews NC
(704) 882-8088   www.thedividegolfclub.com

Charlotte Golf Links

Out of bounds is what you will be if you miss the opportunity to play the Charlotte Golf Links on the Carolina Trail. Experience the challenge and charm of Scottish links-style golf. The Charlotte Golf Links is an 18-hole championship golf course designed by Tom Doak, one of the most popular golf course architects in the country. The landscape is beautiful and challenging. A game of golf here will take you alongside ponds, streams and heather. Voted Charlotte's Number One Public Course, the Charlotte Golf Links has three sets of tees for every skill level and a par of 71. The clubhouse is bordered by the 18th green for exciting views as you enjoy lunch from the Squires Grill. The driving range is night-lighted for your enjoyment throughout the season. For a tough yet enthralling round of golf, tee off at Charlotte Golf Links.

11500 Providence Road, Charlotte NC
(704) 846-7990
www.charlottegolflinks.com

The Green Uptown

Stand on any corner in Charlotte's Center City and you'll see and hear the sounds of a bustling, vibrant city. It's a little-known secret that among this hustle and bustle there is a tranquil, urban park called The Green. A gift from Wachovia Corporation to its surrounding community, the Green is a harmonious interaction of color, light and texture. Wagner Murray Architects' design reflects Wachovia's commitment to children's education. The park is filled with artwork that centers on reading and literature. Serving as the Charlotte Convention Center's front yard, The Green is located between Tryon and College Streets, and is anchored by the historic Ratcliffe Flowers Building, known now as the Ratcliffe on the Green Restaurant and Wine Bar. Listed on the National Register, this historic building with its large bay window is representative of a period when people took leisurely walks and stopped to smell the flowers. Open lawns connect St. Peter's Church and the Ratcliffe Condominiums to the Green. Lush gardens, interactive fountains and animated artwork add to the park's charm, making it an ideal urban escape. Visitors can follow the floating storybook pages that seemingly explode from the grand entry columns throughout the park, solve a literary puzzle, or stroll along the rhythm walk while listening to a playful mix of animal and water sounds. Running the entire length of the park is an enormous game board that includes hand, word and ground games that add elements of fun and entertainment to the unique aesthetic experience that is the Green. The park was thoughtfully designed with a sense of community. Alive with color and imagination, The Green is an oasis in Charlotte's Center City.

435 S Tryon Street, Charlotte NC
(704) 944-1828
www.thegreenuptown.com

Photo © Indigo Photography

Photo by Rolland Elliot Studios

Photo by Jeff Cravotta

Photo by Jeff Cravotta

Photo by Peter Brentlinger

Phillips Place

A complete shopping experience awaits in the SouthPark area, the glittering heart of Charlotte's upscale retail landscape. It is Phillips Place, where shoppers, diners and people-watchers can slow down the pace of life. This unique environment includes a variety of outstanding restaurants and specialty retail. The setting is distinctive and welcoming. Renowned for its design, Phillips Place offers the quality and amenities of a village square.

The tree-lined, pedestrian-friendly main street continues for several blocks, accented along the way by iron lampposts, park benches, sidewalk cafes and bubbling fountains. The retail mix forms a unified and complementary whole of locally owned specialty shops and nationally known luxury brands.

Discriminating shoppers can treat themselves to Jimmy Choo boots and Dolce & Gabbana fashions; Lacoste golf attire and Armani Suits; Prada sunglasses and Vera Wang bridal gowns. Retailers include Smith & Hawken and Restoration Hardware. At Phillips Place, the cuisine is just as varied as the shopping, from the European-style gourmet market Dean & Deluca to the metropolitan sophistication of The Palm. You'll find fresh seafood, Tuscan-style Italian delights and innovative Chinese dishes on the menus of popular cafes and bistros. On the lighter side, Dean & Deluca's Wine Room provides the perfect spot to enjoy wine tasting and hors d' oeuvres. Phillips Place includes salon and spa facilities, art galleries, a 10-screen movie theatre featuring stadium seating, and a beautifully appointed Hampton Inn & Suites. Charming and cosmopolitan, with an abundance of free parking, Phillips Place makes it easy for you to slip away to a world of shopping and dining adventures.

6809 Phillips Place Court,
Charlotte NC
(704) 714-7600
www.lincolnharris.com

Del Frisco's Double Eagle Steakhouse

Brio Tuscan Grille

Piedmont Row West

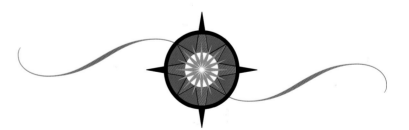

PIEDMONT

TOWN CENTER

Piedmont Town Center

Rising high above the famed SouthPark area of Charlotte, Piedmont Town Center made its market debut in dramatic style. This brand-new lifestyle center complements the upscale excitement of its surroundings. A mixed-use development featuring retail, residential and office space, Piedmont Town Center reflects the vision of some of the nation's leading developers, architects and property managers. The result of their collaboration is a place where you can live, work and play. Anchored by nationally recognized restaurants, including Del Frisco's Double Eagle Steakhouse, Brio Tuscan Grille, and The Oceanaire Seafood Room, Piedmont Town Center is accented by boutique shops that line the pedestrian-friendly street. An executive YMCA features 13,000 square feet of state-of-the-art facilities. Piedmont Town Center is front and center in Charlotte's thriving business community. Piedmont Natural Gas Company chose this site for its corporate headquarters, recognizing the value of a prime location in the second-largest economic district in North Carolina. As a shopping district, Piedmont Town Center has few equals. The circular brick-lined entrance is highlighted by a giant sunburst design and a grand fountain. The center bustles with activity day and night. Terraced restaurant seating gives diners the feel of an open-air Italian piazza. And from the upper floors, panoramic views showcase the city at its sparkling best. Piedmont Town Center is a joint venture between Lincoln Harris and Crescent Resources, two companies that continue to transform the SouthPark landscape. For selection, convenience and all the elements that make a lifestyle center desirable, Piedmont Town Center stands tall—and stands apart.

4620-4625 Piedmont Row Drive, Charlotte NC (704) 714-7600
www.piedmonttowncenter.com

Southern Piedmont
Candies, Ice Cream, Bakeries & Coffee

TEA ReX®

It's all about tea at the TEA ReX gourmet teahouse in Charlotte. Wayne Powers and his sons brew on site, the way fine teas should be brewed. They have been satisfying customers since 1997 with a vast selection of flavorful brews. Whether your taste is for herbal, floral, tannic, grassy, full-flavored, mushroomy, smooth or sharp tea, you'll find your niche. Describe what you like, they will brew it for you. Also on hand are natural juices and energy drinks, plus energy bars and other healthy nibbles. TEA ReX is the place to pick up teaware and accessories, such as kettles, strainers and teapots. All TEA ReX teas are available in airtight quarter-pound packets to take home. Make a point to stop in to TEA ReX at 4 pm for the daily serving of scones, jam and Devon clotted cream.

2102 South Boulevard, Charlotte NC
(704) 371-4440
www.tearex.com

S&D Coffee

In 1927, S&D Coffee began with a single roaster and a large dream. S&D Coffee has persevered throughout the years by never wavering from the initial core values that J. Roy Davis, Sr. instilled in his company. Now, more than 75 years later, S&D continues to grow and change. S&D has extended its service beyond the small mom-and-pop grocery stores to include large regional and national chains. In 1987, S&D opened a Retail Market Center due to public demand. Customers were stopping drivers trying to purchase S&D coffee blends off the back of their route trucks. Since that time, the Retail Market Center has grown significantly, moving from its original plant location to a beautiful new shop in The Village in Concord. They specialize in the freshest coffee and tea products available anywhere, as well as gift baskets and coffee-related items. Customers can purchase products from their homes and offices at the S&D website. Visit them at their new location or on the web.

280 Concord Parkway S, Suite 119, Concord NC
(888) 225-8055
www.sndcoffee.com

Edible Art of Charlotte

Edible Art is a family-run business that uses recipes dating back through generations. Owner Cathy DuFault and her husband David run this wonderful shop where you can actually drop in and get a slice to go. The guiding principles behind their accomplishments are to listen to their customer's needs, focus on details and produce the highest quality cakes at the best possible value, a perfect recipe for success. Wedding and birthday cakes are the focal point of the shop's creativity, but you can get a cake or special dessert for any occasion, from a corporate celebration to a tailgate party, decorated to your individual preferences. One customer drove all the way from Ohio to pick up a baby shower cake and carried it on to the shower in Atlanta. If that isn't a ringing enough endorsement, visit the shop to see some edible art for yourself.

2906 Selwyn Avenue, Charlotte NC
(704) 342-2253
www.edible-art-charlotte.com

The Smelly Cat Coffee House

What arts district would be complete without a funky and fabulous coffeehouse where the locals sit back, sip some brew and shoot the breeze? Fortunately the denizens of NoDa, the art district around North Davidson and 36th Streets in Charlotte won't have to find out. The Smelly Cat Coffee House occupies an historic brick building and has become a local favorite since its opening in 1997. Owner Jolly Dale encourages local artists to display their work at the shop. During NoDa's famous Friday night Gallery Crawls, the coffeehouse offers live music and sometimes even a magician or palm reader. The comfortable atmosphere is inviting and the neighborhood bulletin board, chalkboard menu and cozy booths add interest and a relaxed feel. The beverage menu features a wide variety of organic coffees perfectly roasted and brewed along with hot and cold tea, frappes, smoothies and shakes. Throughout the day they serve freshly made baked goods, such as quiche, muffins and pound cakes. The Smelly Cat is a dog-friendly establishment and four-footed patrons are welcome to come inside or be seated on the patio with their human companions. They will be treated with complimentary biscuits while you enjoy your coffee. Sit back and enjoy the neighborhood with a visit to The Smelly Cat Coffeehouse.

514 E 36th Street, Charlotte NC
(704) 374-9656
www.smellycatcoffee.com

Nova's Bakery

It starts with a nudge from the olfactory system, spreading throughout your body, filling your mind with the desire to find the source of the invigorating, comforting smell of freshly baked bread. If you're in the Charlotte area, chances are that delicious smell is winding its way through the city from Nova's Bakery on the corner of Pecan and Central Avenues in the historic plaza. Sladjana and Vlado Novakovic opened the business in 1996. It quickly grew into the area's most popular bakery, voted The Best in Charlotte for 10 years in a row by all local newspapers. The couple came to the United States from Belgrade in the early 1990s, originally settling in Boston, where they managed a bakery. After a few cold, wet winters, they decided they were better designed for Southern living and made plans to relocate to Jacksonville, Florida and open a bakery of their own. Fortunately, they made a detour to Charlotte to visit a friend, who convinced them of the area's need for good bread. The Novakovics focus on the philosophy that fresh breads made from top-quality ingredients like organic flour, in the traditional Eastern European way, will foster customer enthusiasm. Regular customers have proven this theory true, making Nova's successful year after year. Specialties of the house include delightful cranberry-pecan bread, tender focaccia and fragrant kalamata olive bread that will bring your taste buds to life. Revel in the joy of freshly baked bread at Nova's Bakery.

1511 Central Avenue, Charlotte NC
(704) 333-5566
www.novasbakery.com

Nona's Sweets

Nona means grandmother in Italian. Who bakes a better treat than grandma? Jo-Ann Morlando used to bake for friends and family using techniques learned in her grandmother's kitchen. When the demand grew, Jo-Ann and her husband, Nick, opened Nona's Sweets. Jo-Ann continues to pass down family recipes on a daily basis to her daughter, Dominica, and daughter-in-law, Anne. Nona's Sweets is dedicated in loving memory to nonas everywhere. The Italian specialties, cakes, cookies, and homemade candy recipes are combined with exceptional, warm customer service and nostalgic confectionary flavors. Nona's is also a fudgery, providing 18 flavors of fudge. For your next celebration, try one of their signature cakes, such as the Italian Creama. Raspberry glazed, it's two layers of coconut, pineapple and pecan cake covered in rich cream cheese icing. The Duomo is a truly remarkable confection. Chocolate or vanilla cake is covered with whipped icing and a hollow center filled with strawberry, chocolate, amaretto or peanut butter mousse. Nona's has lots of gift-giving ideas. Choose from buckets of cookies, samplers, boxes of candy and many other sweet treats. Wedding cakes are no problem with Nona's design team. They will make your special day unforgettable. Are you looking for a new way to celebrate? Book a cake decorating party with Nona's Sweets. Their on-site party room and specialist make it a breeze. From breakfast muffins to cookies to pastries, everything is made on-site using the best ingredients. Come on in and remember how well grandmothers bake at Nona's Sweets.

9601 N Tryon Street, Suite H, Charlotte NC (704) 717-6144
www.nonassweets.com

Southern Piedmont Fashion

Bruce Julian Clothier

Bruce Julian has an extensive background in the clothing business. In 1948 his father, Milton Julian, started Milton's Clothing Cupboard in Chapel Hill, and quickly opened branches in Charlotte, Dallas and Atlanta. Bruce started working for his father at the age of 14, and one of his tasks was to dream up marketing ideas for the business. One especially memorable event that Bruce created involved painting the words "Sale at Milton's" on the backs of dozens of turtles who were then set loose on the University of North Carolina campus. In 1977 Bruce was invited by his father to open his own store in Charlotte. In 2001 that store began a new chapter, now known as Bruce Julian Clothier. He soon opened another location, a luxurious, expanded space in the Arboretum Shopping Center. Bruce Julian specializes in styles suited to the man with style and taste. The clothing you can't find at the chain stores are found here. He caters to the needs of individuals as opposed to the masses, focusing on the perfect balance of modern and traditional design. The motto at Bruce Julian Clothier is "Good clothes open all doors," and that's a philosophy that the countless long-term clients enthusiastically endorse.

8128 Providence Road, Suite 300, Charlotte NC
(704) 364-8686
www.brucejulian.com

Old Dog Clothing

"Every dog has his day" is definitely the motto of the Old Dog Clothing store. A friendly golden retriever greets you at the door, making Old Dog feel like a second home. Long-standing customers count on Old Dog to deliver outstanding quality clothing and sportswear for men and women at a fair price, both custom and ready-made. With a master tailor on hand, you can be assured of proper fit. Customer satisfaction is top priority; no request is too large or too small. Custom suits and shirts, weekend wear, blouses, t-shirts or accessories, all get the same attention. All dogs are welcome at the Old Dog. Phillips Place Shopping Center

6822 Phillips Place Court, Charlotte NC
(704) 554-5000
www.olddogclothing.com

Southern Piedmont Galleries

Picture House Gallery

Picture House Gallery in Charlotte is more than just an art gallery. Bob Griffin has been committed to providing a broad array of exceptional fine art services since 1974. Corporations as well as individuals have come to rely on the gallery's superior personalized services. Picture House Gallery is a place where clients can consult experts to find the art that best fits their style. The gallery offers fine custom framing and on-site assistance with installation, lighting and display presentation. Picture House Gallery displays the works of more than 50 artists in a wide variety of media, ranging from original oil paintings and watercolors to ceramics and sculpture. Among them are Jamali, the celebrated mystical artist who creates stunning and innovative works in what he describes as his fresco tempera technique, and sculptor Frederick Hart, well known for his work on the National Cathedral in Washington, DC and the Vietnam Veterans Memorial.

1520 E 4th Street, Charlotte NC   (704) 333-8235   www.picturehousegallery.com

J. Richards Gallery

Whether you are new to the world of art collecting or an avid connoisseur, the knowledgeable staff at J. Richards Gallery of Charlotte can assist you in the acquisition of exquisite original paintings. J. Richards Gallery is proud of its extensive selection and the exceptional quality of its original artwork. The Gallery, located in the Phillips Place Shopping Plaza, is well known for 20th century oil paintings done in the French style. Here, you can view a stunning array of impressionist, realist and contemporary oil paintings, along with gouache and pastel paintings by accomplished European and American artists, including the works of H.C. Pissarro, Yolande Ardissone and Jean Pierre Dubord. At J. Richards Gallery, art transcends mere investment potential, with the primary objective being the pleasure of owning great art. The focus for Director Shelia Spitz and the J. Richards Gallery staff is to enhance their clients' lives with fine, collectible art. The gallery has awe-inspiring creations available in a variety of sizes and price ranges. Their accomplished services extend to at-home consultations, appraisals, custom framing and installation. Enrich your life and your home with fine art available for viewing, by appointment, from J. Richards Gallery.

6800-A Phillips Place Court, Charlotte NC
(704) 554-1881
www.jrichardsgallery.com

Maddi's Gallery

When Diane and Madis Sulg opened Maddi's Gallery in Charlotte, the furthest thing from their thoughts was a second gallery. However, after enjoying a wonderful community reception, plus the involvement of their daughter, Michaella Dalton, and her husband, Jon, opening a second gallery soon seemed like the logical next step. Almost two years to the day after Maddi's opened, they launched a second gallery in Bikdale Village in Huntersville. Handmade glass pieces in riot of colors, sizes and shapes adorn the shelves and hang from the window tops. The spectrum of color carries through to handmade ceramic, metal and wood items. Many of the pieces are very functional. Maddi's is famous for its artist-made jewelry, and the selection here is simply stunning. Works in metal, crystals, beads and stones fill the center of the store. One New York designer, Alexis Bittar, works in hand-carved Lucite. After designing jewelry for the gals on *Sex in the City* and the Estee Lauder ads, his work is very much in demand. Southern folk art is another of Maddi's specialties. Untrained painters, potters and carvers from all over the South are represented here. Their work, sought after by collectors throughout the country, brightens gallery floors, walls and ceilings. With the same commitment to service as the original Maddi's, this gallery loves custom orders. They are happy to gift-wrap and ship. When new customers come in, they usually ooh and ahh over the merchandise, but regulars say they come back because Maddi's makes them happy.

1530 E Boulevard, Charlotte NC
(704) 332-0007
16925 Birkdale Commons Parkway, Suite A, Huntersville NC
(704) 987-7777
www.maddisgallery.com

RedSky Gallery

While you are visiting Charlotte, be sure to stop by RedSky Gallery. An inspiring destination like no other, RedSky Gallery is one of North Carolina's most inviting and imaginative discoveries in the world of fine arts and crafts. RedSky is located to the right of Phillips Place, one of the region's premier shopping areas, in the Allen Tate Building. The gallery features the talents of more than 285 local and nationally known artists. Owner Kellie Scott has established a warm environment that provides visually stimulating settings to maximize the impact of original paintings, sculpture and crafts made from glass, metal, ceramic and wood. At RedSky Gallery, the beauty of the unexpected is to be expected. With uncommon pieces of handmade furniture, unique lighting, jewelry and art to wear, the gallery provides inspiring choices for either design-conscious homeowners or seasoned art collectors. RedSky Gallery will be worth your time.

4705 Savings Place, Charlotte NC
(704) 552-5200
www.redskygallery.com

Center of the Earth Gallery

In 2006, Center of the Earth Gallery will celebrate its 18th year as a dynamic venue dedicated to presenting significant art of our time. The gallery represents more than 50 emerging and established artists. CTE's mission is to discover and showcase high-quality, collectible contemporary art. CTE artists are widely collected and are consistently published in fine art journals. This cutting-edge gallery is located in the historic North Charlotte arts district known as NoDa. This former mill village has become a thriving magnet for the visual and performing arts, and is a must-see destination for travelers to Charlotte. CTE owners Ruth Ava Lyons and J. Paul Sires are professional artists with more than 30 years experience in fine arts. Both earned master's degrees from the prestigious Cranbrook Academy of Art, and their work is found in museum, corporate and residential collections. Along with its reputation for excellent private art placement, the gallery's roster of corporate clients includes the Hearst Corporation, Philip Morris USA and Transamerica. Come and experience the hip NoDa street scene during the Gallery Crawl on the first and third Fridays of each month. Let Center of the Earth bring eclectic and compelling art into your world.

3204 N Davidson Street, Charlotte NC
(704) 375-5756
www.centeroftheearth.com

McColl Fine Art

McColl Fine Art is one of the premier fine art galleries in the Southeast. Through his passion for fine art, owner Hugh L. McColl, Jr. has raised the bar for collectors not only in the Charlotte area, but throughout the Southeast. Director Mark Methner acquires important works both in the United States and Europe for the gallery's inventory. The gallery specializes in fine American and European paintings from approximately 1850 to 1925. It is very selective in its acquisitions, offering top-tier works by the artists it handles. Styles of art represented by the gallery include the Hudson River School, American impressionism, the Barbizon School, French impressionism and post-impressionism. The gallery is firmly committed to the proper presentation of important works of art, and believes the selection of an appropriate frame should reflect the historical context of the painting and be sympathetic to a work's aesthetic qualities. McColl's carries an exceptional collection of American and European frames to present both its paintings, and those belonging to clients, in the best possible light. The gallery exudes a beautiful, museum-like sense. The staff is warm and inviting, freely and generously offering time and expertise to visitors. McColl Fine Art is a must-see for fine art collectors and enthusiasts.

208 E Boulevard, Charlotte NC
(704) 333-5983
www.mccollfineart.com

Foust Studio

Foust Studio displays a lively blend of abstract and figurative canvas and paper artwork as well as handcrafted jewelry and prints. The contemporary mixed media paintings created by Charlotte Foust are brilliantly vibrant. Foust is a native of North Carolina and obtained her bachelor's degree from the University of North Carolina. For 12 years, Foust exhibited throughout the nation. During this time, she built a following for her original art that includes an impressive client list. Foust gained recognition for her work early in her career when she was awarded the Regional Artist Grant for Emerging Artists. Her work was exhibited in 2003 at the International Art Expo in New York. The Mint Museum of Art selected one of her collages for a juried exhibition. Foust has participated in exhibitions every year and has received acclaim in many publications for her outstanding work. Throughout her career, Foust has steadfastly remained true to her personal vision. The art she fashions reflects her love of flowers, color and nature in an extremely personalized yet universal expression. Foust Studio specializes in commissions and displays an oft-changing progression of new works. Visit the studio. There is bound to be a waiting masterpiece destined to fit into your life. At Foust Studio, breathe new energy into your office or home space with an authentic work by Charlotte Foust.

5200 Park Road, Suite 115, Charlotte NC
(704) 525-7989
www.fouststudio.com

Studio 91

Studio 91 is the realized dream of artist and proprietor Annette Girman, who displays an array of canvas art created by such inspiring artists as Thomas Arvid, Jean Abadie and Leonard Wren. Each artist is hand-picked based on style and subject matter. Studio 91 carries originals and limited edition giclees. Housed inside the gallery is another kind of artwork. Annette's husband, Jeff Girman, owns and operates Grand Cru Wine Cellars, which specializes in wine cellar design, construction, decoration and installation. Jeff can transform nearly any room into a showcase for wine storage. Grand Cru can offer everything from large-scale storage, to small and intimate spaces. His work is ideal for both home and commercial venues. Jeff works with various woods, such as heart of redwood, black walnut and mahogany. His creations are as functional as they are attractive. Jeff can also provide detailed features that customize and personalize your cellar further, such as gothic archways, waterfall displays and glass-arched doors. Everyone is invited to visit and view the artwork at Studio 91 and Grand Cru Wine Cellars located in the Meadowmont Village.

606 Meadowmont Village,
Chapel Hill NC
(919) 933-3700
www.studio91fineart.com

Photo by Ray Parrish

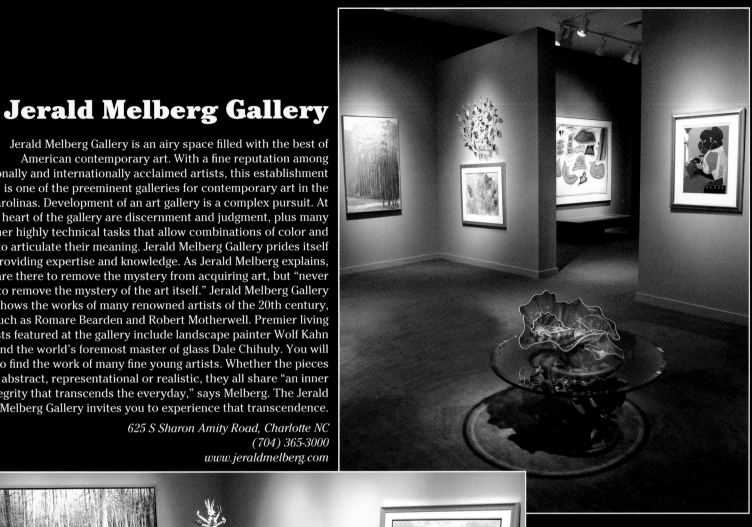

Jerald Melberg Gallery

Jerald Melberg Gallery is an airy space filled with the best of American contemporary art. With a fine reputation among nationally and internationally acclaimed artists, this establishment is one of the preeminent galleries for contemporary art in the Carolinas. Development of an art gallery is a complex pursuit. At the heart of the gallery are discernment and judgment, plus many other highly technical tasks that allow combinations of color and form to articulate their meaning. Jerald Melberg Gallery prides itself on providing expertise and knowledge. As Jerald Melberg explains, they are there to remove the mystery from acquiring art, but "never to remove the mystery of the art itself." Jerald Melberg Gallery shows the works of many renowned artists of the 20th century, such as Romare Bearden and Robert Motherwell. Premier living artists featured at the gallery include landscape painter Wolf Kahn and the world's foremost master of glass Dale Chihuly. You will also find the work of many fine young artists. Whether the pieces are abstract, representational or realistic, they all share "an inner integrity that transcends the everyday," says Melberg. The Jerald Melberg Gallery invites you to experience that transcendence.

625 S Sharon Amity Road, Charlotte NC
(704) 365-3000
www.jeraldmelberg.com

Southern Piedmont Gifts

Clearinghouse South

Clearinghouse South, Inc. is an antique lover's dream if you're looking to buy or sell rare or treasured items. Clearinghouse is a consignment store for the selective shopper and an upscale resale shop that's famous for unusual curios, collector's items, antiques and high-end *objets d'art*. You won't find any run-of-the-mill items at Clearinghouse South. Owner Betty Walsh provides a wonderful setting for your notable items in a 1907 house. Betty stocks fine furnishings from end tables to china cabinets, as well as smaller items, such as silver, china, fine antique linens, crystal, jewelry, glassware and paintings.

If it's a distinctive piece with intrinsic value, you will find it at Clearinghouse South. This is why Clearinghouse South is popular with interior designers and decorators looking for special pieces. If you have a treasure that you just don't have room for, this is the place to take it, as well. Betty will talk to you about the history of your piece, determine its value, set the price and then display it beautifully amidst a backdrop of complementary pieces. Give Betty or one of her friendly staff members a call about their consignment services, but be careful, their items can be irresistible and the stock changes so regularly that you just may wind up with another treasure from Clearinghouse South.

701 Central Avenue, Charlotte NC
(704) 375-7708
www.clearinghousesouth.com

Diamonds Direct Southpark

A diamond might very well be your purchase of a lifetime. Therefore, an informed decision has never been more important. The experts at Diamonds Direct Southpark have been educating customers for three generations. The Diamonds Direct management understands the stress of high-pressure sales. For this reason, the sales associates earn no commission and must complete training in gemology. The store's diamonds come directly from the mines of Russia and South Africa, eliminating wholesale middlemen and allowing Diamonds Direct to concentrate on what it does best. At Diamonds Direct Southpark, you will find a volume 20 times that of other jewelers. Customers make educated decisions and take advantage of exceptional sales services and warranties, such as a 30-day money back guarantee, or a lifetime original purchase price upgrade on a new diamond. Education, guidance, selection and value are the cornerstones of their approach. Someday you will ponder the purchase of a lifetime. The sales associates at Diamonds Direct Southpark look forward to sharing their knowledge with you.

4521 Sharon Road, Charlotte NC
(704) 532-9041 or (888) 400-4447
www.diamondsdirectsouthpark.com

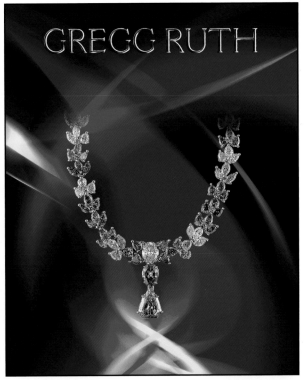

GREGG RUTH

Our Paintin' Place

Whether you're in need of coaching or just a little encouragement, bring along your imagination for an adventure that requires no stress or experience. Our Paintin' Place is an exclusive paint-your-own pottery studio that offers a creative haven where people can experience the revived art of painting ceramic pottery in a friendly and relaxing environment. The family-oriented atmosphere makes this an excellent spot to hide from the outside world or to treat everyone to an afternoon of amusement. With hundreds of pottery items to select from, Our Paintin' Place provides adults, teens and children with an inviting and relaxing setting where imaginations are free to roam. The studio provides a multitude of resources, including tracing paper, stencils, idea books and the Internet for access to a variety of fonts and online clipart. The staff is glad to help you put the art in party. Bring your birthday parties, school field trips or friendly gatherings and let them host your event. You bring the refreshments and guests, and they will provide the fun and the clean up. If you can't make your way to them, Our Paintin' Place will bring the excitement to your home, day care or wherever your heart desires. This studio is becoming a highly sought-after destination with an increasingly faithful client base. Visit Our Paintin' Place for family fun that will last.

2914-A Mt. Holly-Huntersville Road, Charlotte NC
(704) 391-PYOP (7967)

Douglas Furs

Douglas Furs is a timeless and elegant fur, leather and cashmere shop in Charlotte with a fascinating history. Their story began in 1935, when Ben Douglas, Sr. won the first of his three terms as Charlotte's mayor. He had already built a formidable reputation by doubling the water system, founding the Charlotte Memorial Hospital, funding Charlotte's first municipal airport and campaigning against heavy opposition to establish a main thoroughfare into town. In addition, Douglas owned a dry cleaning business. The war was raging in Europe and Ben was a personal friend of President Franklin D. Roosevelt, who had a problem to solve. The jackets worn by pilots in the war were fleece-lined and trimmed in fur. FDR posed the problem of cleaning these jackets to Ben, who not only solved the jacket cleaning dilemma, but in the process established Douglas Furs in 1946. Douglas Furs now carries many elegant and savvy designer lines, including Blackglama, Musi and Louis Feraud. There is a certified cold storage on the premises protected by a secure vault. The staff of tailors and professionals is eminently capable of performing the cleaning, conditioning, restyling and repairing necessary to keep your life-long purchase in optimal condition. Douglas Furs is located in the Courtyard Mall, and their staff will always greet you with a smile.

2400 Park Road, Charlotte NC   (704) 333-5161   www.douglasfurs.com

Jesse Brown's Outdoors

In the heart of the Southeast lies everything you need to get started on your next outdoor adventure. Welcome to Jesse Brown's Outdoors. With two Charlotte locations, shoppers have the recreation and travel gear they need within easy reach. Jesse Brown, a former pilot for CC Air, was dismayed that he couldn't find specialty stores featuring outdoor gear in the South. After seeking and finding such a store in New York City, he decided to open one of his own more than 30 years ago, and the rest is history. Current owner Bill Bartree shares this immense love of outdoor recreation, and says he enjoys the freshness of getting to deal with folks who like to do the fun things in life. Outdoor enthusiasts will be delighted with the large and varied inventory. Top-notch clothing lines, such as Filson and Barbour, will keep you comfortably protected in any weather. Fly fishermen can choose from an extensive variety of fly rods and reels made by industry greats, including Winston and Sage. Mountain climbers, kayakers, hikers and bikers will find an extensive inventory of vital gear. Whether you are venturing into the rolling hills of North Carolina or gearing up for an assault on Mt. Everest, Jesse Brown's Outdoors has the gear you need. The store aims to provide the best gear and customer service available, so its customers can pursue the activities they love. Stop in and see the selection at Jesse Brown's Outdoors before departing on your next outdoor adventure.

4732 Sharon Road, Suite 2M,
Charlotte NC
8929 J M Keynes Drive, Suite 400,
Charlotte NC
(888) 8GO-HIKE
www.jessebrown.com

The Cubbyhole

Tom and Carolyn Turner and their business partners Charlotte, Geralyn, Donna and Elizabeth have created an exciting store that is operated by mothers. Carolyn and the ladies have eight children between them and are all dedicated to motherhood first. However, as we all know, dedication alone doesn't pay the bills, so these mothers partnered to open a business that allowed them to balance motherhood with career. The Cubbyhole in Charlotte is a fabulous gift shop that carries an extensive and eclectic collection of amusing gifts and home décor items. You'll find jewelry, clothing, garden items and a Brighton store inside. Running a popular and diverse shop such as The Cubbyhole would be a full-time-plus job for any one person. However, these innovative matrons have devised a plan where they each work two days a week with extended but flexible hours during the holiday season. The Cubbyhole sells a whimsical array of prints, clocks and lamps. Look for kitchen entertainment items, a baby bath-and-body section, books, cards, stationery and more. The Cubbyhole has faithful followers who shop there not only for the great products and frequently changing inventory, but for the warm atmosphere of comfort, joy and celebration. Discover this paradise of a boutique on your next excursion to Charlotte and find out what retail therapy is all about.

Ballantyne Commons East, 15235-M John J Delaney Drive, Charlotte NC   (704) 759-0017

Perry's Fine, Antique and Estate Jewelry

Perry's At Southpark is in its 30th year of business, and business is as good as ever. Perry's has seen changes in the industry and has met the challenges and changes by adhering to traditional business practices and the philosophy that if you give a customer quality and lasting value for their money, they will return again and again. A trip to Perry's at Southpark attests to Mr. Ernest Perry's preference for tradition over trend. Massive, elegantly carved 100-year-old, 12-foot-tall oak and mahogany jewelry cases line the perimeter of the store. The cases were manufactured by Wade Manufacturing of Charlotte and reportedly delivered to Van Sleen Jewelry Store in Gastonia by mule team. When Van Sleen went out of business, Mr. Perry bought the cases to complement his store's vast inventory of fine, antique and estate jewelry. Among the oldest pieces to grace the store's cases was a diamond, pearl and emerald necklace which had been owned by a Russian Czar. The piece was acquired at an estate auction. Though Mr. Perry no longer conducts estate auctions, he conducts frequent charity auctions to raise money for the city's needy. Perry's at Southpark greeted the new millennium with a much needed expansion to accommodate. The massive wooden cases still line the walls of the store; the store's inventory is as eclectic and exotic as ever; but while his neighbors in the mall have moved around, Perry's at Southpark is right where it was 20 years ago. Recently completed mall renovations have made the store more accessible than ever. Perry's at SouthPark buys and sells jewelry every day at all price ranges. "But I've found that jewelry rises to its greatest value when it has been given as a gift and has collected lots of memories. That's when it's worth the most," says Mr. Perry.

4400 Sharon Road, Charlotte NC   (704) 364-1391   www.perrysjewelry.com

David's Ltd.

David's Ltd. in Charlotte's Cotswold Village Shops has been known for more than 30 years as North Carolina's source for distinctive fine jewelry. With three generations of family history rich in jewelry tradition, David's Ltd. is a cornerstone in the Charlotte community. Owners David and Sandie Rousso have spent their adult lives building their business around the finest jewelry designers and Swiss watch manufacturers in the world. Adorning their showcases are prestigious timepieces from Rolex, Breitling and Baume & Mercier, just to name a few, along with exclusive jewelry collections from Mikimoto, Scott Kay, Charriol, Lagos, Kwiat and others. In the history of David's Ltd., couples in love have looked to the store for the finest in diamonds and bridal jewelry. David's association with Hearts on Fire, creator of the world's most perfectly cut diamond, has taken its clients to a new level of appreciation. David's Ltd. is proud of its membership in the American Gem Society. Its staff of certified gemologists and certified sales associates is a testament to the company's honesty, knowledge and adherence to a strict code of ethics. David's Ltd. is a full service jeweler offering watch and jewelry repair on site, and if you want to create the jewelry of your dreams, a custom designer is available to make it happen. Whether you are visiting Charlotte for a short time, or planning to make it your new home, David's Ltd. should become your family jeweler.

310 S Sharon Amity Road, Charlotte NC
(704) 364-6543
www.davidsltd.com

Scott Jaguar

For three generations spanning more than half a century, the Scott family has been selling cars in Charlotte and building lifelong relationships with car lovers. William Scott came to Charlotte in 1954 and acquired a Dodge dealership. Even while building up a successful business, William always had time to assist others, and his efforts on behalf of other local car dealers earned him the Ambassadors Club Award from the National Automobile Dealers Association. In the 1980s, William bought the land on Tyvola Road where Scott Jaguar sits today. Though the area was far away from downtown, he foresaw the eventual expansion of the city; as Jim Scott puts it, "The fact that my grandfather moved the business to this location 20 years ago shows what a visionary he was." Towards the end of the decade, the Scotts added a Jaguar franchise. When Ford acquired Jaguar and retooled the design into a quality performance vehicle, the Scotts decided to drop all of their other franchises and focus on Jaguar sales. With the idea that for the Jaguar lover there simply is no other car, it was a gamble that paid off. With outstanding sales, Scott Jaguar has customer satisfaction ratings that are the 11th highest in the world. Jim, who everyone calls Scotty, took over as manager in 1999, operating it as a family business and maintaining the high levels of service that have made Scott Jaguar's name so trusted.

400 Tyvola Road, Charlotte, NC
(704) 527-7000
www.scottjag.com

Party Reflections

In 1958, Wayne and Sue Hooks started a business supplying tables and chairs to the people of Charlotte for events. The business grew to include various products, such as medical equipment. In 1983, the company split its resources and staff to become two entities. Chair and Equipment Rentals, Inc. became the medical supply business, and Party Reflections, Inc. served the special event market. In the next 15 years, inventory and business volume quadrupled. The Hooks gifted stock to their children, and Dan Hooks went to college. He attended Wake Forest University and worked in the business, starting at the bottom as chair washer, in keeping with his father's philosophy of working your way up in order to know how to lead. He graduated with a Bachelor of Science degree in business administration. Over the next several years, Dan was given more responsibility. He is now president of the organization and is not able to participate in the hands-on work as much as he once did. However, he still steals away sometimes to install a tent, just to make sure his crew doesn't think he has gone soft. The Party Reflections staff works to create smiles on people's faces and to invent unforgettable party experiences while keeping up with current trends. With Party Reflections, the chair you are sitting in may once have been occupied by Billy Graham or Mohammed Ali, you never know. For your next event, rest easy while Party Reflections makes it magical. They put the special in events.

3412 Monroe Road, Charlotte NC
(704) 332-8176
www.partyreflections.com

Christie's On Main Antique Mall

Popularly deemed the fun place to browse and discover hidden treasure, Christie's On Main Antique Mall features a grand variety of antiques and fine collectibles to suit any style. The shop is very eclectic and has gained much acclaim in the area. It is very well known for the largest selection of vintage costume jewelry in Charlotte. Set in historic downtown Pineville, Christie's On Main Antique Mall features quality consignments and multiple dealers, each with their own showcase of fine wares. Owners Chris and Paul Schafer are constantly buying estates, ensuring not only a diverse assortment of collectibles but a continually changing inventory as well. The regular customers are pleased to always find something new each time they visit. If you are seeking something in particular, call and they will try to find it for you. From fine European furnishing to retro 1950s and shabby chic décor, Christie's On Main Antique Mall seems to specialize in just about everything. If you're looking for a one-of-a-kind item, such as a piece of gorgeous 19th century majolica, a sparkly piece of vintage jewelry or even a historical political button, it's worth the trip to Christie's On Main Antique Mall. You might even get to meet Stella, the store's adorable gremlin.

318 Main Street, Pineville NC (704) 889-5525
www.shoppecharlotte.com

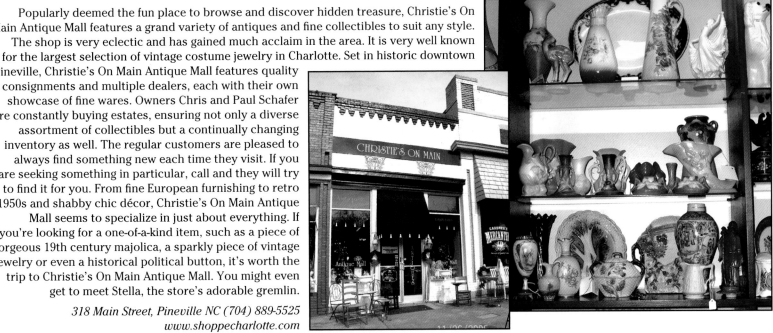

City Art Works

A visually stimulating artistic experience surrounds all who step into City Art Works. Vibrant colors and designs invite you to delight in the eclectic. Creative and distinctive handmade jewelry, gifts and *objects d'art* are highlighted by non-traditional fixtures which draw even more attention. Owners Susan Sloan and Alan Goldstein wanted to create something extraordinary. With such an exciting environment, they've certainly succeeded. A fanciful mixture of art abounds, from folk to retro to contemporary. In addition to the whimsical, City Art Works is an exclusive vendor in the Carolinas Piedmont area of Sticks, handmade, wood-burned and painted furniture from Des Moines, Iowa. Customers can special order and customize their Sticks furniture. In addition to positive and friendly customer service, customers are welcomed by Schmutz, a King Charles spaniel, who is not only the official greeter, but also head of security. Artsy and awe-inspiring, City Art Works gives the same attention to detail and beauty to the gift wrap that it does its collection. City Art Works is a singular art and gift gallery. Susan and Alan invite you to experience and enjoy the shopper's paradise they have created at City Art Works.

1630 E Woodlawn Road, Suite 267, Charlotte NC
(704) 527-1300
www.cityartworks.com

Sports Warehouse

Allen and Kelly Haseley, owners of the Sports Warehouse, met at a recreational volleyball game while in college at University of North Carolina, Chapel Hill. Volleyball remained a shared passion after they moved to Charlotte, and in the fall of 1995 they leased a warehouse and founded Volleyball Unlimited. In 1997, they decided to expand their horizons and create a larger facility dedicated to multiple activities, and the Sports Warehouse was born. Since its opening in November 1998 the Sports Warehouse has provided indoor and outdoor sports leagues for thousands of kids and adults in the Charlotte area. The Sports Warehouse is home to the Charlotte Sports Connection and Carolina Juniors Volleyball Club. In addition to many exciting sports leagues, the Sports Warehouse offers an indoor skate park and laser tag arena, as well as facilities for birthday parties and summer camps. Volleyball was how the Sports Warehouse began, but the Haseleys continue to expand and add different sports, leagues and activities based on what the Charlotte region needs. Their next expansion in the fall of 2006 will include a health club, rock climbing walls, basketball courts and many other sports and activities.

10930 Granite Street, Charlotte NC   (704) 583-1444   www.sportswh.com

Southern Piedmont Health & Beauty

Charlotte Laser Center and MedSpa

Upon entering the doors at Charlotte Laser Center and MedSpa, you are enveloped in a warm and friendly atmosphere. Charlotte Laser and MedSpa is among the most advanced non-surgical cosmetic medical spas. As specialists in non-invasive cosmetic and anti-aging medicine, they offer the perfect blend of aesthetics and science. You can enjoy luxurious treatments that have genuine medical value, as well as long lasting aesthetic benefits, such as botox, microdermabrasion, chemical peels, IPL photorejuvenation, laser hair removal, collagen treatments and laser vein treatment. Their facials reduce wrinkles, improve sun damaged skin, lighten sun spots and help blemish-prone skin. At Charlotte Laser and MedSpa, professionals employ various FDA-approved hair removal systems. In this way, they are able to tailor a program specific to your needs, independent of your skin color. The staff at Charlotte Laser and MedSpa is committed to providing an enjoyable and relaxing environment while you receive the highest quality, clinically supervised treatments, as well as professional skin care products to aid your beauty plan.

11220 Elm Lane, Suite 102, Charlotte NC
(704) 369-0429
www.charlottelasercenter.com

The Crown Athletic Club

Charlotte's business and civic leaders agreed that keeping up with their health-conscious colleagues required a private fitness facility par excellence. The Crown Athletic Club premiered its 18,000-square-foot masterpiece in 1992, exceeding all expectations. State of the art throughout, the widest range of equipment and activities cater to every interest, ability and skill level. Certified instructors of diverse expertise create personalized exercise programs that offer ongoing support. Before your session, choose the latest CD or movie. Personal entertainment centers are found on all cardiovascular equipment. Saunas, steam rooms and whirlpools reward every workout in the luxurious and meticulously maintained locker rooms. Members and guests may enjoy a massage by a licensed therapist. Private business meetings or entertaining are accommodated in the boardroom and balcony. The Crown Athletic Club was created for the comfort and enjoyment of its members. Individual attention and the finest facilities make it the ultimate in health and fitness.

100 N Tryon Street, Suite 350, Charlotte NC
(704) 331-0777
www.crownathletic.com

a

Euphoria Salon & Spa

The motto for the stunning city of Charlotte is *Esse quam videri*: To be, rather than to seem. Euphoria Salon & Spa takes this concept to heart. Here is where the ladies and gentleman of Charlotte come to pamper and rejuvenate themselves. Owner and color correction specialist Yana Dudko came to the United States from Russia, where she acquired European styling skills and techniques. She opened Euphoria Salon & Spa in 1999 and offers a full spectrum of services and products. Inside the salon, Yana is known as the Goddess of Color Correction. She also specializes in the latest hair-straightening technique from Japan. This process allows clients the freedom of wash-and-go hair, freeing them from lengthy morning bathroom regimes that require extensive time and hair products. Yana's fantastic and friendly staff presents guests with broad regimen of spa treatments to rejuvenate their bodies and free their minds. The treatments include facials, massages, body treatments and ear candling. What makes a treatment from Euphoria Salon & Spa so magical and rewarding is that they use innovative services, with the help of naturally grown plants, to help you achieve total relaxation. Some of the products available include Kerastase, Phytologie and the exclusive Matis skin care line from Paris. The warm, European-inspired salon and spa welcomes you in with subtle lighting, graceful sculpture and elegant art work throughout. Euphoria Salon & Spa is exactly what it wants to be, an exemplary salon and spa.

3904-D Colony Road, Morrocroft Village, Charlotte NC
(704) 367-9112
www.euphoriasalon.com

Modern Salon and Spa

Modern Salon and Spa is one of the premier salons and spas in the Charlotte region. Beginning in 1990, Arsalan and Arezo Hafezi put their vision to work when they opened the first Modern Salon and Spa location at Colwick Towers. Arezo's passion for cutting hair along with Arsalan's love for business created a very successful team. The Hafezis' goal is to educate, inspire and maintain a close culture for all family members and guests. The Hafezis have worked together for the past 15 years, balancing their personal and professional lives to create a successful business. For the past five years, *Salon Today* has listed Modern Salon and Spa as one of the top 200 salons in the nation. They entered the list at number 87, and in 2005 ranked at number six. Modern Salon and Spa incorporates unique spa services to provide for a more relaxing experience. Spa services are customized for each guest. Relax and enjoy a custom massage or facial based on the Aveda Elemental Nature philosophy and your signature Aveda aromas. Packages are available, including your choice of massage, body wrap, facial, manicure, pedicure and makeover. Modern Salon and Spa is not just a haven for women. The salon and spa services cater to men, as well. Men can indulge in an old-fashioned hot shave or receive a haircut and head massage. Enjoy a visit to Modern Salon and Spa, a retreat that brings beauty, relaxation and well being into perfect balance.

Phillips Place, Hearst Tower, Birkdale Village,
Ballantyne Village, Mantra Salon and Spa
(704) 339-0909 or (888) 339-1009
www.modernsalonandspa.com

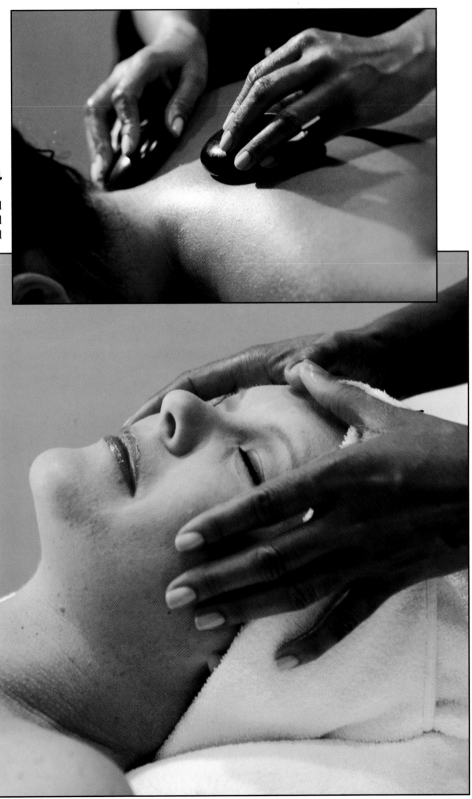

Voci Spa

Voci Spa in Charlotte provides clients with the extra special services needed for rewarding and rejuvenating cosmetic procedures and surgeries. This extraordinary renewal center was the ingenious invention of Elaine Voci, R.N. The idea was conceived while Elaine was working in the medical practice of her husband Vincent E. Voci, M.D., FACS. She took a phone call from one of their patients who needed some post-surgery psychological boosting. Elaine realized that patients needed a place designed to nurture a positive self-image while retaining dignity. Voci Spa shares space with a medical practice and works in collaboration with doctors Vincent Voci and Thomas Liszka to assure that clients receive expert medical attention in conjunction with services that will emphasize total body renewal. Elaine considers the spa's greatest strength to be its highly qualified staff, which focuses completely on providing exemplary patient care. The spa is known for its BioMedic micro-peels and facial treatments, as well as micro-pigmentation and tinting services. The spa offers manicures and pedicures, waxing, massage, medical skin care and cellulite treatments. It specializes in treatments that are based on sound medical principles and uses only products that contain the highest quality, medically formulated ingredients. Voci Spa has the quiet, gentle and comforting atmosphere needed to heal body and mind.

7808-G Rea Road, Charlotte NC (704) 752-8030 2620
E 7th Street, Charlotte NC (704) 333-9211 www.vocispa.com

Palestra Skin Care Center

The ancient Greeks took time to revitalize their minds and bodies in rejuvenation rooms called *palestras*. Steam and herbal baths coupled with massage were believed to be the foundations for good health. Reminiscent of the ancient Greeks, Palestra Skin Care Center strives to help each individual client achieve the inner balance and outer health that creates true beauty. Coupling the ancient knowledge of the Greeks with the very latest in modern skin care science, Palestra offers an extraordinary range of unusual skin-care therapies geared for each client's particular needs and desires. The salon uses only the finest international skin care products from Murad, DDF and Sothy's, plus the latest state-of-the-art equipment and techniques. Facials, masks, peals, exfoliation and ultrasonic skin resurfacing are just a few of the services offered. Full body treatments include wraps, cellulite reducing thermals and massages with everything from feathers to hot stones. European-owned and operated, Palestra is one of the only eight skin and health care spas in the country to be accredited by CIDESCO, the world's major international beauty therapy association. The staff prides itself on creating a peaceful environment and an atmosphere of quiet care filled with relaxation. Come to Palestra, where the client's needs are first, and the goal is total relaxation.

210 S Caswell Road,
Charlotte NC
(704) 342-4660
www.gopalestra.com

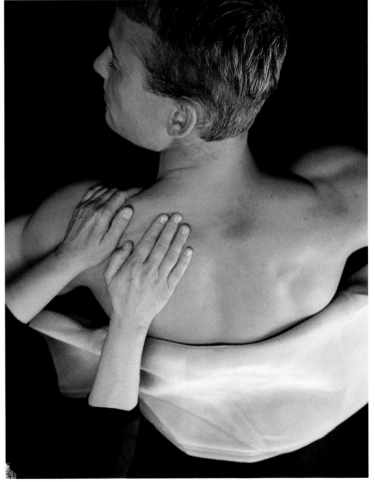

Carmen! Carmen! Salon é Spa

Carmen! Carmen! Salon é Spa exists for the sole purpose of serving clients with the best possible hair care and spa services. Under the direction of Carmen Cutrona, North American Hairstylist of the Year and Global Master of the Arts winner, Carmen! Carmen! has achieved international status. In August 2005 Carmen celebrated his 30th year in business. The full service spa relaxes guests with massages, facials and nail care. Even when you are not visiting the spa, your service is accented with a touch of relaxation. Every haircut begins with a consultation with your stylist, followed by a signature stress relieving treatment. Color services include a soothing hand massage with Aveda's Hand Relief. Every guest is a VIP at Carmen! Carmen! Salon é Spa. Your experience is both comforting and luxurious. During your service, enjoy a complimentary cup of Aveda's Comforting Tea. Every service at Carmen! Carmen! ends with a complimentary skin care analysis and makeup touchup.

Cotswold Village Shops (707) 364-0270
Mallard Point/University Area (704) 549-9778
Ballatyne Commons East (704) 540-5640
Jetton Cove/Lake Norman (704) 892-9411
www.carmencarmensalon.com

ReGenesis Medical Spa

At ReGenesis Medical Spa in Charlotte, your quest for a new beginning can become reality. Their personal treatment plans and clinically proven techniques are all overseen by a highly trained staff that is dedicated to the simple goal of improving your appearance and giving you a fresh, new start. By using state-of-the-art technology, their physicians achieve the extraordinary results you desire. Owner Donald J. Sudy, M.D., with his wife and clinical director, Sarah Yousuff, M.D., opened the clinic in order to ensure their patients received the proper education, tools and insight needed to maximize clients' potential for success without the constraints placed by managed care insurance programs. Yousuff is certified in both Anesthesiology and Pain Medicine and has received extensive training in laser medicine and facial aesthetics. Dr. Sudy has an impressive medical resume that includes awards received during his service as flight surgeon at the Little Rock AFB, as well as an Air Medal for missions served in the Bosnia-Kosovo conflict. Additionally, he was activated to serve as flight surgeon in the Middle East, earning a second Air Medal and an Air Force Commendation Medal. Sudy was awarded a Certificate of Recognition, for service to his nation, by the American Academy of Emergency Medicine in 2004, and is also an active member of the American Academy of Aesthetic Medicine and the American Society for lasers in Medicine and Surgery. ReGenesis offers a variety of treatments including Botox®, Wrinkle Therapy/Photorejuvenation, Chemical Peels, Laser Vein Treatments and Microdermabrasion Skin Resurfacing. Let the beauty within emerge at ReGenesis Medical Spa and Wellness Center.

4423 Sharon Road, Charlotte NC
(701) 362-2232 or (888) 481-2232
445 N College Street, Morganton NC
www.regenesismedicalspa.com

Varji & Varji Salon

Whether you need a style boost or just a moment to pamper yourself and restore your energy, visit Varji & Varji Salon. Opened in 2000 by Max and Susan Varji, the shop has become one of Charlotte's premier AVEDA Concept salons. Varji & Varji is an innovative salon committed to providing a unique guest experience designed to both enrich and enhance. The focus on continuing education at Varji & Varji ensures that their creative team of talented professionals is always a step ahead of the trend. Max and Susan love working together and it shows. The salon has a comfortable and friendly atmosphere that specializes in creative styles, color treatments and, of course, Aveda products. These plant-derived, organic aromatherapy products are renowned for their quality and are never tested on animals. Located in the historic Dilworth district, just minutes from downtown Charlotte, this distinctive and colorful salon offers more than just a wash and cut.

A visit to Varji & Varji is a holistic experience for the senses. Scalp massages, waxing, great styles and exemplary service are just a few of the positive aspects of this salon. Upon arrival, customers are offered refreshments by an upbeat and personable member of the staff. The great working relationships and positive atmosphere keep clients feeling pampered and beautiful. For a refreshing, invigorating break from shopping or just an excuse to take time out of a busy day, Varji & Varji Salon is a treat.

911 E Moorhead Street, Charlotte NC
(704) 333-1957

Performance Pilates

Joseph Pilates once said of his exercise program, "You will feel better in 10 sessions, look better in 20 sessions and have a completely new body in 30 sessions." True to his predictions, his program has made that happen for thousands of individuals who maintain a Pilates lifestyle. At Performance Pilates in Charlotte, you too can learn this dynamic, intelligent form of exercise and improve mind, body and spirit while you work out.

Liz Hilliard opened her studio in 2002 with the focus of providing a place where clients could gain a sense of well being. All of her sessions are either private or duet. Located in the Historic Myers Park area one mile from the popular South Park district, the Performance Pilates program offers clients a way to sculpt and tone their entire body through Joseph Pilate's techniques, which meld physical and mental conditioning with the principles of concentration, control and centering, along with precision, flow and proper breathing. Practitioners

experience a multitude of benefits, including greater mind/body awareness, improved balance and core stability, relief of pain and tension, stronger, leaner muscles, increased circulation, and flatter abs and stomach. Additionally, Pilates offers enhanced performance for those involved in other physical outlets, such as yoga, tennis and gymnastics, and provides increased flexibility, mobility, and agility. Live healthier and feel better with a Pilates' program that is tailored to your needs at Performance Pilates.

(704) 236-3377
www.performancepilates.com

Country road in the foothills

Southern Piedmont
Home Décor, Flowers, Gardens & Markets

Fifteen Ten
Uncommon Home Antiques

You'll fall in love with Fifteen Ten Uncommon Home Antiques. Here you will find an extensive and eclectic array of valuable antique consignments and collectibles. Fifteen Ten works with 150 consigners to provide the Charlotte area with a cornucopia of collectibles. Visitors will find one-of-a-kind furniture, art and other vintage pieces to add to their homes. Located in the heart of Plaza-Midwood in Charlotte, this elegant shop has something for everyone. The friendly and knowledgeable staff pride themselves on top-quality service to go along with their top-quality merchandise. Allow them to help you find the perfect occasional table, mirror or piece of glassware to complement any room of your house. Radiance and luminescence can easily be added to any space with clever lighting. Fifteen Ten Uncommon Home Antiques has an extensive and decorative selection of chandeliers and lamps to help you create a happy glow throughout your home. These uncommon and memorable pieces arrive weekly, so the selection is always changing. Find your can't-live-without-them collectibles at Fifteen Ten Uncommon Home Antiques.

1510 Central Avenue, Charlotte NC
(704) 342-9005
www.1510-antiques.com

The Blossom Shop

Charlotte has long boasted a fine tradition of style. For over 75 years, The Blossom Shop has held the honor of being the preeminent florist in The Queen City, sharing in generations of treasured memories. This full service florist specializes in creative design and takes the art of floral arranging to new heights. Their designs and displays for weddings, anniversaries, banquets, dinners, business openings and sympathy enable them to create exquisite settings for all occasions, large and small. The Blossom Shop carries a delightful selection of home accessories and giftware to add a finishing touch to your home, or to present a lovely housewarming gift. Their designs range from contemporary to traditional English or French Garden style. They also offer notable designs that utilize flowers, mosses, branches and other woodland materials to make a realistic and natural looking composition. The Blossom Shop carries a large selection of flowers, non-flowering plants and gift/gourmet baskets. The baskets are filled with selections of the shop's most popular gifts for new homes, anniversaries, students, business colleagues and others. Visit The Blossom Shop at one of three convenient locations.

2242 Park Road, Charlotte NC   (704) 376-3526
Shops at Founders Hall, Charlotte NC   (704) 373-1090
617 Providence Road, Charlotte NC   (704) 372-4447

The Majestic Bath

The Majestic Bath in Charlotte is a place of inspiration, knowledge, and service. Not only can you find the latest and most artistic fixtures for kitchen and bath, you can experience the "red cow" factor. When you drive down the road and see one black cow after another and then you spot a red cow, that's the red cow factor. Owners and sales associates Wanda Jackson, Victoria Ruotolo and you spot more than the mere unusual. Their over 50 years of combined experience in the plumbing industry gives them an understanding of the need for hardworking fixtures that blend beauty and durability for building the bath or kitchen of your dreams. Co-owner Erika Dubois puts equal energy into the accounting end of the business for an efficient, customer-friendly experience. In the spectacular showroom you will find the clean, classic lines of Toto's Lloyd Collection, decorative cabinet knobs with Swarovski crystals from Edgar Berebi, and fine Lalique crystal faucets from THG. The experts at the Majestic Bath specialize in the artistic tailoring of kitchens and baths to every customer's needs and fantasies. For a glimpse at the possibilities, visit The Majestic Bath showroom, where extraordinary bathroom and kitchen fixtures are gathered together for your inspiration.

621 S Sharon Amity Road, Charlotte NC
(704) 366-9099
www.themajesticbath.com

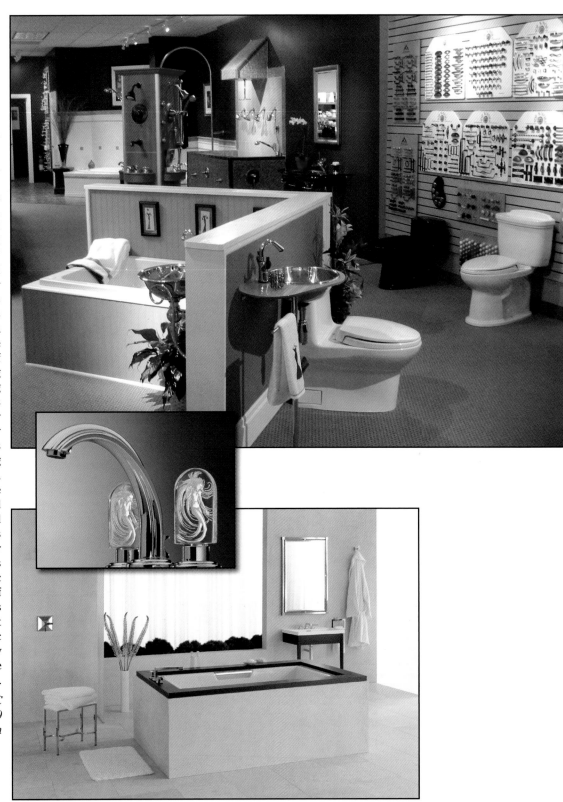

Heritage Stone

Heritage Stone is an interior stone fabricator that believes strongly in the beauty and esthetics of natural stone. Owner Dan Gotte brings more than 20 years of experience to his company, which he opened in 2001. Heritage Stone offers more than 7,000 square feet of natural stone in the striking showroom, which is housed in Charlotte's historic South End. The company's state-of-the art-facility provides competitive pricing, guaranteed delivery and on-site fabrication featuring cutting edge CNC equipment. Because they are a locally based company, they have an efficient and timely installation process so you won't have to wait weeks or even months for your stone to be installed. One of Charlotte's best-kept secrets, Heritage Stone offers a more superior selection and quality of natural stone than what you would find at big name improvement companies. Their stone and craftsmanship have been used in high-profile projects across the city, including the Piedmont Town Center and the condominium project on the corner of West 5th and South Poplar streets. Dan and his knowledgeable and friendly staff are happy to answer all of your natural stone questions and assist you in making the selection that best suits your taste and lifestyle. Granite, marble and limestone will add the beauty and endurance of natural stone to your home. Heritage Stone will provide the rest.

1215 S Graham Street, Charlotte NC
(704) 331-0022
www.heritage-stone.com

The Stone Library & The Stone Gallery

Len Malavé has a true love and appreciation for natural stone, which is only natural; he's a third generation stonemason. "Stone is one of God's wonderful creations," says Len, who started out as a helper with the D'Ambrosio Ecclesiastical Art Studio and has worked for more than 20 years with some of the best stone artisans in the country. When Len went into business on his own, he started out with a set of buckets, a granite slab and two filing cabinets. Today, besides his state-of-the-art manufacturing facility in Greensboro, he has opened a magnificent Stone Library in the Design Center of the Carolinas in Charlotte. Combining Old World quality with the latest technology, Len specializes in custom fabrication and installation of interior natural stonework, including floors, tables, bathrooms, countertops, carvings, fireplace surrounds and mantels. Exterior stonework in the form of pools and patios is another Malavé specialty. He uses all forms of natural stone, including granite, marble and limestone, and features a huge selection of European, domestic, Canadian, South American and Asian stones. In his high-tech showroom The Stone Library, architects and designers can show clients the difference between granite and marble, which stone would be the best to use in a kitchen or bath, or even how stone is quarried in different countries and shipped to America. Len is not just a businessman and artisan, he's truly a creative visionary who is setting the standard for his industry at The Stone Library & The Stone Gallery.

101 W Worthington Street, Suite 116, Charlotte NC
(704) 372-0104
www.malavegranite.com

Charlotte Marble and Granite, Inc.

Building, renovating or remodeling a home can be stressful. You want everything to be perfect, and it can be difficult choosing materials and contractors. However, when it comes time to choose your countertops, vanities, fireplace surrounds and tiles, relax and turn to Charlotte Marble and Granite. With more than 20 years of stone fabrication experience, business partners Shanon Heldreth and Brent Trimble have gained a reputation for excellence based on their exemplary customer service, quality products and professional installation. Charlotte Marble and Granite is known for its timeliness and overall professionalism from start to finish. With true dedication to their work, Shanon and Brent are always personally involved in every project and are on hand to answer all of your questions.

Charlotte Marble and Granite carries natural stone, including travertine, limestone and slate. Granite is ideal for the serious chef, as it can withstand temperatures

up to 1000 degrees Fahrenheit. It is easy to clean and nonporous when polished and sealed, making it impervious to most household food stains. Marble has long been revered by pastry chefs around the world and is ideal for rolling dough, because it naturally stays cool to the touch. Charlotte Marble and Granite can furnish bathroom vanities or household furniture tops, balustrades and custom fabrications. Its mission is to consistently provide quality workmanship, professional service and a wide selection of natural stone options. Create the look you've always wanted with the wonderful staff, experienced designers and magnificent stone selection at Charlotte Marble and Granite.

215 Foster Avenue,
Charlotte NC
(704) 523-5005

Carolina Cabinet Refacing

John Marino, president of Carolina Cabinet Refacing in Charlotte, places total emphasis on customer satisfaction for each project the company undertakes. He greatly looks forward to each customer seeing their finished project and saying, "I love my cabinets, I love my cabinets, I love my cabinets." At Carolina Cabinet Refacing, they offer only the finest grade, Amish-select hardwoods, and provide uncompromising Amish craftsmanship, which has led to the company's outstanding reputation for excellence. All of Carolina Cabinet Refacing's crews are experienced and dedicated professionals. Amish craftsmen make all of the company's products, and expert finish carpenters install all of the refacing. Carolina Cabinet Refacing's commitment to quality is reflected in their promise of providing only authentic products that are backed by an industry-leading lifetime product warranty which is supported by a 10-year workmanship warranty that is unparalleled in the industry. Carolina Cabinet Refacing uses time-honored, authentic Amish cabinet refacing techniques to transform your existing cabinets into exquisite, custom show pieces. The cost to you is far less than what you would pay for all new custom cabinetry, while the finished product exquisitely reflects your personal taste and style. The friendly and product knowledgeable staff members truly love what they do and that love resonates in every aspect of every project. Enhance your kitchen, bath area or formal rooms with a whole new look by way of custom refacing available only at Carolina Cabinet Refacing.

2229 Village Lake Drive, Charlotte NC   (704) 531-9224   www.ilovemycabinets.com

Charlotte's Garden

After coming to Charlotte years ago to be near family, Mignon and Ron Hooper ran into a dilemma. They couldn't find what they considered to be the perfect flower shop. So they partnered with Mignon's sister, the talented Kori Bolles, in 1994 to create Charlotte's Garden. In the shade of a stately 1920s mansion that evokes a sense of timeless beauty, a true family business sprang to life. They infused their business with a love of superb flora and a flair for creating exquisite arrangements all occasions. Their spark remains today, flowing not only from the minds and hearts of those who brought it forth, but from the boundless energy of younger family members who have joined the business. Kori's children and Mignon's daughter bring the sweet kiss of a new generation, spending many of their days in the shop, lending their own brand of energy to the blooming life and beauty surrounding them. Charlotte's Garden meets the call for your flowers, fund-raisers or special events with arrangements destined to bring smiles of appreciation.

715 Providence Road, Charlotte NC
(704) 343-5353
www.charlottesgarden.citysearch.com

Campbell's Greenhouses & Nursery

Campbell's Greenhouses and Nursery, located in Charlotte's historic South End district, is a full service retail shop that specializes in orchids, bonsai, tropical foliage and outdoor ornamental plants. The variety and quality of plants, along with knowledgeable staff, has allowed owner Jesse P. Campbell to build a thriving business serving the public since 1986. Seasonal changes allow shoppers and visitors to continuously discover different plants to accent and beautify their homes or offices. For even more home, garden and office accents and accessories, you can visit Campbell's second location, Dilworth's Little Secret, a shop located on the trolley line and specializing in hard goods for the home and garden, along with unique gift items for all occasions. Discover the difference at Campbell's Greenhouses & Nursery.

209 McDonald Avenue, Charlotte NC   (704) 331-9659
2000 S Boulevard, Suite 530, Charlotte NC   (704) 333-0995

Daniel Stowe Botanical Garden

Open to the public since 1991, Daniel Stowe Botanical Garden grew out of the generosity of Daniel Stowe, a native North Carolinian and a magnate in the textile industry, who wanted to provide a gift for future generations. He donated $14 million and 450 acres of rolling meadows, woodlands and shoreline tracts to create a world-class botanical garden. Located in an historic area along the Catawba River near the border between North Carolina and South Carolina, the Stowe Garden features nine themed spaces, including the tropical Canal Garden, the Conifer Garden and the Four Seasons Garden. These garden rooms are accented with a dozen sparkling fountains. The Garden provides a dual focus, with an emphasis on Southern horticulture and the natural beauties of the Piedmont region. At Daniel Stowe Botanical Garden, visitors may take self-guided tours or arrange for tours. Tours begin at the 13,500-square-foot Robert Lee Stowe Visitor Pavilion, a wonder in itself, featuring a magnificent colonnade and an entryway crowned with a beautiful antique stained-glass dome 22 feet in diameter.

6500 S New Hope Road, Belmont NC   (704) 825-4490   www.dsbg.org

Oak Street Mill Antique Market

Cornelius is a rapidly growing city with the charm of an old town. It sits on a lake and features brick sidewalks and quaint shops. Cornelius is an old cotton mill town, named after J.B. Cornelius, who built the city's first mill. The Oak Street Mill Antique Market, a medley of 50 charming antique dealers, is located in an old cotton mill which started out as Gem Yarn Mills. The building, which was built of common bond brick in 1906, is now owned by Nan Fabio and Beth Phillips. The Oak Street Mill features more than 10,000 square feet of nostalgia and boasts a stunning array of every imaginable antique, including furniture, china and glass, rugs, pottery, jewelry and linen. Oak Street Mill will let you take a new purchase home for a 24-hour home trial period. A trip to the Oak Street Mill Antique Market provides a calm, therapeutic shopping experience where you are invited to browse the cornucopia of enchanting delights at your own pace.

19725 Oak Street, Cornelius NC (704) 895-2653

Mamalu Antiques & Specialty Shop

Winston Thomas was not impressed with his first viewing of the space for his new shop. The dirt floor and weeds in the walls gave no clue of the transformation that would transpire over the next year. Winston and Gwendolyn Thomas are now ensconced in an eclectic bit of paradise in the hub of Charlotte's prestigious NoDa district. The store was named after Winston's mother Lula. Brother-in-law Larry helped to set up the shop and is now a buyer for Winston. Winston chose to deal in antiques because of the craftsmanship and intimacy built into these pieces. He points out that there was no mass production when these were made; instead, a person or a family put their personal efforts into the creation. The store stocks items for collectors, interior decorators and many infatuated repeat

customers. Lamps, furniture, special glassware and items from Paris, Honolulu, Africa, India and all over America mingle together in happy harmony. Thomas loves meeting people and will travel the world in search of an incomparable item. Antiques have the distinction of being functional, decorative and a good investment. People slow down and browse here. The inventory includes a fine series of reproductions made in various states, including New England and North Carolina. Thomas is aware that North Carolina is still the furniture capital of the United States. Walking through this captivating showplace is like traveling the world. Bring yourself in, and the staff will show you around.

3120 N Davidson Street, Suite 100, Charlotte NC
(704) 332-3686
www.mamaluantique.com

Custom Interiors

With a classic eye for detail and a love for antiques, David Smith and his company Custom Interiors can help you turn your home into a haven. Custom Interiors was opened in 1993 by Sueanne Smith and is now owned and operated by her son, David. With a strong interest in 18th and 19th Century European antiques, David often traverses the cities of England and France in search of quality furnishings craved by his discerning clients. The retail store offers new and antique European-style furniture, along with a plethora of accessories and textiles that will let your decorating ideas take flight. For those who know they want something extraordinary, but aren't sure how to achieve the desired effect, David has interior designers on staff. Stunning armoires, banquettes, tables and secretaries greet visitors in the showroom along with richly textured fabric settees, chairs and couches. On every wall you will find charming prints, sconces and mirrors that will add interest and depth to any room. The showroom itself is warm and inviting and allows clients to feel at home while they browse and admire the treasures before them. Small vignettes and elegantly grouped displays of furniture make it easy to imagine how something may look in your home. The friendly and very knowledgeable staff is always on hand to answer any questions you may have about style, origin and care of a particular piece. Trust Custom Interiors to help you with all of your design and furniture needs.

19700 W Catawba, Cornelius NC
(704) 892-4040

House of Andrachelle

Haute Couture for your home. Margaret Fergusson opened the U.S showroom in 1995, after the success of Andrachelle Interiors, a residential and commercial design company based, in Kent, on the outskirts of London. Even if you are not familiar with Gloucester goblets, Tewksbury triple pleats, Suffolk hand-smocked or Gothic Triple Crown heading for draperies, you will feel right at home here. Andrachelle strives to achieve perfection in the execution of fine silk drapery design and complementary room interiors. Their talent lies in creating window treatments for the discerning, with an eye for detail. House of Andrachelle's showroom is frequented by homeowners and trade professionals looking for the finest textiles, passementerie and custom-made draperies. Andrachelle also carries exceptional hand-finished window hardware, tablecloths, pillows and lampshades. Exquisite components are the ingredients of a signature room, and you will find them at House of Andrachelle.

1230 W Moreland Street, Suite 106, Charlotte NC   (704) 342-3106
www.houseofandrachelle.com

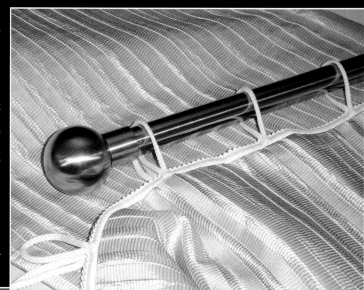

Elizabeth House Flowers

Want to express your love or affection for someone special? Elizabeth House Flowers has been a great place to order flowers for any occasion since 1987. Owners James David Wynn and Cecil Sherin provide innovative designs using quality materials. They provide delivery of stunning arrangements appropriate for Charlotte and North Carolina's many venues, from skyscrapers to seaside county chapels. The industry's best European growers provide Elizabeth House with an endless supply of fresh seasonal flowers, plants and orchids. The florists are known for setting and carrying out themes for parties, weddings and memorial services. Whether you are looking for pastels or bright colors, Elizabeth House can accommodate your needs. They sell designs for the home, such as art prints, toile planters and candlesticks. Elizabeth House specializes in funeral presentations, offering a wide variety of casket sprays, wreaths and baskets. The owners received the Best of the Best award from *Charlotte City Magazine* in 2005. They were praised as one of the top 250 teleflorists in the country in 2005 and continue to win coveted awards for their creative designs. No matter how small or large your special occasion, Elizabeth House Flowers can help.

1431 S Boulevard, Charlotte NC
(704) 342-3919
www.elizabethhouseflowers.com

Royal Gardens

Royal Gardens is located minutes from downtown Charlotte in the historic Elizabeth District. Housed in a charming, two-story, 1913 Arts and Crafts home, this enchanting shop is a wonderland of delightfully eclectic home and garden treasures that will warm your heart and put a smile on your face. Since 1993, this family-owned and operated business has been gaining a reputation for exemplary service, stunning design and top-notch quality. The Sweet family specializes in landscape installation, maintenance and ornamentation of your garden. The family is firmly committed to making Charlotte a more beautiful place. Royal Gardens offers a diverse mix of home and garden accessories, including antique roses, collector's items, fountains, statuary, sculptures, incredible yard art and birdhouses. They carry a fabulous selection of herbs, glazed and stone containers, and everything necessary to create a peaceful water garden. In 2003, Royal Gardens won the Best Full Color Retail Advertisement award in the North Carolina Press Association's advertising contest. When Royal Gardens handles your property, an expert in the field accompanies each step of your landscaping journey, from design through installation and maintenance. Sit back, relax and enjoy the rewards of their hard work, knowing that every detail has been seen to, then browse through the shop for any finishing touches that you just can't live without. Ensure peace in your kingdom with landscaping, maintenance and accessories from Royal Gardens.

1733 E 7th Street,
Charlotte NC
(704) 334-FROG (3764)

Purple Picket Furniture Store

Have you been searching for the exact piece of furniture to pull a room together? Perhaps you want to replace that creaky, 1970s-era, bed-frame? Maybe you just want a whole new look, but you really don't want to spend thousands of dollars. Take time to visit the Purple Picket Furniture Store. This amazing store offers an eclectic collection of furniture to suit any style. Scott Edwards began this business with the idea that people want furniture that is classic, romantic and, above all, that makes a statement. Just as importantly, he saw no reason that his customers should pay a fortune to make their home décor dreams come true. He began by finding auction pieces and progressed to wholesale and closeout items. Snatching these up at bargain prices, he and his staff of craftsmen restore and repair the furniture. His ideas and concepts have worked beautifully. Edwards says loyal customers will stop him in the streets to passionately describe a piece of furniture they bought from Purple Picket. Visitors to the showroom are treated to a plethora of high-end, designer and one-of-a-kind home furnishings. Magnificent bed-frames, cozy settees and couches with matching ottomans, an extensive collection of tables and curio-cabinets await the intrepid furniture hunter.

The next time you are looking for the perfect accent to a room, stop by and see the friendly, knowledgeable staff at the Purple Picket Furniture Company.

601 N Polk Street, Pineville NC
(704) 889-DEAL (3325)
www.purplepicket.com

Black Lion

The settlement of Charlotte was named in the Colonial era after the wife of King George III of England. Today, Bob and Nita Emory and daughter Elisabeth offer a treasure trove of gifts and furnishings fit for royalty in Charlotte. Bob Emory was the regional sales manager for a national agency, selling gifts to the trade. He traveled the Southeast selling Buyer's Choice, Ralph Lauren, and hundreds of products, such as Christopher Radko articles from Europe. After 20 years, Emory opened his fist retail Black Lion store in 1995. In 2000, he purchased the old Pineville K-mart that had been vacant for three years. From there, his venture expanded to include five establishments. Now there's no need to go to New York or Europe when remarkable home accessories are at hand in the Black Lion. The Black Lion carries more than 500,000 items. Worldwide and one-stop shopping make this upscale creation a convenient alternative for the discriminating shopper. Five locations and more than 150 shops under one roof, with a 2,000-square-foot interior design house located inside, provide a plentiful array of select furniture. Year-round Christmas inventory and chandeliers can all be found here. Retail public space is available for entrepreneurs starting out in the business world. Save your airfare, and come to Black Lion for that dazzling, hard-to-find gift or home furnishing item.

10605 Park Road, Charlotte NC
(704) 541-1148
www.blacklion.com

Antique Kingdom

When Philip Highsmith retired from teaching physics at Converse College in 1982, he opened Antique Kingdom. Located in a rambling white house with a covered porch, in one of Charlotte's earliest streetcar suburbs, the business is now owned by Philip's son, Steve. The Highsmiths purchase original antiques and solid pieces of enduring beauty. The pieces speak for themselves. Colorful glassware and one-of-a-kind finds, all well crafted, fill the store. Shopping in this antique paradise is an adventure. The building holds three levels of wonderful discoveries, with a knick-knack room on the first floor and larger furniture on other floors. Antique Kingdom has received praises from many publications, including a mention in the *Southern Living* Shop Til You Drop column, and an article in the *Charlotte Business Journal.* The owners are the first to tell you if the showy piece that catches your eye is not an actual antique in the strictest sense of the word. There are consignment pieces here, and finds from New York and elsewhere. They offer layaway, and a pickup and delivery plan. Antique Kingdom has carved a solid niche for itself in a city that knows antiques. Customers appreciate their honesty, friendliness and consistent quality. The store is located in the old Plaza-Midwood neighborhood. Come by and explore Antique Kingdom. They might even let you sit on the porch.

700 Central Avenue, Charlotte NC
(704) 377-KING (5464)   www.antiquekingdom.biz

Shirestone of the Carolinas

Located in the historic South End Design District of Charlotte, Shirestone of the Carolinas is a remarkable specialty countertop company known for its commitment to quality, exemplary customer service, and the ability to offer the unique. Shirestone of the Carolinas has become a respected part of the region's building community. Owner Inga Barnard has taken on the responsibility of creating exclusive countertop designs and employs a gifted staff that possesses more than 55 years of cumulative experience. Her background has given her the expertise to provide the necessary guidance to any customer seeking an alternative to the "common kitchen" and "everyone else's style." To that end, she and her staff endeavor to always go above and beyond the expectations of those who have, as she says, "honored us with their patronage." As the exclusive Shirestone products dealer in the Charlotte area, everyone in the shop works diligently to offer a unique style that is customized to fit your individual needs. In the past, their product was traditionally found only on the West Coast, but it has become quite popular in the American Southeast in recent years. With a hand-crafted process using a proprietary formula that is designed to create both a unique and durable surface, Shirestone will continue to grow in popularity as more builders and remodelers learn about its distinctive look. Please come by and look for yourself, or visit the website. You will know why the products offered by Shirestone of the Carolinas continue to grow in popularity.

2809 S Boulevard, Charlotte NC
(704) 340-1491
www.shirestone.net

Design Upholstery

Mike and Sabrina Polly began Design Upholstery in 1983 and they have been located in the historic Plaza-Midwood section of Charlotte since 1985. Their are planning to change their name to Design Services of Charlotte to reflect the broad range of services they provide. Design Upholstery specializes in custom headboards, cornices, and wall upholstery, as well as custom-built and re-finished furniture. They offer receiving, delivering, and temporary storage for designers, as well. Design Upholstery sells foam replacements for cushions and offers a wide array of fabrics. Mike grew up in the upholstery business, working closely with his grandfather, Rufus Stanfield. His grandmother, Ethel Stanfield, was a seamstress. His uncle, Everett Stanfield, owns a furniture and maritime upholstery company in Pensacola, Florida. The Pollys understand that furniture upholstery is an art, and that what is under the fabric, the foundation, is at least as important as the fabric itself. When you have a piece of furniture custom built at Design Upholstery, it will be constructed of the highest quality springs, foam and wood frames. Mike was recently featured in two shows on the Discovery Channel's *While You Were Out* series that were filmed in Charlotte. From ornate wall upholstery in Historic Georgetown to fine furniture ordered from Germany and Paris, designers trust Design Upholstery with the care of all their furnishings, and you can too.

1315 Central Avenue, Charlotte NC
(704) 376-7754
www.designupholstery.com

after

before

Bedside Manor

French, Italian and Portugese linens are just a few of the fine goods you will find at Bedside Manor. The largest linen store in Charlotte, Bedside Manor was opened by Laura and Jeff Fitch in 1994. With the help of Anna Castilow, store manager since 1998, Laura and Jeff offer a rich selection of rare discoveries in bed linens, tablecloths, bath towels and other useful, beautiful items, including reproductions of 19th century bed frames and armoires. You can find wonderful, plush Egyptian cotton towels and a world of other items for the bath and the rest of your home. They carry a selection of children's and baby bedding, as well as sleepware, robes, soaps, body care products, and superb wedding gifts. Laura and Jeff have traveled around the world attending everything from elegant European design shows to exotic bazaars in pursuit of the finest offerings. They've built a devoted clientele through both their unparalleled selection of wares and their commitment to customer service. As Laura says, "Service is our number one priority; we go the extra mile for our customers."

6822 E Phillips Place Court, Charlotte NC
(704) 554-7727 or (866) 554-7727
www.bedsidemanor.com

Powell Antiques and Interiors

The South End design district in Charlotte is home to Powell Antiques and Interiors, a true innovator when it comes to Southern-heritage home decoration. The Powell family business, three generations young, features over 3,600 square feet of investment-grade antiques. Hoke C. Powell II, and partners Mike and Martha Schreier, offer a modern combination of antiques sales and home decorating services. You will find considerable variety at Powell's. Inventory is rotated through stores in Georgia and South Carolina. Martha Schreier offers a consultation service through her business MSJ Interiors. By blending style, class and dramatic atmosphere, she can help you customize a room or your entire home. The store displays a large selection of unmatched home décor items and accents, including vintage pillows by Belle Designs, art, prints and exquisite furniture. First impressions are important at Powell's, where superior expertise, selection and services are bound to impress you.

1719 S Boulevard, Charlotte NC
(704) 371-3117

Bella Casa

Bella Casa has what everyone wants, fine home furnishings at great prices. Owner Kitty Vadini and buyer-manager Layton Campbell form a winning team and it shows. Bella Casa is a specialty boutique without the stratospheric prices attached. Their one-of-a-kind reproductions include eclectic, Old World items and sometimes even reclaimedwood pieces. Items can come from as far away as France, Spain, England and South America. The earthy ambience takes you to another world as you enter this enchanting shop. Exquisite furniture and eye-catching home accents and gifts vie for your attention. The upscale merchandise carries a downtown price, and inventory has a reputation for moving fast. Buy it when you find it, because it is not likely to be there next time. Everything needed to create or enhance your comfortable, luxurious abode can be found at Bella Casa. The bed you choose can be accessorized with comforter, pillows and pajamas without ever leaving the store. You can pick up French-milled soap for the bath and a candle holder for that bookcase or end table you found. Bella Casa also carries those hard-to-find gifts for the people in your life. Bella Casa means beautiful home. After a visit to this exemplary treasure store, that is exactly what you will have.

10225 Park Road, Charlotte NC
(704)759-9449

Wooden Stone

Have you ever called a neighbor to tell them about a great new set of dishes you picked up only to find they recently acquired the exact same set? The carbon copy accessories and home décor items that line department store walls today have long since passed interesting or artistic, but hope is not lost. You can add flair and excitement to everyday things in your home with a trip to Wooden Stone in Davidson. This fabulous shop opened in 2004 and has since become the destination store for those in the know who are looking for engaging new home or gift items. Wooden Stone offers a terrific collection of handcrafted furniture, jewelry, glassware and metal work. This store, reminiscent of a gallery, features numerous artists from all across the Untied States and Canada, with approximately a quarter of them residing in North Carolina. Owner Drew Crawford, with the support of his parents Van and Evalyn, opened the store with an eye toward offering quality useful pieces that are as beautiful as they are functional. Wooden Stone offers customers a gift registry suitable for any occasion along with professional photography for special events. They are also happy to take orders for custom furniture or other specially commissioned items. Because of the large and ever-changing inventory, Wooden Stone is an excellent resource for homebuilders and interior designers. Add original, whimsical touches to your home with the wonderful, useable furnishings and décor items waiting to charm you at Wooden Stone.

445 S Main Street, Davidson NC
(704) 892-1449
www.woodenstonegallery.com

Southern Piedmont Museums

Charlotte Museum of History & Hezekiah Alexander Homesite

In the late 1760s, Hezekiah Alexander, a colonist of Scots-Irish descent, moved his family down the Great Wagon Road to the frontier of Mecklenburg County. Hezekiah prospered in his new home, becoming a leading member of the community. In 1774 he completed an imposing two-story stone house. Still standing, Hezekiah's rock house is the oldest structure in Mecklenburg County, a fitting centerpiece for the Charlotte Museum of History, which relates stories of the people who shaped one of the South's most interesting and dynamic cities. In the 36,000-square-foot museum, four galleries lead visitors from early settlers and 18th Century freedom fighters to gold mines, slavery, the Civil War, and the rise of textiles, transportation and commerce. Visitors can literally walk back in time while exploring the eight-acre site, which includes the 1774 Hezekiah Alexander house, the American Freedom Bell, the Backcountry Patriot statue, and historic American Indian and Colonial gardens.

3500 Shamrock Drive, Charlotte NC
(704) 568-1774
www.charlottemuseum.org

Backing Up Classics Motor Cars

America's love of the automobile is renowned. People from every generation, culture and region in this country share this passion for cars. With this in mind, Jimmy Morrison purchased Backing Up Classics, 18,000 square feet of space dedicated to displaying wonders of the motor age. He and his brother Gary grew up around cars, so it is not surprising that the brothers went on to open their own dealership in the 1970s, specializing in exotic, rare and pre-owned cars and motorcycles. Despite a rural location, loyal customers and word-of-mouth advertising kept the unusual lot busy. Not everyone stops in to buy a classic; many folks just want to look at the beautiful examples of automotive engineering. A shiny red 1913 Ford Speedster, for example, or a '69 Z28 Camaro with a fiberglass hood and rear disc break option. They have a Delorean DMC-12, a 1926 Ford Model T, and the 1936 Ford Roadster featured in the movie *Chiefs*. The museum features race cars, muscle cars and a selection of motorcycles. Banquet, meeting and party facilities are available. Backing Up Classics invites you to stop in and browse the gift shop, fully stocked with NASCAR and other automobile memorabilia.

4545 Concord Parkway S, Concord NC
(704) 788-9500
www.backingupclassics.com

Discovery Place and Charlotte Nature Museum

Discovery Place makes it possible to visit astonishing frontiers without ever leaving Charlotte. This avant-garde science center is educational fun at its finest. From outer space to the depths of the ocean, no realm is left unexplored via the adventurous Discovery Place presentational journeys. The Discovery Halls showcase both permanent and feature exhibits, with a variety of programs and events that run the gamut of interest and entertainment. The Dead Sea Scrolls, for example, have been displayed here. As has Action! An Adventure in Moviemaking. The IMAX Dome, another feature attraction at Discovery Place, presents larger-than-life images in an intriguing, up-close and personal way. The nearby Charlotte Nature Museum, located next to Freedom Park, is an urban science center that exhibits plants and animals of the Piedmont, including an ever-changing Butterfly Garden that comes to life through the hued wings of its aerial guests. Show your support by becoming a member, and enjoy convenient discounts as you continue to explore the phenomenal variety offered by Discovery Place and the Charlotte Nature Museum.

301 N Tryon Street, Charlotte NC
(704) 372-6261 or (800) 935-0553
www.discoveryplace.org

Levine Museum of the New South

At the Levine Museum of the New South, visitors can walk through a tenant farmer's house, run their hands across a pile of seed cotton, and sit at a 1960s lunch counter and listen to personal accounts from leaders of the sit-in movement. The museum began in 1990 as an idea shared by Duke University Trustee Sally Dalton Robinson and Anne Batten of the Mecklenburg Historical Association. Following a successful $8.2 million capital campaign, the museum was able to move into a state-of-the-art facility on 7th Street in the heart of Charlotte's burgeoning uptown cultural district. The museum's centerpiece is its 8,000-square-foot exhibit, Cotton Fields to Skyscrapers, which includes interactive displays and exhibits. Public programs and events have been an important aspect of the museum since its founding. Youth programs offer children from age two and up the opportunity to learn history through storytelling, dance, music and art. The museum's distinguished lecturer series brings renowned historians and journalists to Charlotte, while its annual Taste of the New South fundraiser, featuring cuisine by outstanding regional resorts and inns, is eagerly anticipated. Relive the history of the South and enjoy the Levine Museum's emphasis on Charlotte and the Piedmont Province.

200 E Seventh Street, Charlotte NC
(704) 333-1887
www.museumofthenewsouth.org

Southern Piedmont Restaurants

The JFR Barn

The JFR Barn has a warm, rustic atmosphere conducive to settling in for a first-class meal. Open since 1974, the JFR Barn is the oldest restaurant in the Sandhills area. Its goal is to make your dining experience exceed any of your expectations. *Wine Spectator, Wine Enthusiast, Food and Wine, The Pinehurst* and *Southern Living* magazines have all showered awards and accolades on the JFR Barn, a clear indication the Barn has met its goal. Hundreds of spectacular selections grace the wine list. Recommended entrées include grilled duck with a raspberry glaze, succulent grilled salmon or grilled veal liver. The JFR Barn's varied menu includes a tantalizing jumbo lobster tail, tender filet mignon, grilled shrimp and lamb chops. All in all, its steaks, chicken, seafood and chops are considered second to none. Private rooms accommodate 30 to 120 guests, with the ultimate dining experience being the wine room and cellar. Call for a schedule of the monthly dinners or take advantage of the catering service. Make plans to visit The JFR Barn. You'll see why they have garnered so much attention.

305 Rothney Avenue, Southern Pines NC
(910) 692-7700

Cosmos Café

Bartenders in Barcelona covered drinks with little plate lids known as tapas, and placed small servings of food on the plates to accompany the drink. Cosmos Café in Charlotte celebrates tapas. Food choices include full meals, wood-fired pizza, sandwiches, an extensive mezes and tapas menu, and a comprehensive wine list. The tapas dishes feature a treasure trove of flavors, such as sautéed blue mussels, or brie en croute served with pomegranate syrup and crusty French bread. Crab con queso is served with tricolored tortilla chips. Heartier fare like bison filet mignon, Maryland crab cakes and a seared Magret duck breast are part of the entree portion of the tantalizing menu. Chefs at Cosmos Café are pioneers of the James Beard Foundation Dinners. The host chef of Cosmos will coordinate with 10 other chefs to create a full 10-course culinary event.

This benefit dinner will showcase the work of interesting local artists in their Microcosm Art Gallery. Specialty martinis and fine cigars are served in the Thirsty Camel Lounge. A Latin Dance instructor gives free instruction Thursday nights, and a daily happy hour includes two-for-one mezes and tapas. Gus and George Georgoulias, and partners Andy and Tom, invite you to share a selection of tapas and drinks with friends late into the night at Cosmos Café.

300 N College Street, Charlotte NC
(704) 372-3553
www.cosmoscafe.com

Bojangles Famous Chicken 'n Biscuits

The first Bojangles' Chicken 'n Biscuits was opened by Jack Fulk and Richard Thomas in 1977. Named after the legendary New Orleans singer, dancer and vaudeville artist Bill Bojangles Robinson, the business has grown to be nearly as famous as its namesake. The menu boasts spicy cajun chicken that is never frozen but always fresh, made with the secret spices and seasonings of the original recipe. Buttermilk biscuits are made fresh every 20 minutes. Coffee is made from freshly ground beans each time, while sweet tea is brewed and steeped the Southern way. Breakfast is served all day. Sides such as dirty rice, seasoned fries with the skin on, and cajun pintos are traditional favorites. The sausage is of the highest quality. Everything about Bojangles belies the fast food image. This locally-owned wonder is active in many local organizations and charities, including sponsorship of an annual golf tournament, the Muscular Dystrophy Association's top fundraising event in Charlotte. The company also sponsors the Carolina Panthers, the Charlotte Bobcats and Lowe's Motor Speedway. With more than 350 restaurants, Bojangles' serves a lot of its Famous Chicken 'n Biscuits. If you haven't tried them yet, drop in. You'll feel like you came home.

9432 Southern Pines Boulevard, Charlotte NC
(704) 940-8661 or (800) 366-9921
www.bojangles.com

Wolfman Pizza

Wolfman Pizza has been a Charlotte legend since 1991. Originally created by Barry Wolfman, it is currently owned and operated by Cameron McRae. Famous for California-style pizzas, Wolfman's specializes in nontraditional homemade sauces and toppings. Dough is made fresh daily and only the best ingredients are used. You can choose from approximately 40 different toppings. They offer a dozen different sauces, ranging from traditional to marinated black bean sauce. The menu also includes jumbo chicken wings with your choice of sauce, to-die-for-salads, unique pastas, and panini sandwiches. Once you bite into the homemade Styx, you will be back whether the moon is full or not. Romano-and-herb topped bread sticks are served with a tangy marinara, sundried tomato pesto, and a creamy-cheesy artichoke dip. Wolfman Pizza offers a great dining experience whether you eat-in or order takeout. Many of the five locations, in Charlotte, Cotswold Mall, Providence Commons (Ballantyne Area), Myers Park Center, Quail Corners and Mooresville deliver. Wolfman's also sells take & bake pizzas. Wolfman's Pizza was voted Best Pizza in Charlotte for 11 consecutive years. The clientele can attest to the fact that nothing has changed over the past 15 years regarding the taste and popularity of their masterpiece pizza. Remember your experience at Wolfman Pizza with "glow in the dark" t-shirts that can be purchased at any location. Visit their website for more details.

Cotswold: (704) 366-3666
Providence Commons: (704) 845-9888
Myers Park: (704) 377-4695
Quail Corners: (704) 552-4979
Mooresville: (704) 662-9727
www.wolfmanpizza.com

The Dog Bar NoDa

If you think you overhear someone say that the North Davidson area in Charlotte is going to the dogs, you may have misunderstood them. What they were really saying was everyone in the NoDa is going to the Dog Bar, one of the historic area's newest hotspots. The Dog Bar is Charlotte's only dog friendly bar, as long as your pooch is well behaved and has proof its free of rabies. This popular spot in the NoDa arts district is the place to see friends bumping elbows with local celebrities, where business suits and future bright stars can share a colorful cocktail or satisfying meal. When warm weather beckons clientele outside, an umbrella-shaded patio accommodates those who want to be seen but not burned. The Dof Bar is owned by Charlotte native J.P.Brewer with partners Dan Morgan and Will Witherspoon, two members of the Carolina Panthers football squad. Next time you're in NoDa, unleash your fun side at the Dog Bar. It's sure to get your tail wagging.

3307 N Davidson Street, Charlotte NC
704-370-3595
www.dogbarnoda.com

Coach's Sports Bar and Grille

Where can you go to see any sporting event at any time? Coach's Sports Bar and Grille, the original sports bar in Pineville, opened with the sports fan in mind. Jim "Spanky" Sprowles purchased Coach's with the idea to give his customers what they want, when they want it, where they want it, and at a price they can afford. Spanky was working as an electrical engineer when he was offered the opportunity to open a restaurant/bar, and he took it. He bought Coach's and dedicated it to sports and family. Coach's has it all: brew, Buffalo wings and ballgames. The prices are extremely reasonable on the American-food based menu. What more could a sports fan ask for? There are three 100-inch projection screen televisions, three large plasma high-definition televisions and 36 other variously sized television screens scattered around the spacious main dining room, as well as in the large game room and special private rooms for catered events. The family-friendly atmosphere offers a unique Carolina sporting experience. At Coach's Sports Bar and Grille, you will have no problem finding your big game to watch on C-Band, Direct TV and digital cable.

10403-J Park Road Extension, Pineville NC
(704) 544-0607

Charanda Mexican Grill and Cantina

To many people, Mexican cuisine is nothing more than a never-ending parade of taste-alike tacos and burritos, with the occasional fajita thrown in for variety. Luckily the truth of the matter is far different at Charanda Mexican Grill and Cantina in Concord. Mexican food, much like the varied and delicious dishes of the Mediterranean countries, is as diverse and inspiring as the regions of Mexico themselves. In Charanda (which means rich-red soil in the

Tarasco dialect of central Mexico), people use traditional family recipes to offer fabulous dishes that reflect influences from the southern United States and northern Mexico that are anything but commonplace. This popular eatery opened in 2002 under the ownership of Freidy and Juan Ramirez and his two partners, Francisco Olea and Juan Chamochumbi.

Begin your meal with one of Charanda's festive appetizers, such as the delicious nachos or the chicken wings. A favorite entrée not to be missed is the steak relleno, which is masterfully prepared from a recipe created by Juan and Freidy's mother, Dona Juve, and served with rice topped with charro beans and a cactus salad. Additional menu delights include the mango salmon and the tamarindo pork chops. The four partners pride themselves on offering a varied and interesting menu served at reasonable prices with unsurpassable customer service. Come in and discover your new favorite Mexican restaurant with a visit to Charanda Mexican Grill and Cantina.

8626 Concord Mills Boulevard, Concord NC   (704) 979-3366

Stacy's

The town of Denver and its Lake Norman businesses have experienced much growth over the years, and Stacy's is no exception. The restaurant has accumulated a very loyal following as new people flock to this rising city. Owner Stacy Pitsikoulis came from Island Chios in Greece in 1969 to visit his uncle and ended up staying, although he still goes home to visit his mother every year. Since 1971, Stacy and Fay Pitsikoulis have offered a great variety of freshly made steaks, seafood, Greek and Italian dishes to their anticipating customers, along with a popular, homemade peach cobbler. Originally called Denver Restaurant, the restaurant has expanded to a 5,000-square-foot location and acquired a new name. Located 25 miles north of Charlotte, Stacy's is a popular eatery. Since it's near Dale Jarrett Racing Adventure, Harry Gant and many other racecar drivers stop by to eat. Even Burt Reynolds frequented the restaurant in the old days. On your next visit to Charlotte, Stacy's invites you to enjoy a great meal in a friendly family-owned restaurant. Who knows, you might even get to see a star.

3790 Highway 16, Denver NC (704) 483-5811

Courtney's BBQ

Called the Home of America's Best Ribs, Courtney's BBQ will knock your socks off. Since its inception in 1999, owners Gene and Janice Courtney have garnered local and national acclaim. Courtney's won a championship in Beef Brisket at the Tryon Ridge Festival, and took first place in the Tarheel Barbecue Festival's Hog Happenin' Contest. They continually supply their succulent fare for competitions led by Team Captain Marty Woolbright, who brings the honor back for Courtney's time and again. Courtney's BBQ is known for their Lexington-style sauce, which they bottle and sell. They're also famous for their St. Louis trim spare ribs, pork, and a full line of seafood, including oysters, devilled crab and fried flounder. The Courtney's and their daughters, Lee and Rae, are active in their community, sometimes serving up 25,000 fundraiser plates in a season. Courtney's BBQ is popular for catering. As the locals say, "If you haven't tried Courtney's, you haven't tried award-winning barbecue." If you're going to be anywhere near Clover, Courtney's will be worth your time.

1166 Highway 55 E, Clover SC (803) 222-5900 www.courtneysbbq.com/new

Cuisine Malaya

Does the thought of being able to get true ethnic Malayan, Japanese and Thai cuisine all at one location intrigue you? Owner Teik Chan and Executive Chef Jeffery Ho promise you won't be disappointed at Cuisine Malaya. Located in the historic Elizabeth district on the south end of East Trade Street, Cuisine Malaya is a popular dining destination for locals, as well as out-of-towners. Many short-term residents of Singapore and Malaysia, upon returning home to North Carolina, insist on eating at Cuisine Malaya to get a taste of the flavors they enjoyed during their time in a different culture. From roast duck spring rolls to mango shrimp, it isn't often that you get to savor true ethnic specialties served on the eastern side of the Continental Divide. Try it, and you're sure to like the choices at Cuisine Malaya.

1411 Elizabeth Avenue, Charlotte NC (704) 372-0766 www.cuisine-malaya.com

Bentley's on 27

Send your senses on an excursion of bold flavors, intoxicating aromas and glorious vision with a trip to Bentley's on 27. Owner Jim Emad and his wife Kay invite you to experience a whole new level of fine dining. Lose yourself in the romance of warm gold ceilings, elegant chandeliers and relaxing handmade leather chairs from Italy. Three fireplaces and wall niches help to showcase a stunning collection of blown-glass artwork from well known artisans around the world. While enjoying an incredible meal, patrons can indulge in a spectacular view of Charlotte. Executive Chef William Schutz is a Long Island, New York native who came to the Charlotte area after 20 years of working in some of the best kitchens in Manhattan. His experience and attention to detail is echoed in every meal he presents. The menu, inspired by American and French cuisine,

has a delicious assortment of appetizers to begin your meal, such as scampi sautéed in brandy, parsley, lemon and garlic and served over angel hair pasta. Following Emad's vision to include classic French dishes, several items, including Chateaubriand Bouquetiere and Holland Dover sole, get an Old World twist with tableside preparation using a *gueridon*. Seldom used in this day and age, a *gueridon* is a mobile cooking cart that allows a chef to prepare a meal right in front of the diner. To end your business day or begin your evening, stop by Bentley's lounge to enjoy a glass of wine or cocktail from Jim's tastefully selected collection. With exemplary service, exquisite cuisine and intimate dining areas, Bentley's on 27 is the right place for a memorable evening.

201 S College Street, 27th Floor, Charlotte Plaza, Charlotte NC
(704) 343-9201
www.bentleyson27.com

T-Bones on the Lake

Similar to many lakeshore destinations, Lake Wylie's focus is water recreation, whether it be fishing, sailing or water skiing. Living it up in fine restaurants is on the menu when visitors are off the lake, with popular T-Bones offering relaxing dining for families and business people alike. Lake Wylie's shores are in both North and South Carolina, just 20 miles south of Charlotte. Owned by the Presley family since 1985, T-Bones is famous for its slow-cooked baby back ribs, steaks and seafood. Guests say it's like being on vacation at the lake regardless of whether you're just stopping by for a meal or you actually are on vacation, which is a great idea since this is prime touring country. T-Bones on Lake Wylie opened in 1994 with 500 seats, four bars, and 38 boat slips for lake lovers. The Drunken Parrot Bar serves up live regional entertainment for an unforgettable and enjoyable evening. Whether you're an avid water skier in search of a stunning getaway, a visitor seeking new lakeside treasures, or are just looking for great dining for the evening, make sure to include T-Bones on Lake Wylie in your plans.

3990 Highway 49, Lake Wylie SC
(803) 831-0170
www.tbonesonthelake.com

Cantina 1511

In Charlotte, an exceptional experience in Mexican dining awaits you at the distinctive Cantina 1511. Frank Scibelli and Dennis Thompson, two of Charlotte's distinguished entrepreneurs, developed the concept for this cantina. Scibelli, the owner, focuses on the authentic Mexican cuisine of the Yucatan peninsula. The indigenous ingredients of the region include habanero chiles and epazote. Meat is often cooked in open fire pits, marinated with nuts, spices, sour fruit juices and chiles, and sometimes wrapped in banana leaves. Cantina 1511 may not offer the banana leaf, but the menu still provides a glorious array of tasty, satisfying Yucatan-inspired delights, such as the famed Red Snapper Veracruz, which showcases the lighter, citrus palette of the Yucatan coast. Recipes use an array of imported chiles and can be made mild or spicy at your request. Outside patio seating provides a fresh air alternative to the pleasant indoor seating. A fun cantina atmosphere contributes to making your meal a festive occasion. The menu includes margaritas, 35 brands of tequila and a brief wine list. Pottery punctuates the setting-sun color scheme. In the main dining room, cozy booths sit beneath windows. There is also banquet-table seating. At Cantina 1511, you will be warmly greeted and then treated to your own culinary Mecca.

1511 E Boulevard, Charlotte NC   (704) 331-9222

Cajun Yard Dog Restaurant

The Cajun Yard Dog Restaurant in Charlotte offers New Orleans-style cuisine with a mixture of country classic dishes served up in a casual, fun and relaxing atmosphere. Chef Jeff Parsons has continued to add creative and exciting Creole-influenced dishes since the popular eatery opened in 2001. House specialties include country-style pork roast, lemon-herbed half chickens served with bourbon sauce, étouffée dishes, and fresh blackened seafood entrées. Cajun Yard Dog's po'boy sandwiches are not to be missed; they are made with various savory fillings from oysters to barbecued pork. Further traditional favorites are bacon and black-eyed peas, okra soup and rattlesnake bean chili, each served with a choice of two sides.

The menu offers daily specials, terrific desserts and take-out choices. The whole family can enjoy dinner and live entertainment, featuring a distinctive blend of jazz and classic rock. The inviting strains of that old style Mississippi River music encourage patrons to sit back, relax and enjoy the sensational food and company. The restaurant's cheery and dedicated staff, in conjunction with Chef Jeff's truly fabulous food, is what really keeps folks coming back again and again. It's also why you should come early. There is often a line of customers that runs out the door and halfway down the block. Owner Ron Atherton and staff encourage you to treat the whole family to a down-home meal, toe-tapping music and an overall rousing good time at the Cajun Yard Dog Restaurant.

8036 Providence Road, Suite 900, Charlotte NC
(704) 752-1750

Trio

Trio, an upscale casual restaurant at the intersection of McMullen Creek Parkway and Route 51, was built by the owners of Charley's Restaurant in 1992. The architectural features offer a variety of dining experiences to suit everyone's needs. You may choose to dine in a comfortable bar area, in cozy booths with views of the landscaped outdoors, in an open central area with linen-dressed tables, at the pizza bar in full view of the wood-burning oven, in a semi-private room, or under the umbrellas on the outdoor patio. Trio provides a blend of traditional and contemporary foods and gives you options to select light fare or a full course meal. The menu includes sandwiches, soups and salads, pizza, fresh seafood entrées, pasta, steaks and outstanding homemade desserts. Diners can choose from a monthly selection of specials created around regional themes. Trio restaurant is an ideal destination for an after-work cocktail, a quick bite to eat, a romantic evening meal, a lively dinner with a group of friends or a relaxed family gathering. The experienced, friendly staff and management team work together to serve every customer. You will be impressed with the quality, variety and prices of their food. Customers keep coming back to Trio to sample great food at reasonable prices in a comfortable, casual environment where each person feels special. Trio accepts advanced reservations for tables of six or more. Call-ahead seating is also available. When you enter Trio, a world of dining experiences opens for you.

10709 McMullen Creek Parkway, Charlotte NC
(704) 541-8000
www.trio-charlotte.com

Charley's

Charleys, an upscale casual restaurant in the Cotswold Village Shops, serves a blend of traditional and contemporary foods. The menu includes sandwiches, entrée-size salads, barbecued ribs, seafood, pasta, steaks and pizzas. Diners choose from a selection of monthly specials, plus can be assured of finding old favorites from Charley's original menu. Customers keep coming back to Charleys because of the great food served at reasonable prices in a comfortable, casual environment where each person feels special. Charleys restaurant opened in the SouthPark Mall in April 1985 as part of a chain of nine restaurants of the same name in Virginia and North Carolina. In 1986, a group of investors purchased the SouthPark restaurant and, in 1992, built a second restaurant, Trio, on Route 51. In 2001, Charleys moved into a newly renovated site in Cotswold. You may choose to dine in the lively indoor or outdoor bar areas, at tables or booths in the main room, in a popular semiprivate room, or in their outdoor patio, where you also enjoy summer entertainment. Charleys is an ideal destination for an after-work cocktail, a quick bite to eat, a relaxing evening meal or a dinner with family and friends. Charleys accepts advanced reservations for tables of 10 or more. For groups of fewer than 10, call Charley's 15 to 20 minutes before your anticipated time of arrival to be put on the waiting list.

274 S Sharon Amity, Charlotte NC
(704) 367-9500
www.charleys-charlotte.com

Jackalope Jacks

Do you believe in jackalopes? You don't have to, as long as you love a great burger and enjoy the idea of choosing from 18 draft beers to wash it down. In Charlotte, Jackalope Jacks is the place you'll find them, at the sign of the mythical mammal, said to be half jackrabbit and half antelope. Under the ownership of Robert Nixon and Andy Wilson, Jackalope Jacks maintains a great pub atmosphere. A large patio allows you to dine outdoors for eight or nine months of the year. When not eating or imbibing, there's a full-size shuffleboard court and a large game room. Now and then there's a bingo game, and locals say the Sunday Brunch is the best in town. House specialties include roast pork loin, fish and chips, shrimp pasta and meatloaf. Chicken comes grilled, country fried or done in Monterey or parmesan styles. There is, however, no jackalope meat on the menu. You say you're a doubter when it comes to jackalopes? Well, maybe they're easier to believe in after a cold beer.

1936 7th Street, Charlotte NC
(704) 347-1918
www.jackalopejacks.com

Zebra Restaurant

Cuisine is a fine art at Zebra, a restaurant run by Jim Alexander, a graduate of the prestigious Culinary Institute of America. He received Certified Executive Chef status in 1991 and served on the U.S. Culinary Olympic Team in 1996. Few could be better qualified to bring the best in fine dining to Charlotte's SouthPark district. Jim's accomplishments have been recognized by the *Charlotte Observer*, which bestowed its highest rating on Zebra, and AAA, which has given Zebra a four-diamond rating for three years in a row. Zebra's wine list boasts 800 selections in a 10,000-bottle cellar and is an award-winning attraction in its own right. A la carte contemporary French cooking is the order of the day at Zebra. From the hors d'oeuvres to the dessert, this is definitely an experience worth every minute of your time. Be sure to try one of the delectable soups for which Jim is justly celebrated, or try the 12-course chef tasting menu, and don't hesitate to ask the wait staff for recommendations if you're having trouble making up your mind. Zebra is as committed to making you comfortable in an unpretentious environment as it is to satisfying your gourmet cravings.

4521 Sharon Road, Charlotte NC
(704) 442-9525
www.zebrarestaurant.net

Bonterra Dining & Wine Room

Did you know that red wine should be stored and served at 68 degrees and that white should be kept and served at 42 degrees? They know it at Bonterra Dining & Wine Room in Charlotte. These folks are serious about wine, serving over 200 wines by the glass. You'll be amazed at the difference in taste when wine is served at the optimum temperature. At Bonterra, owner John (J.D.) Duncan and his staff go beyond your normal expectations to accentuate their unique, wine-friendly atmosphere. Their efforts have won a *Wine Spectator* magazine Award of Excellence, a DiRona award, and an AAA Four Diamond award. Bonterra flies its lobsters from the cold waters of South Africa, and has fish flown in daily from Honolulu. Guests are served in a building that served as a church from 1895 through 1987. The church provided food and shelter for farm workers for many years. Now it's your turn to have the best food and wine provided to you. Take the time to enjoy a visit to Bonterra Dining & Wine Room.

1829 Cleveland Avenue, Charlotte NC (704) 333-9463 www.bonterradining.com

Red Rocks Café, Bar and Bakery

Founded in 1992 by Ron Herbert and John Love, Red Rocks Café, Bar and Bakery has become locally famous. You'll find great food, personalized service and a jazzy dining atmosphere. The Birkdale Village location is owned and run by Ron with Domenic Battiste as executive chef. John owns and runs the SouthPark location with Ron Brown as executive chef. No matter which location you visit, you will discover quality steaks, ribs, pasta and seafood. Every menu item has been named for a past customer, some famous and some not so famous. The comfortable booths, low lighting and jazz music playing in the background add enjoyment. The brick walls and dark hardwood floors also add a touch of class to the dining experience. You can choose your favorite wine from the café's distinctive wine cellar and end your meal with a dessert made from scratch. No need to get a babysitter, Red Rocks has a children's menu. Reservations are suggested, but not required. Red Rocks also offers catering and private dining for any of your special occasions. Visit Red Rocks Café for personalized service in an upscale atmosphere.

8712 Lindholm Drive, Huntersville NC   (704) 892-9999
4223-B Province Road, Charlotte NC   (704) 362-0402
www.redrockscafe.com

Tavern on the Tracks

At Tavern on the Tracks you'll find equal parts northern fare and southern hospitality. Built in the 1930s as a warehouse, this brick building has been a bar since the late 1990s. The building is large and open, but there's a welcoming feeling from the moment you enter. Owners Greg Roderick and Bill Acquario worked many years in the restaurant business in New York. In 1995 they brought their western, New York-style cuisine to Charlotte. The Tavern is the home of Buffalo Bills fans in Charlotte. However, North Carolina Panther's players often come in after games for the famous buffalo wings and, of course, fun. All food at the Tavern is homemade. Beef on a Weck is very popular. This is slow-cooked roast beef served on a kimmelweck roll. Stuffed banana peppers are another popular item. Sunday brunch is not to be missed. Crab cakes benedict and filet mignon with eggs are among many entrees and superb desserts that are special. Enjoy your brunch out on the sun deck with a beautiful view of downtown, or inside the cozy restaurant. Whether you are a fan of the Buffalo Bills or the Panthers, great food and hospitality in a fun relaxed atmosphere awaits you at the Tavern on the Tracks.

1411 S Tryon, Charlotte NC (704) 372-0782

Harry & Jean's Passionate American Food

Meet Ralph Meranto, a man who is passionate about American food, so passionate, in fact, that he opened Harry & Jean's, a restaurant dedicated to Passionate American Food. Ralph's two restaurants, named for his Holland Dutch and Scotch-Irish grandparents, have a relaxed, mid-upscale, family-influenced atmosphere. Guests will find the dining room, parlor and family room reminiscent of visiting a home from the early 1900s. Each dining space offers its own ambience through varied color schemes defined by wood and fabric. Every room features photographs of Ralph's family from the early 1900s. The menu at Harry & Jean's is based on home-style cooking, each meal created with unique flavors and presented with an upscale flair. The restaurant is open seven days a week and features a jazz brunch on Sundays. Harry & Jean's offers tasty appetizers to begin your meal, such as crispy calamari, stuffed mushrooms or lobster bisque. Some of Ralph's favorite entrées include smothered chicken, lasagna and the Monte Cristo sandwich. The restaurant's house-made desserts, such as the caramel apple crisp and gooey brownie, are family favorites that were traditionally made only on holidays. You can complete your meal with fresh ground coffee in one of the restaurant's specialty coffee drinks, such as Gatsby's Grand Finale. Bring your family to meet Ralph's family; you'll discover pride and passion in every detail of each Harry & Jean's dining experience.

201 S Tryon Street, Charlotte NC
(707) 333-4300
www.harryandjeans.com

Greek Isles Restaurant

Head for the Greek Isles Restaurant, voted Best Ethnic Restaurant in 2005 by the *Observer*. Owner Panos Photopoulos and family serve seafood, chicken, chops and steaks prepared in the styles of the Greek Islands with names like Santorini, Mykonos and Crete. Customers use words like "spectacular" to describe the food. The family and staff often greet customers and friends with "yiassou" and say "opa" (cheers) as regulars come and go. You can enjoy the food and atmosphere outside on the patio, if you like, with a view of the Charlotte skyline as you watch trollies go by. Panos was born in a small Greek town near Mt. Olympus and moved to Chicago at age 25. There he met and married Toula, and they had three sons while working in the restaurant business. Tiring of Midwestern winters, they moved to Charlotte because it offered a climate similar to that of Greece. In 1985, they bought the French Quarter, which they still run while splitting their time with the Greek Isles. Sons Greg, George and Frank round out the family business lineup. The food you want is at Greek Isles Restaurant. It's authentic, and it's waiting for you.

200 East Bland Street, Charlotte NC
(704) 444-9000

Dressler's Restaurant

Eat well, laugh often, live long. That's the motto at Dressler's Restaurant, where owners Kim and Jon Dressler believe in taking care of guests and having fun. Jon started in the restaurant business in 1983. He and his staff focus on quality food in a relaxed atmosphere. You can dine on the patio, in the bar, or inside where earth tones and warm stones accentuate the walls. Jon describes the food that chef Scott Hollingsworth prepares as "upscale contemporary American." Appetizers include the popular crab dip, which combines jumbo lump crab with a warm béchamel sauce. Salads include the G's House, a mix of mesclun greens with goat cheese, caramelized onions, sugared walnuts, and homemade balsamic vinaigrette. Entrées include a wide variety of fresh seafood imaginatively prepared. The house favorite is the halibut topped with jumbo lump crab. Steaks are all certified Angus beef. Meat selections include Filet Imperial, rack of lamb and a mouth-watering pork chop. With a wine list featuring 175 bottles, there is a bottle of wine to go with every meal. Desserts are all made in house. The crowd pleaser is the cheesecake, crafted with loving care by Jon's mom, Joan Dressler. For a comfortable, stylish meal in Birkdale Village, Dressler's is absolutely perfect.

8630-1A Lindholm Drive, Huntersville NC   (704) 987-1779   www.dresslersrestaurant.com

Southend Brewery & Smokehouse

For the number one rated microbrewery in the South, look no further than Southend Brewery and Smokehouse in Charlotte. Here you'll enjoy hand-crafted beers, house-smoked pork, chicken and oven-baked pizzas in a 100-year-old building that was a cotton mill. The center of attention is a functioning brewhouse encased in glass. Or you can move to the patio, enjoy the food with live acoustic music and a spectacular view of uptown Charlotte. Joe Ryan and his staff focus on producing quality beer and excellent American fare. Vats are visible behind glass walls, with each tank producing 15 barrels of beer during a 14-day brewing cycle. The results are lights, blondes, pale ales, wheats, red and brown ales, and stouts. Whatever your taste, you'll like what you find brewed here. Southend is a fun place, where you can enjoy a premium cigar or try your hand at a stock car racing simulator. Visit soon to discover why they are number one.

2100 S Boulevard, Charlotte NC   (704) 358-4677   www.southendbrewery.com

The Meeting House

In a quaint, historic Charlotte house built in 1905, Christopher Zion produces an epicurean delight at The Meeting House. Christopher, trained at Cordon Bleu in Paris, showcases upscale American fare rooted in traditional, regional ingredients. Here you'll find the best pork chops served over white beans with collard greens and a molasses sauce. The Meeting House is known for rock shrimp, and Johnny Cakes made with blue crabs, shrimp, potatoes and corn meal. The signature dessert is molten chocolate cake. *South Carolina Weekly* awards five stars to the Meeting House and the *Wine Spectator* has recognized it for its 60-plus vintage wines available by the glass. Says Christopher, "I try to appeal to our diner's senses by complementing my dishes with the best wines from around the world. For instance our Simply the Best Pork Chop, with brown butter-braised Great Northern, candied shallots and collards, pairs perfectly with Silverado Sangiovese." If you want that kind of concern and care going into a wonderful meal, head for The Meeting House.

801 Providence Road, Charlotte NC   (704) 334-6338   www.meeting-house.com

Maharani

Maharani's mission is to provide Charlotte with the most authentic Indian food available. This goal is easily reached thanks to the skills of restaurateur Amandeep Singh, who hails from New Delhi, and his secret weapon, executive chef Kehar, who was trained in the Punjab. Maharani has become a very popular dining destination in Charlotte thanks to the superb cuisine praised both by locals and by natives of India living in the area. Amandeep has shown a real talent for running a restaurant. In the past this talent enabled him to operate two successful Indian restaurants in northern Germany and one in New York before he and his cousin Inderpal came to Charlotte and launched Maharani in 2002. Among the house specialties are tandoori clay oven dishes and fresh baked Indian breads such as naan. Those who love spicy food won't be disappointed, and those who are wary will be pleased to know that dishes are offered in a range of spices from cool to hot. Maharani also offers a selection of the finest imported beers from India, which go exceptionally well with the hotter dishes, and a fine selection of wines for the milder fare. The aromas and spices of India await you at Maharani in the midst of the Queen City.

901 South Kings Drive, Suite 115, Charlotte NC
(704) 370-2455

Penguin Drive-In

The revitalized and thriving Penguin Drive-In stands sentry over the charming and highly desirable Plaza-Midwood neighborhood. Born in the 1950s and originating as an ice cream shop, the Penguin Drive-In has earned a place in the hearts of local families. This became the ideal place for ice cream after a Sunday drive and for neighborhood kids to hang out after school. In its early days locals called it the Bird. Soon the little drive-in became popular for those of all ages and walks of life. Now the friendly and cheerful staff promptly serves quality meals filled with Southern flair and flavor. A popular snack is their fried pickles, deep-fried and served with creamy ranch dressing. Also offered is a nice selection of fresh salads and homemade soups and stews. The Bird offers a diverse and tasty selection of sandwiches, including such favorites as fried bologna and the grilled cheese pita. They also have great hamburgers and hotdogs, such as the full blown hemi and the winky-dinky dog. Alongside traditional French fries and onion rings you will find the oh-so-good sweet potato fries and scrumptious hushpuppies. The next time you're in the Plaza-Midwood area, stop in for some great food, exemplary service and an old-fashioned dose of fun at the Penguin Drive-In.

1921 Commonwealth Avenue, Charlotte NC
(704) 375-6959   www.penguindrivein.com

Arpa Tapas Wine Bar & Grill

At Arpa Tapas, Wine Bar & Grill in downtown Charlotte, you find a Mediterranean theme with a wine list to rival any European restaurant. You find authentic Spanish cuisine, with ingredients grown locally or imported from Spain. Pick several menu choices or full catering; they are served on plates you and your guests can share. That way you can each sample several items. There is an international wine list, with a concentration on Spanish vintners, of course. It's all done in an atmosphere that's playful, but luxurious, with edgy elegance. Come on in and celebrate with the Croquetas de Pollo y Jamon and a glass of Maso Canali's Pinot Grigio. Or head for a table for two and relax over a Requeson con Tomate and a bottle of Marques de Caceres Tempranillo. In addition to being cozy and intimate, this establishment has the rare quality of being stylish without being trendy. Arpa is part of the Harpers group of restaurants, owned by Tom Sasser and presided over by executive chef Tom Condron. John Jackson is the proprietor at Arpa; Warren Baird is the chef de cuisine.

129 W Trade Street, Charlotte NC   (704) 372-7792   www.arpawinebar.com

Zink

Are you feeling cool tonight? Do you want to see and be seen? Do you want superb food at your table while you're drinking in the atmosphere? Then Zink in Charlotte is where you want to be. Zink is part of the Harpers group of restaurants owned by Tom Sasser and presided over by executive chef Tom Condron. Here deep crimson decoration soothes you while the subtle and modern design elements accent the restaurant with elegance. Brass-railed staircases and glass shelving, quiet tables or sushi bars all have the effect of spoiling you at Zink. You feel very exclusive without being intimidating. There is an aura of cozy high society here. Proprietor Nasser Razmyar and chef de cuisine d' excellence Paul Cruz see to it that you find the menu items superb and affordable. Full catering is also available. The main courses range from salmon and trout to duck and pork, as well as Southern favorites like chicken and dumpling. With lobster, wild boar and more, the menu is exotic as well as comforting. You'll like tasting, seeing and being seen here at Zink.

201 N Tryon Street, Charlotte NC
(704) 444-9001
www.zinkamerican.com

Harper's

At Harper's Restaurant in Charlotte, you find classic, casual American cuisine. Enjoy hickory-grilled fish, beef and chicken, plus a variety of salads, sandwiches and pastas. Or try a gourmet wood-fired pizza. Harper's is the flagship concept of the Harper's group of restaurants. North Carolina native Tom Sasser opened Harper's in 1987, offering a relaxed atmosphere and a memorable culinary experience. Each of the Harper's restaurants features a beautiful patio and landscaping, brick and stone construction, brass detail and local artwork. The style incorporates the local flavor with decorative murals painted by local artists. Area microbrews are served on tap, and regional favorites appear as special menu items. Enjoy it all at this Charlotte landmark.

Charlotte (Woodlawn): (704) 522-8376   Charlotte (SouthPark): (704) 366-6688
Greensboro (Friendly Center): (336) 299-8850   Charlotte (West Trade): (704) 371-8774
www.harpersrestaurants.com

Ratcliffe on the Green

Southern hospitality blended with Old World standards and charm gives guests reason to make Ratcliffe on the Green a regular destination. Diners feel like invited guests to a friendly home, not just customers. Ashli Wilson and her staff make certain no detail is left undone, yet nothing seems pretentious in this circa 1920s building. Originally built as Ratcliffe's Flowers, partners John Duncan and Ashli Wilson reinstated the historical name and brought magic back to this amazing site. Together, they introduce Charlotte residents and the world to the new era of Ratcliffe. Preparing contemporary American cuisines, the dedicated culinary staff uses resources from around the world to bring you the freshest and highest quality ingredients possible, ensuring you an incredible, memorable dining experience. Fresh, innovative cooking comes to new light in this dramatic setting. The professional service staff is well trained and ready to make your time at Ratcliffe on the Green more than a great meal. Proud to offer more than 100 wines by the glass and an additional 200 wines from the wine cellar, you will find the wine journey a much appreciated part of your dining experience. Ratcliffe on the Green is proud to be the sister restaurant of Bonterra, one of Charlotte's most acclaimed restaurants by the local and national press. Drop in for a dining experience like no other.

435 S Tryon Street, Charlotte NC
(704) 358-9898
www.Ratcliffedining.com

Ho Ho China Bistro

Ho Ho China Bistro is a dream come true. It all started when four young people from China met while working in a Charlotte restaurant. The four, two men and two women, became close friends. Then the friends became partners, in more ways than one. Qing Lin, who trained in the culinary arts in China's Fun-Jian province, married Tracy Yang. The other young man, Jason Jeng, married Tracy's sister, Carol Yang. Then, in July 2003, they became business partners with their opening of Ho Ho China Bistro. Located in the Queen City's original restaurant row, Ho Ho China Bistro offers authentic Chinese cooking with special essences from secret recipes. The food is characterized by diversity in the use of seasonings, unique culinary skill, great variety in the use of ingredients, and changes in styles. The house specialty is Ho Ho Shrimp, which features crispy jumbo shrimp in a sauce that is sweet, sour and spicy, with a dash of Grand Marnier. Ho Ho Duck is a famous Peking dish cooked by pot-stewing and oil scalding. For the calorie-conscious, Ho Ho offers dishes from the steamer. The owners of this marvelous family-owned restaurant pride themselves on adaptability. So whatever your taste buds desire, you are sure to find satisfaction.

1742 Lombardy Circle, Charlotte NC
(704) 376-0807
www.hohochinabistro.com

Mimosa Grill

At the Mimosa Grill in Charlotte, you find a showcase of Southern signature dishes planned with a global twist by celebrated executive chef Tom Condron of the Harper's group. Proprietor Mark Darville and Mimosa chef de cuisine Jojo Alexander welcome you to a world of fine dining in downtown Charlotte. Mimosa has an atmosphere of bold, timeless elegance, employing a warm combination of Tennessee fieldstone and rich cherry hardwoods. Join the staff for a dining experience you'll long remember. This establishment is warm enough for an intimate dinner for two and impressive enough for your most special occasion. The Mimosa offers full-service catering and event scheduling. Do you have a business party, wedding reception, wine tasting or state dinner in mind? You name it, the Mimosa staff will impress everyone with its Southern graciousness paired with New World influence. The Grill can accommodate groups of up to 100 people. A private dining room handles up to 50 people, and the patio handles up to 50 for a sit-down dinner or 100 for a reception. Mimosa is part of the Harpers chain of restaurants, owned by Tom Sasser and presided over by executive chef Tom Condron.

327 S Tryon, Charlotte NC
(704) 343-0700
www.mimosagrill.com

Mama Ricotta's

Mama Ricotta's was voted Best Italian Restaurant in 2000 by the *Best of Charlotte*. Meals at Mama Ricotta's are made from scratch, evoking the aroma and taste of the Old Country. Mama Ricotta's is owned by entrepreneur Frank Scibelli and exemplifies his reputation for quality. Eclectic, colorful and casual, the eatery is close to Charlotte's uptown NoDa art and street scene. Meal portions are generous to the extreme, and diners have the option to "family size" an entrée for plates that feed two or more. The mozzarella is made in house, and desserts are worth saving room for. A catering service offers comprehensive event planning and food from around the globe to groups from 15 to several hundred. The catering service offers, as a starting point, a four or five *prix fixe* menu with alcohol included. The restaurant's private dining area accommodates lunch or dinner events for 25 to 50 people. The menu supplies an agreeable combination of succulent comfort food and authentic Mediterranean fare. While dining, ask about the featured quartino, an exquisitely Italian method of sampling one-quarter liters of wine not usually available on the regular menu. Mama Ricotta's is one of the few restaurants in town that caters to both the hungry child and the connoisseur gourmand. The chef invites you to sink into a booth and pamper your taste buds with the signature penne alla vodka and top your meal off with chocolate nutella pie. You will be gratified.

601 S Kings Drive, Charlotte, NC
(704) 343-0148

Picasso's Sports Café

Legend has it that Don Burgoon, owner of Picasso's Sports Café, is a descendant of Gen. John Burgoyne, the British officer who was defeated at the battle of Saratoga in 1777. When he fled to Philadelphia, the family subsequently changed its name. A graduate of the University of North Carolina, Don worked as a career counselor in Charlotte, but when he had the opportunity to invest in his favorite bar on South Boulevard, he jumped at the chance. Under his management the former steakhouse has become the most successful sports bar in the city. The original bar has relocated to the historic Dilworth Brewery building, and two more locations are now open: one near the University, managed by Don's son, Don Burgoon III; and the other at Elizabeth Billiards on Central Avenue. The University location features plenty of memorabilia associated with UNC, whose exploits can be watched on the 52-inch television and two 24-inch sets. Each location features an open living room style, 14 kinds of pizza, and chicken wings prepared 13 different ways. It's a lucky 13 for Picasso's, which was Voted Best Sports Bar and Best Chicken Wings in the *Charlotte Observer*.

1301 E Boulevard, Charlotte NC
(704) 331-0133
230 E WT Harris Boulevard
(University),
Charlotte NC
(704) 595-9553

Tyber Creek Pub

If you're feeling a little bit Irish and a little bit Rock and Roll, head over to Tyber Creek Pub; the dream child of three friends (two from Queens, New York and one from Ireland) who relocated to a whole new kind of borough. Located in Charlotte's South End, which has gone from industrial neighborhood to trendy hotspot, this pub offers patrons an eclectic mix of music, pub grub and brews. Boasting the best Guinness on-tap, the folks at Tyber Creek also serve 17 other on-tap varieties, mixed drinks and a nice wine selection. You will find a diverse blend of traditional Irish fare, New York deli-style sandwiches and a few old time favorites. Tyber Creek partners Tommy Timmins, Maynard Goble and Kevin Devin are, more often than not, found behind the bar serving drinks or out on the floor visiting with patrons. The pub provides a choice selection of musicians and entertainers nightly and also has a dance floor upstairs for those who need to move to the rhythms. Tyber Creek Pub, originally named in honor of an Irish community by Washington D.C. police officer Tim Krott, offers dim light and intimate, interior seating along with a generous outdoor area that doubles as a great place for people watching. The comfortable, friendly and spirited atmosphere makes this little pub the perfect place to relax and down a pint with your mates.

1933 S Boulevard, Charlotte NC
(704) 343-2727

Upstream

The headwaters of a stream are the freshest and cleanest, right? That's the philosophy of Tom Sasser, owner of Upstream in Charlotte. "It (the beginning of the stream) is a good little metaphor for what we are trying to do here," says Tom. A recent review in the *Charlotte Observer* notes, "Much about Upstream is refreshing, but nothing more so than its moving against the fine-dining current to keep good food accessible and easy to enjoy. These guys have the passion of the proverbial salmon going–well, you know." Approximately 85 percent of the menu is devoted to a variety of seafood items. Says Tom, "I read cook books like other people read novels. I like everything on the menu. If I don't like something, I take it off." As a result of this passion and dedication, Upstream has won many awards, including a listing in *Esquire* magazine's Best New Restaurants of the Year, *Zagat's* Most Popular Restaurant award, and *Charlotte* magazine's Best Seafood award. In Charlotte, this is the place for seafood and full-service catering in a gorgeous setting at the water's edge. Upstream is part of the Harper's group of restaurants, owned by Sasser and presided over by Executive Chef Tom Condron.

6902 Phillips Place, Charlotte NC (704) 556-7730 *www.upstreamseafood.com*

Sir Edmond Halley's Restaurant & Freehouse

For an authentic English pub experience and a touch of Southern charm, Sir Edmond Halley's Restaurant & Freehouse has the best of both worlds. Chef and owner Tobin McAfee has added a creative spin to the traditional English pub. The mouthwatering menu includes all the pub classics from England and Ireland, including Irish Guinness stew, shepherd's pie and fish and chips. It also features new classics, like ostrich meatloaf from Australia. Halley's Eight Dollar Parliment lunch is famous in Charlotte for lunch meetings. Its lunch menu features dishes that appeal to everyone, from traditional pub fare to specialties like Halley's famous black bean burger. Come for the food and stay for the spirits. The pub features 11 taps of British beers, pale ales and cider, as well as Guinness. It also carries an array of single malt scotches, small batch bourbons and a well rounded wine list. Chef Tobin has trained in kitchens all over the world and has brought a multicultural gathering place to Charlotte. In the backroom, you'll find a jukebox, darts, checkers and backgammon. Even Haley's desserts will leave you weak. The specialty is a flourless chocolate cake. Sir Edmond Halley's Restaurant & Freehouse was named the best place for Late Night Dining in the South by Turner South's *Blue Ribbon* television show. Come in for an Old World pub experience in the heart of the new South.

4151-A Park Road, Charlotte NC   (704) 525-2555   www.halleyspub.com

The Roasting Company

Housed in a building that combines the styles of a Mexican cantina and a classic art deco diner, The Roasting Company offers a unique take on rotisserie chicken. Poultry grown on local farms is delivered fresh daily, marinated, and cooked with a special Costa Rican recipe. It is then served with a superb selection of fresh vegetables, from Southern standards like sweet potatoes and collard greens to more exotic fare like black bean salad and pineapple casserole. Chicken is the mainstay, but The Roasting Company's pork dishes are prepared with a special jaco sauce that makes them another favorite. Doug Bell, owner of The Roasting Company, started in the restaurant business in Nashville. In 1991 he moved to Charlotte, where he opened his new business after a friend raved about the chicken he'd had while on vacation in Costa Rica. The customers share the friend's enthusiasm.

1521 Montford Drive,
Charlotte NC (704) 521-8188

Pier 51 Seafood

Cousins Billy, Vaki, and Demetri are ready with seafood at a great price and service with a smile at Pier 51 Seafood in Charlotte. The cousins use family recipes to prepare 13 different varieties of fish plus the best shellfish. You'll find an abundance of menu choices served in large portions. The fried favorites include lightly breaded fried fish, clam strips and oysters, all served with a mound of hush puppies. The spicy fried catfish is a must-try favorite. If you have a smaller appetite, Pier 51 offers broiled fish or crab cakes that'll give you a taste of Pier 51 without filling you up. Vaki's family has been in the seafood business since 1968. They invite you to bring an appetite to Pier 51.

8332 Pineville Matthews Road, Charlotte NC   (704) 752-5151

Pasta & Provisions

Tom George, his wife, Debbie, and son Max have been providing fine food on the fly for over a decade. Tom lived in Boston's North End while attending college and worked at the Al Capone Cheese Company for 12 years, where he was Al Junior's right hand man. In 1992, Tom brought his wife and family back to his hometown of Charlotte and opened Pasta & Provisions. The store is known for its Italian imported groceries and daily preparation of fresh foods. Fresh pasta and sauces are made on the premises. From marinara to pesto to seafood Newburg, Pasta & Provisions has a sauce available to make any meal delicious. You'll find freshly prepared foods, ravioli by the pound, fresh mozzarella and a splendid variety of artisan cheeses. Pasta & Provisions crafts its legendary artichoke gorgonzola spread from the richest cream cheese, artichoke hearts, imported gorgonzola, basil and garlic. Focaccia bread is made from an age-old recipe and baked on-site daily. Pasta & Provisions has a large selection of Italian wines and a staff with the knowledge to help make your choice the best. Pasta & Provisions offers catering for all occasions.

1528 Providence Road, Charlotte NC   (704) 364-2622   www.pastaprovisions.com

The Palm Restaurant

The Palm Restaurant is the oldest family-owned, white tablecloth restaurant to expand across the United States and still maintain family ownership. Pio Bozzi and John Ganzi's original New York City steakhouse has grown into a thriving empire of more than 25 restaurants. The residents of Charlotte are fortunate to have their own Palm with a vaulted ceiling and intimate booths. The Northern Italian entrepreneurs who began the Palm tradition in 1926 intended a restaurant specializing in cuisine from their native Parma. Steaks and seafood were not part of the original concept, but began out of an effort to cater to a clientele of artists and writers. Third generation owners Wally Ganzi and Bruce Bozzi introduced gargantuan four to eight-pound lobsters in the 1970s, disproving the theory that large lobsters are tough. Almost overnight, the Palm went from selling 150 pounds of lobster a week to 25,000 pounds a week. Even with these additions, The Palm honors its roots with some of John Ganzi's original dishes, thus reinforcing its reputation as an Italian steakhouse. Celebrities frequent all Palm locations, because of the fine food, casual setting and accommodating service. The walls of each Palm are covered with caricatures of local notables and national celebrities, a tradition that started when John and Pio didn't have money to decorate and invited local newspapermen to draw cartoons in exchange for plates of spaghetti. The Charlotte Palm invites you to reserve a table or private dining room and experience Italian food coupled with the South's notable hospitality.

6705 B Phillips Place, Charlotte NC   (704) 552-7256   www.thepalm.com

The Captain's Cap

In 1981, family-members John Hondros, Steve Kakouras and Spero Stathopoulos opened the doors to The Captain's Cap Family Seafood Restaurant. This original eating establishment offered the people of Gastonia and its surrounding areas the very freshest seafood, consummately prepared and beautifully served. The concept worked magnificently. Fresh fish and seafood, in an all-you-can-eat fashion, turned out to be just what the folks of Gaston County wanted. The partners often said, "Just give us a try, and we know we'll see you again." The management and staff of The Captain's Cap have a goal that they strive toward each day, which is to serve the best possible food at a reasonable price in a clean and friendly atmosphere. The Captain's Cap has been doing that in grand style for more than 25 years. This popular restaurant has the feel of a vintage fish camp complete with wooden booths. The restaurant's full menu features a connoisseur's salad bar, as well as signature seafood dishes and fabulous beef and chicken. The partners first visited North Carolina in the 1970s and were inspired by Pat and Mick's Seafood Restaurant in New London. They later moved from Greece to Gastonia and opened their first restaurant. They opened a second restaurant in Belmont in 1994 with partners Kostas Zahapopoulos and John Mageras. They opened a third restaurant in Denver in 2001. The Captain's Cap invites you to visit and dine with them or order your meal to go. Either way, you will know it was prepared with care.

3140 Linwood Road, Gastonia NC
(704) 865-7433
670 Park Street, Belmont NC
(704) 825-4103
1218 N Highway 16, Denver NC
(704) 483-2121

Connolly's Pub

If you've been looking for a relaxing, comfortable place to unwind after a hard day, look no farther than Connolly's Pub in downtown Charlotte. Kevin Devin, who left school in County Galway, Ireland, to become a plumber and worked in bars part-time, and his partner Tommy Timmins, originally from Queens, New York, opened this delightful ode to the Emerald Isles in 2000. Connolly's meets all the basic requirements of a good pub, such as a witty Irishman, complete with brogue, behind the bar; dark, gleaming wood; and a mix of Irish music playing in the background. Wednesday evening's get rolling with live music in the party room upstairs. This delightful Irish pub was named after notable Irish patriot James Connolly, who is remembered for the key role he played in the Easter Rising, which began on Easter of 1916 in Dublin. It is here where neighborhood workers come to let off steam after a long day and grab a bite from Connolly's hearty menu. Patrons can choose from the traditional serving of Boxty, a dish of tender braised beef surrounded by a light Irish pancake; or a savory spinach salad overflowing with bacon, eggs and dressing. Corrina, the head bartender, is on hand to pull you a pint of Guinness or serve you one of the many imports, draughts or bottled beers available. Stop in at Connolly's on your next visit to downtown Charlotte.

115 E 5th Street, Charlotte NC
(704) 358-9070

The Melting Pot

For a new eating adventure, try the casually elegant atmosphere of The Melting Pot. The Melting Pot's great fondue begins with the finest quality cheeses, carefully aged to the restaurant's demanding specifications. Your server prepares each fondue tableside and seasons it to your taste. It's a true Swiss fondue, rich in flavor and smooth in texture. Fresh breads, vegetables and apples are served for dipping. Choose from a list of fine wines and relax while the staff provides attentive service. Owners Todd Dennis and Brian Neel are proud of their loyal clientele and staff. They guarantee that once you've had your initial experience at The Melting Pot, you'll be back for more. The Melting Pot experience isn't complete without the specialty dessert, chocolate fondue. Strawberries, bananas, pineapple and other fresh fruits, plus cheesecake, nutty marshmallows, pound cake and brownies are served for dipping into any one of their decadent chocolate fondue recipes. Try either one of The Melting Pot's Charlotte locations for a fondue dinner that always hits the spot.

901 S Kings Drive, Suite 140B, Charlotte NC   (704) 334-4400
230 E WT Harris Boulevard, Suite C1, Charlotte NC   (704) 548-2432
www.meltingpot.com

City Tavern

John Weinbrenner owns the City Tavern on East Boulevard, and Brant Polzer has been his right-hand man since it opened in 1999. City Tavern offers a chef-driven menu, and as waiter, owner and chef, John has developed his menu from his own collection of favorite recipes from both New York and Atlanta. The atmosphere at City Tavern combines the feel of a cozy neighborhood restaurant with casual elegance, and the food served is simply irresistible. From comfort foods such as gourmet meatloaf with parmesan mashed potatoes to cutting-edge cuisine such as Asian sea bass with spinach and sticky rice, the food and the ambience merge into a truly enjoyable experience. To go with their delicious menu, City Tavern's full service bar offers 40 wines by the glass or 45 specialty martinis. City Tavern can also cater anything from a wedding to a corporate function. Whatever you're looking for, City Tavern has probably won an award for it. The Best Martini Bar, the Top 25 Restaurants Under $25, and the Best New Neighborhood Hangout are just three of the distinctions the restaurant has earned. If you're in doubt about where to go, City Tavern is the place to try.

1514 E Boulevard, Charlotte NC   (704) 575-0146

Mert's Heart and Soul

As a regular at their former restaurant, Miss Myrtle Lockheart used to bend James and Renee Bazelle's ears with fascinating stories of the old bootlegging days, when she was known as Mert. In 1998, when James and Renee decided to open a new down-home Southern restaurant, they honored their favorite storyteller by naming it after her. Mert would be proud of Mert's Heart and Soul. The genuine low-country and Southern country fare will keep you busy and satisfied. As you'd expect from any respectable Southern kitchen, cornbread is made fresh from scratch all day and the fryers are where most of the action is. Traditional favorites include chicken, catfish and green tomatoes, blackened pork chops, red beans and rice, salmon cakes and fresh collard greens. The brunch menu includes plenty of omelet and egg combos, with your choice of toast, biscuits, homefries or grits. For dinner, sample the aforementioned staples or try soft shell crab on a hoagie bun, ribs, meat loaf or the veggie plate. For dessert, an absolute must is banana pudding. Give your mouth a real taste of the South in a down-home atmosphere that makes you feel like you're being served by long-lost family.

214 N College Street, Charlotte NC   (704) 342-4222   www.mertsuptown.com

Ciro's Italian Ristorante

Italy comes to North Carolina via Brooklyn at Ciro's Italian Ristorante. Art Ciro Corniella and Paola Caruso own this little bit of Italy in Harrisburg. The name "Ciro's" comes from Arty's middle moniker, and most of the recipes come from an old cookbook given to Arty by his Sicilian friend's great grandmother. You will definitely want to try the famous whiskey shrimp and chicken. They also offer veal classics and Zuppe De Pesce. Ciro's specialty pizzas include the Pizza Bianco, and they offer numerous traditional pasta dishes to tempt you. For the perfect finish, savor the flavor with one of Ciro's authentic Italian desserts. This is a family establishment. Lucia, Arty's wife, keeps it all together and running smoothly. By popular request, Paolo plays the accordion nightly at the University location. *Buon' Appetitio.*

4351 Main Street, Suite #111, Harrisburg NC
(704) 455-7400 8927
J.M. Keynes Dr. #100, Charlotte, NC
(704) 510-0012

The Big Chill

You can dance the night away at The Big Chill, a fine-dining establishment with an opulent atmosphere that is reminiscent of a 1940s supper club. The Big Chill is one of the newest nightspots in Charlotte, designed to bring you all the glamour, elegance and excitement of the perfect evening. You can pamper your palate with superb cuisine, and cut a rug to time-honored classics seasoned with rhythm and blues performed by world class musicians. The Big Chill's talented chefs offer an exceptional menu presented by a dedicated, trained professional staff. Owner Darcy Donovan has created visual grandeur, sophisticated fare and spectacular entertainment at The Big Chill in Charlotte. Private hire for functions only. Call for reservations.

911 E. Morehead, Suite 100, Charlotte NC
(704) 347-4447
www.thebigchillcharlotte.com

Lupie's Café

The owner of the Carolina Panthers enjoyed his favorite lunch so much, he gave the shirt off his back to the staff at Lupie's Café. For a generation, Lupie Duran has been serving up the freshest, rib-stickin'est comfort food to be found in Charlotte. She opened this famous eatery in the old Martin's Grocery in historic Griertown at the hub of five of Charlotte's most interesting neighborhoods. A lively mix of clientele is drawn to the consistently delicious Texas, Cincinnati and vegetarian chilies, daily specials like meat loaf or chicken and dumplings, as well as the rest of the mouthwatering, all-American menu available every day. Lupie makes no secret of her most important ingredient. It's her warm and delightful staff of professionals with the knack for cooking. Expanding the family circle, daughter Larkin operates Lupie's in Huntersville. Lupie's has won several awards, including 2001 Best Home Cooking Restaurant and 2000 Best Inexpensive Restaurant from *Creative Loafing*. In 2001, Charlotte *Citysearch* gave it the Best Comfort Food award. Lupie's makes many contributions to the diverse community it serves. For 15 years, it has supported Hospice of Charlotte with an annual chili cook-off. For an excellent meal at a one-of-a-kind eatery, visit Lupie's.

2718 Monroe Road, Charlotte NC
(704) 374-1232
www.lupiescafe.com

Barolo Tuscan Grill

Tuscany is a region of Italy that brings to mind glowing landscapes of sun-drenched hills, friendly people and wonderful food. Tuscan cuisine is known for its delicious simplicity, and the Barolo Grill is a marvelous example of the best that Tuscany has to offer. With signature dishes like Portobello Mangione, mushroom sautéed in rosemary cognac cream sauce; or Tortellini di Alessandra, made of spinach and potato in tomato cream sauce with sundried tomatoes, who could ask for more? Yet, there's still dessert. Barolo serves a chocolate cream filled cannoli with cherries and fresh whipping cream. Barolo's founder Alberto Mangione was born and raised in Italy, and came to Barolo after working with his Uncle Roberto in Mangione's Restaurant. Alberto's guiding principle, developed over years of restaurant experience, is "Some see eating as sheer necessity. At Barolo Tuscan Grill we see it as pure pleasure. You will feel very comfortable and special here." One visit will convince you that Barolo lives up to Alberto's pledge.

7708 Rea Road, Charlotte NC (704) 752-9797

Big Pinnacle of Pilot Mountain as seen from Little Pinnacle

Madison's

Bustling Charlotte is home to a thriving community of professionals in nearly every field. At the end of a long and weary working day, it's nice to know that the perfect place to start or finish your evening is right downtown. Madison's, an upscale, members-only club, comes complete with behind-the-bar waterfall and executive leather couches. Rich mahogany fills the room, offering a warm, luxurious backdrop for intimate conversation. Thursday through Saturday, members can enjoy live jazz while sipping on one of 50 martini varieties, a bottle of fine wine or one of several classic cocktails. If nothing in the bar meets your fancy, you can bring your own bottle and store it on the premises. Owners Tom Timmins and Kevin Devin have a distinguished selection of fine cigars available for your enjoyment. Tom, who originally hails from Queens, New York, gave the club its

notable name. Club amenities include pay-per-view boxing events, Monday night football and other sports related pastimes. The club also has billiard tables to help you relax and pass the time. Madison's is geared toward the younger professional crowd, has a business-casual dress code, and is open seven days a week. Guest memberships vary and are available for both corporations and individuals. Please telephone for inquires about membership.

115 E 5th Street, Charlotte NC
(704) 358-4244

La Bibliothèque

Dine on the garden terrace or amongst the books at La Bibliothèque, Charlotte's oldest fine dining institute. The restaurant has a reputation for excellence going back more than 20 years and has been the proud recipient of AAA's four diamonds for the past 10 years. Founder and owner Brenda Bowling started her career in West Virginia in the interior design business, and her expertise is reflected in the ambience of La Bibliothèque. The classic décor includes antiques, shimmering chandeliers, rich oil paintings and more than 1,500 books. Brenda wants to give her clientele the experience of dining in a theater-like and sophisticated environment. She offers fine French and continental cuisine with plentiful sauces and distinct American touches. Expect handpicked wine selections and such specialties as duck salad, veal medallions and pheasant breast. Finish your elegant meal with mousse cake, fresh fruit or a special cheesecake created daily by the chef. You can also enjoy a flaming dessert made at your table. La Bibliothèque's location makes it a perfect setting for a business group or a romantic dinner for two. The restaurant will custom design its menu for your special occasion. Visit La Bibliothèque for a private tour, a complimentary glass of wine and suggestions for making your special event memorable.

1901 Roxborough Road, Charlotte NC
(704) 365-5000
www.labibliotheque.net

Stool Pigeons

Cameron McCrae opened the original Stool Pigeons in Myrtle Beach as an upscale sports bar with 32 draughts on tap. There are now eight locations, each carrying its own distinctive signature style. Four locations are managed by Jason Smith. The other four are in the capable hands of Jim Brown. All of them feature music and late night service. Stool Pigeons serves a tasty lunch and dinner, and is open for happy hour. The menu contains favorites such as cheesecakes, chicken wings and fish 'n' chips, but also boasts some original fare. The "sliders" are mouth-watering mini-burgers made with Black Angus beef. Crispy salads make a fresh accompaniment, and desserts such as the brownie sundae await selection to finish off the meal. Stool Pigeons is a bustling gathering place for sporting events, boasting a premium audio/visual system for fans. Special events such as trivia night offer fun activities for groups, or an easy way to meet new friends. Events are often punctuated with drink specials and promotions. The uptown Charlotte location contains 17 televisions and three big screens, and is located close to the Panther's Stadium and the Bobcat's arena. Stool Pigeons welcomes you to the next big game. Stop in, sit down, order your favorite food and drinks, and enjoy a carefree game day.

214 N Church Street, Charlotte NC
(704) 358-3789
www.stoolpigeons.biz

Pewter Rose Bistro

Charlotte's South End is a popular historic district, and it's easy to speculate that the Pewter Rose Bistro had a hand in making it so. Susie Peck and Kevin Diffley co-own this bit of eclectic paradise. Longtime chef Blake Dewey and his cohorts are not bound by any particular food category, so their imaginations and resulting creations run deliciously rampant. International cuisine and an ultra-creative, relaxing atmosphere form both a culinary and visual delight. Pewter Rose mixes fine dining with a metropolitan nightclub that sings out for repeat visits. Exposed brick walls and airy 30-foot ceilings form a backdrop for whimsical sculptures, original artwork, thousands of tiny sparkling lights and lighted paper stars. The bistro offers 10 to 12 types of wine by the glass each month, drawn from an extensive, evolving wine list, an in-progress labor of love credited to Peck. Chef Dewey can develop amazing culinary feats for any special dietary consideration with advance notice. Vegetarians are always considered in the incredibly original, artistic and extensive menu developments. Pewter Rose takes a distinctly holistic approach, with a focus on organic and earth-friendly ingredients, a penchant for jumping in with community fund-raisers and a knack for staying with or ahead of the times. The Tutto Mundo nightclub inside of Pewter Rose offers refined entertainment for 30-something professionals. Come and revel in the extraordinary sensory extravaganza at Pewter Rose Bistro.

1820 S Boulevard, Charlotte NC
(704) 332-8149   www.pewterrose.com

Photos by Dustin Peck

Yellow Rose at Touchstone

When owner Jim "Spanky" Sprowles opened the Yellow Rose at Touchstone tavern and pub, his friends knew it would be something special. Opened in 1999, Spanky's Yellow Rose has exceeded all expectations. The original grilling sauce for the wings and baby back ribs was invented by John Boy and Billy. Executive chef Will creates culinary magic in the kitchen. The pub is a popular location for local stag and birthday parties, karaoke nights and other exciting events. Yellow Rose at Touchstone is integrally involved in the community, largely due to the generous heart behind the business. Spanky is a retired electrical engineer from Square D and knows all of his customers. If he doesn't know you, it is only a matter of time before he will. The men of Yellow Rose compete in all the local fishing tournaments, donating all winnings to charity. When tragedy struck in New Orleans, three Yellow Rose meals per day were donated for refugees. Sergeant Mike Dover took Spanky's flag to Iraq and had it signed by the 101st Airborne's D company. Carolina Panther's fans show up regularly for the food and fun, enjoying the big-screen televisions and pool tables. If you have never experienced a first-class neighborhood pub, this is the place you have been looking for. Come to Yellow Rose at Touchstone for the unbelievable food, stay for the incredible fun.

9217-F Baybrook Lane, Charlotte NC
(704) 542-2033

Splash Restaurant & Bar

Karim Ghaibi is a true renaissance man. He came from France to study electrical engineering at the University of North Carolina at Charlotte. He is an accomplished horseman, as well as a buyer, trainer, rider and seller of quality horses. He even toured the world pursuing his dreams. Karim enjoys a successful career in the horse world, and owns a horse farm in Huntersville. Karim and his wife, Jasmina, also own and operate a beautiful upscale restaurant in Cornelius. This restaurant, Splash, specializes in Mediterranean cuisine, recipes from Morocco and Southern France in particular. The menu features Spanish, Greek and Italian specialties, as well. Karim wanted to share the food knowledge he gleaned from his travels. He and Jasmina personally designed the restaurant and serve exceptional foods, such as sea bass with lobster and artichoke, and grilled portobello with Gorgonzola pecan sauce. The restaurant is designed to reflect an enjoyable yet distinctive ambience. It is reminiscent of Casablanca, Karim's hometown. Splash offers live jazz weekly. A convivial atmosphere reigns here with a warm overtone that is intensified by the superb menu. With a late night menu offered on weekends, entertainment on Wednesdays and weekends, there are many reasons to come to Splash. The main reason is that you will enjoy exotic food, exquisitely prepared and formally served in elegant surroundings. Come and experience the easy comfort and the gourmet wonders found at Splash.

19501-4 W Catawba Avenue, Cornelius NC
(704) 894-0026   www.splashfoodwine.com

Monticello Uptown

Monticello Uptown is located in the historic Dunhill Hotel, a quality hotel located in the heart of the financial and art district of uptown Charlotte. The Dunhill successfully combines the elegance of luxury European hotels with an American sense of comfort and service, creating a place where the guest experience is unsurpassed. The restaurant shares the Dunhill's dedication to one-on-one service and attention to detail. Monticello Uptown is a very popular meeting place for uptown executives. Breakfast, lunch and dinner are served in a refined and convivial atmosphere. Personalized service includes chef-prepared specialties, outstanding desserts and a fine wine list. The private dining room is decorated with magnificent chandeliers and antiques and can accommodate parties from 20 to 200. These private rooms are in great demand because of their setting in the elegant hotel. Visit Monticello Uptown for international cuisine in a lavish setting.

237 Tryon Street, Charlotte NC
(706) 342-1193
www.dunhillhotel.com

Augusto Conte

Augusto Conte, voted Charlotte Restaurateur of the Year in 2005, is a native of the Italian island of Ischia. He came to the United States in 1989 and settled with his uncle in Connecticut. He soon found a job in a family-owned and operated restaurant where he worked his way up from bus boy to manager, learned to speak English, and met his wife, Christine. The couple moved to Charlotte in 1995 and opened the first of what would become a quartet of critically acclaimed eateries.

Luce, an Augusto Conte Restaurant

For an exceptionally fine dining experience, go to Augusto's flagship restaurant Luce, named in Zagats *2006 America's Top Restaurants* book. Luce offers superb Italian cuisine and wines in an exquisite Renaissance setting with opulent gold chandeliers, Italian marble tiles, imported limestone columns, and hand-painted frescoes by Ben Long. Located Uptown in the Hearst Tower courtyard.

214 N Tryon Street, Charlotte NC
(704) 344-9222   www.luceristorante.net

Coco Osteria, an Augusto Conte Café

Relax with friends at Augusto's casual Italian café located in the heart of Uptown at the entrance of the Hearst Tower. Coco Osteria offers traditional, simple Tuscan cuisine. See how dry pasta pales in comparison when you experience your first bite of executive chef Gabriele Grigolon's tender Ravioli alla Ligure or the melt-in-your-mouth delicious Maccheroni con la Salsicca, tubular pasta served with sweet Italian sausage in a tomato cream sauce. Call ahead for seating.

214 N Tryon between, Charlotte NC
(704) 344-8878   www.cocoosteria.com

Il Posto, an Augusto Conte *Osteria*

Il Posto is Augusto's latest *osteria*. With a city chic atmosphere and elegant two-story interior, you can savor wining and dining at charming sidewalk tables while watching the world pass by. Try the Osso Buco d'Agnello or the Spezzatino di Manzo.

6908A Phillips Place Court, Charlotte NC
(704) 643-6070

Toscana, an Augusto Conte Restaurant

Located in the SouthPark district is Augusto's classic original restaurant Toscana, which has wooed a steady following of regulars since 1995. Executive chef Gabriele Grigolon offers his loyal patrons authentic Italian dishes, all freshly prepared from the finest ingredients and expertly served in a contemporary atmosphere.

6401 Morrison Boulevard, Charlotte NC
(704) 344-9909

McIntosh's Steaks and Seafood

In Charlotte's historic SouthEnd, you will find the original Chain of One, McIntosh's Steaks and Seafood restaurant. This casually elegant establishment offers locals and out-of-towners alike a perfect place for special dinners or formal business meetings. McIntosh's has been awarded *Wine Spectator* magazine's *Award Of Excellence* for nine consecutive years and has been voted best steakhouse for five consecutive years. Its menu offers an exquisite variety of appetizers, such as fried lobster tail or seared yellowfin tuna. Crisp salads and savory soups are the perfect accompaniment to succulent entrées, such as Chilean sea bass with grilled vegetables and roasted garlic parsley oil, or any of McIntosh's prime steaks or chops. The restaurant uses

only the finest quality USDA prime grade, specially aged, corn-fed beef. Choose from perfectly cooked New York strips, filets or a 24-ounce Porterhouse. McIntosh's also has tender lamb loin, chicken or the popular McIntosh's mixed grill with rack of lamb, boneless duck breast and a petite filet mignon. The side dish menu features several delicious options, including sautéed spinach and mushrooms or broccoli with hollandaise. You will want to be sure to save room for one of the fresh and scrumptious creations from the bakery, such as dark chocolate cake or smooth crème brulee. If you are hosting a private event, McIntosh's has two smaller dining rooms available that can each seat 25 guests or be combined for 50 with a separate bar for a truly private, comfortable experience. Enjoy a one-of-a-kind experience at McIntosh's Steaks and Seafood.

1812 S Boulevard, Charlotte NC
(704) 342-1088   www.mcintoshs1.com

Patou Bistro

Laura and Rachid Ouchou have created an extremely popular, chic meeting place in the historic Dilworth neighborhood of Charlotte. Since 1995, Patou Bistro has been offering French cuisine at its best, a tapas menu, fine wines and a cozy bar. *SouthPark* magazine describes their food as "seductively simple and delicious," and customers at the popular bistro agree. The restaurant features an exemplary outdoor patio. You'll find a friendly wait staff, well versed in the subtleties of French food. Specialties include grilled fish, chicken breast stuffed with goat cheese, and carrot soup with a touch of cream that gained rave reviews from the editorial staff at *Citysearch*. Belgian specialties include waterzooi, a creamy seafood stew and Prince Edward Island mussels steamed in white wine. Irresistible desserts are made on-site, such as flaming crepes suzettes, crusted crème brulee or fruit tarts. Chocolate lovers will be well satisfied with such delights as mousse cake and rich marquise. The dessert house favorite is profiteroles, cream puffs served with ice cream and chocolate sauce. Whether you are planning a special family occasion or a romantic evening, make Patou Bistro your first choice.

1315 E Boulevard, Charlotte NC
(704) 376-2233
www.patoubistro.com

Boone Fork Creek Photo by Marty Hulsebos HighCountryImages.com

Southern Piedmont Lifestyle Destinations

The Dorchester

The Dorchester, located in Pineville, is one of the South's established senior living communities. Designed to meet the needs of residents 55 years of age and older, the community provides distinctive senior living unlike any other facility in the area. A rental plan is offered that affords a unique freedom and choice approach for seniors. The Dorchester is a community where you can enjoy life to its fullest. Imagine living where you are located within walking distance of a variety of fun activities, including gala food functions. The Dorchester is minutes from Carolinas Medical, Pineville and several specialty hospitals, as well as the library, golf course and uptown events. The staff and residents believe that friendship and social interaction are important factors in promoting a healthy lifestyle. In order to create a place where residents can enjoy friendships, freedom and choice they have developed their friends-and-neighbors concept. The Dorchester offers a monthly calendar of interesting and fun activities. Some of the popular clubs include the healthy living club and the Red Hat society. Planned trips and activities are coordinated by the program pirector, a.k.a. Ambassador of Fun. The staff and community are dedicated to providing encouragement for their residents that will empower and enhance their lives. They do this by promoting independence, a positive outlook, social interaction, continuing education and fun. Visit The Dorchester and discover senior living in an active and enjoyable environment.

12920 Dorman Road, Pineville NC
(704) 541-0016
www.dorchestercharlotte.com

The Cypress of Charlotte

The Cypress of Charlotte retirement community not only offers residents comfort, luxury and beauty, it offers them peace of mind. The Cypress is a continuing care retirement community where members purchase their own residences, thus securing the economic benefit of individual home ownership. The community has many different villas and cottages from which to choose. Each member pays a monthly membership fee based on the type of residence they purchase. The fee covers monthly meal plans and service, allows residents access to activities and amenities within the community, and includes 90 days in the health center at no additional charge. Also included are building and ground maintenance, laundry services, trash pick-up, weekly housekeeping, security and transportation. The Cypress was developed by The Cypress Company, whose purpose is to offer the very best residential community and quality services. Life Care Services Corporation, nationally recognized as one of the leaders in continuing care community administration, manages the day-to-day operation of The Cypress. Residents will be delighted by the available activities, such as tours, shopping excursions, and art or fitness classes. Other amenities include an elegant clubhouse, indoor pool, home delivery of meals, beauty and barber shops, valet service, plus beautiful walking paths, lakes and flower gardens. Active seniors who are searching for retirement as it should be will want to consider The Cypress. Here, compatible individuals can share common interests without compromising lifestyle.

3442 Cypress Club Drive, Charlotte NC
(704) 714-5500 or (800) 643-1665
www.TheCypress.com

Wilora Lake Lodge

Wilora Lake Lodge provides the comforts of home with the peace of mind in a community designed for every level of retirement living. The quality of life and integrity of personal spirit is preserved at this friendly lodge, and all-inclusive monthly rent and a one-time community fee allows for preservation of personal assets. As an American Retirement Community, they are committed to offering a living environment that maintains the highest standards in the industry. Wilora Lake residents not only enjoy the wide array of care levels present in American Retirement Communities, but also a Red Hat Society, where members wear purple attire and red hats to the monthly meetings. Recently Wilora Lake's Marjory Shelton hosted a luncheon for Charlotte-area chapters of the famed Red Hat Society. Guests shopped the Red Hat Boutique and planned an upcoming purple pajama breakfast. Benefits of living here include a chef-prepared meal every evening, continental breakfast on weekdays, cable television hookup and private mailboxes. Apartment dwellers have the choice of a patio or balcony, spacious closets and individually controlled heat and air-conditioning. A puzzle room, crafts room, woodworking shop and billiards room are available to all residents. Housekeeping and transportation services provide additional convenience. Residents are accommodated according to their needs with various levels of independent, assisted or nursing care. New residents are warmly welcomed into this lively, caring community.

6053 Wilora Lake Road, Charlotte NC
(704) 537-8848 or (877) 422-5042
www.arclp.com

Southminster

Founded with pride by two local churches, Southminster is a nonprofit, continuing care retirement community committed to helping people maintain an active lifestyle with dignity, privacy and peace of mind, while ministering to their spiritual needs. Located in popular south Charlotte, Southminster's intimate, 26-acre campus is home for about 300 residents and a preferred employer with more than 180 staff members. The community opened in 1987 with cottages and apartments for residents on the go, plus assisted and nursing care for residents who experience changes in their health. The community is poised for a major expansion to include new, larger apartments, an indoor pool and wellness center, renovated medical clinic, underground parking and other amenities. An active resident's association provides a wealth of activities for personal growth and individual expression. Visitors are invited to sample a complimentary meal in the formal or informal dining rooms, meet the residents and learn more about the carefree Southminster way of life. Southminster is nationally accredited through the Continuing Care Accreditation Commission.

8919 Park Road, Charlotte NC
(704) 554-0141
www.southminster.org

The Cottages

If you like Charlotte, you will love the Southern homespun feel of The Cottages, an active-living senior community that features both custom-built, craftsman-style homes and condominiums. Located in the fastest growing part of town, just south of Carolina Place Mall, this quaint village will remind you of towns from your childhood.

As you enter the village gates, you are welcomed by the stately beauty of tree-lined streets, the serenity of a peaceful neighborhood, and a feeling of the friendships that are built one sweet tea at a time. You will find residents lounging on the front porch with friends, taking a walk in the neighborhood, or playing bridge at the clubhouse while grandchildren swim in the pool. The village contains a fitness pavilion and spa, indoor and outdoor pools, a walking trail and horseshoe pits.

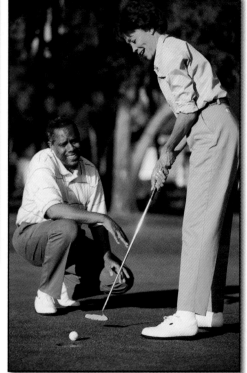

Those who prefer the security and intimacy of condo-style living will have plenty of choices at The Cottages. You may enjoy a fourth-floor home with a balcony view. Or you may decide that a first-floor home with an inviting patio is more your style. Whatever your lifestyle preference, the active adult community at The Cottages will allow you to own a home your way.

13020 Park Crescent Circle, Pineville NC
(704) 544-8889
www.thecottagescharlotte.com

Carriage Club of Charlotte

In beautiful tree-filled Charlotte, the Carriage Club has found the perfect setting for retired people to live in care-free ease and comfort. Carriage Club is set apart from other full service retirement communities by its well planned, supremely compassionate concept. For instance, the Club operates as a senior residential community with a safety net of service and support. They offer housekeeping, full maintenance, security and a wellness program. Many different levels of care and service are available, allowing residents to maintain the utmost independence. Living quarters include a choice of floor plans in a villa, spacious apartment, or Carriage House. Tucked among 44 acres of mature trees and two lakes in a naturally landscaped setting, the winding walking trails provide access to nature. The community atmosphere makes it possible to make plenty of new friends. The staff is caring and full of energy. Special needs get the attention of staff in many different programs.

The Arbors Memory Care serves residents with dementia or Alzheimer's, while Coach House Assisted Living offers assistance with activities of daily living. The Carriage House provides long and short-term nursing and Medicare rehabilitation services. Add to this restaurant-style dining, activities, entertainment, transportation, pool, exercise facilities, library and a meditation chapel, and you begin to understand the thoughtfulness of this community. Carriage Club of Charlotte strives to set higher standards of support and service for their residents.

5800 Old Providence Road, Charlotte NC
(704) 366-4960
www.arclp.com

Aldersgate, A United Methodist Continuing Care Retirement Community

How do you imagine the second half of your lifetime? Do you envision leisure time for activities such as gardening and golf, or time to finally pursue dreams and interests long delayed? Aldersgate understands your vision. This non-profit, United Methodist retirement community in Charlotte has been dedicated to serving older adults for 60 years. Sitting on 227 beautifully wooded acres, Aldersgate is an ingeniously planned campus, designed to meet the diverse physical needs of a mature community at every stage of life. Innovative residence plans include cottages with porches, apartments with fireplaces and balconies, an assisted-living center, a nursing center and a unique memory support center. This safe and secure continuous-care environment features courtyards, gardens, walking paths, a three-hole, par-three golf course and even a lake stocked with bass. Caring and committed staff are ready to assist you personally and relieve you of the burden of home maintenance. The Ray Hall Community Center was inspired by the traditional feel of life in small-town America; it houses Aldersgate's own chapel, bank, library, general store, and a wellness facility with indoor heated pool and spa. Aldersgate is meant to enhance the priceless years when there is time for your personal aspirations to take the lead, for you to re-discover the world around you and enjoy the gentle art of living well. Life is your greatest work of art. Let it be a masterpiece at Aldersgate.

3800 Shamrock Drive, Charlotte NC
(704) 532-7000
www.aldersgateccrc.com

Ayrsley

Imagine living and working where you have all of the convenience of a bustling city and the charm of a small town without the commute. At the Ayrsley campus in southwest Charlotte, you can live that dream. This 140-acre planned community, strategically located in the Lake Wylie corridor, is designed to be pedestrian-friendly and self-sufficient. The town center incorporates residential, business and retail needs along with entertainment and recreation options. Ayrsley is re-introducing the concept of the traditional American neighborhood where life can be enjoyed without owning a car. The community incorporates a high-tech infrastructure. Wireless Internet is available throughout the campus, along with web hosting and seamless telecommunications. There is continuity in data services and state-of-the-art voice, data and broadband technologies available for all communications needs. Here you will be able to find more hours in the day, because everything you need is within walking distance, such as the extended stay and business hotel, technology stores, retail shopping and a slew of restaurants to suit every schedule and budget. Residents and workers of the Ayrsley can enjoy arcades, bike paths, lighted walkways and Steele Creek YMCA. If you have grown tired of endless commutes, then consider a place reminiscent of yesterday's Main Street USA. Combined with the conveniences and technologies of today, Ayrsley Town Center is designed to bring better tomorrows.

Corner of S Tryon and the 485 Beltway, Charlotte NC
(704) 643-4148
www.ayrsley.com

Triangle Area

The Capitol Building

Triangle Area Accommodations

Windy Oaks Inn

Chapel Hill's only bed-and-breakfast inn, Windy Oaks Inn, is located five miles from the University of North Carolina campus. The Piedmont T-style house is the former home of Pulitzer prize-winning playwright Paul Green. Newly restored, the beautiful 1890s farmhouse is nestled on 25 acres amid the towering oak trees for which it is named. Explore the grounds, relax on the patio under the shade of the 200-year-old oaks or curl up with a book in front of the fireplace in the cozy, wood-paneled library. The Inn features five comfortable, beautifully decorated rooms full of antiques and art. Let your imagination roam with the names of the suites. There's the Paul Green Suite, the Highland Call, the Lost Colony Suite, Dog on the Sun, and Abraham's Bosom. All full-rate reservations include breakfast and evening hors d'oeuvres and beverages. A special business rate is available most weekdays. Well behaved pets and older children with responsible parents are welcome. Windy Oaks is a full-service event facility for groups of 10 to 250. They offer on-site catering and create one-of-a-kind customized menus for your occasion. Repeat guests at the inn appreciate the tranquility and outstanding service. With all of these amenities, this is the perfect setting for your wedding, anniversary or weekend getaway.

1164 Old Lystra Road, Chapel Hill NC
(919) 942-1001
www.windyoaksinn.com

William Thomas House Bed and Breakfast

If the walls of the William Thomas House could talk, they would tell of the prominent families who have dwelled here, of the fascinating people who visited, of a struggle for survival and the changes in a growing capitol city. One resident was writer Frances Gray Patton, who became famous for her short stories and the book *Good Morning, Miss Dove*. The William Thomas House was also home to Mug Richardson, who became known as Arthur Godfrey's girl Friday. Mug was crowned Miss North Carolina of 1934. Owners Sarah and Jim Lofton invite you to enjoy comfort and charm in deluxe accommodations and finely appointed surroundings. They provide personal attention with respect for privacy. The house reflects the genteel glow of Southern hospitality and the practical comforts of 21st Century hostelries. Located in downtown Raleigh, the William Thomas House is within easy walking distance of the Governor's Mansion, state capitol, museums, shopping and restaurants. Many other points of interest are just minutes away. Stay at the William Thomas House Bed and Breakfast for a dose of history and luxury.

530 N Blount Street, Raleigh NC
(919) 755-9400 or (800) 653-3466
www.williamthomashouse.com

B&B's Country Garden Inn

Enjoy the secluded country setting of B&B's Country Garden Inn and still be within easy reach of all the city's conveniences and attractions. Surrounded by ponds and gardens and complete with a Jacuzzi gazebo, this cozy bed and breakfast is perfect for romantic and weekend getaways, company retreats and other special occasions. You will be greeted in the beautiful sunroom each morning for a home-cooked breakfast by owners Bud and Beth McKinney. The McKinneys are both top area realtors who love sharing their knowledge of the area with guests as they enjoy the tranquil setting. The McKinney's have turned their home into a very unique place. A lot of love and personality is what you will find at this special inn. The rooms are dedicated to McKinney family members, and it is obvious that each guest is considered a member of the family. While visiting you must meet the inn's beautiful pet swans, Romeo and Juliet. Explore their website to see visual tours of the Inn and learn the history of the rooms.

1041 Kelly Road, Apex NC   (919) 303-8003 or (800) 251-3171   www.BnBcountryinn.com   www.budandbeth.com

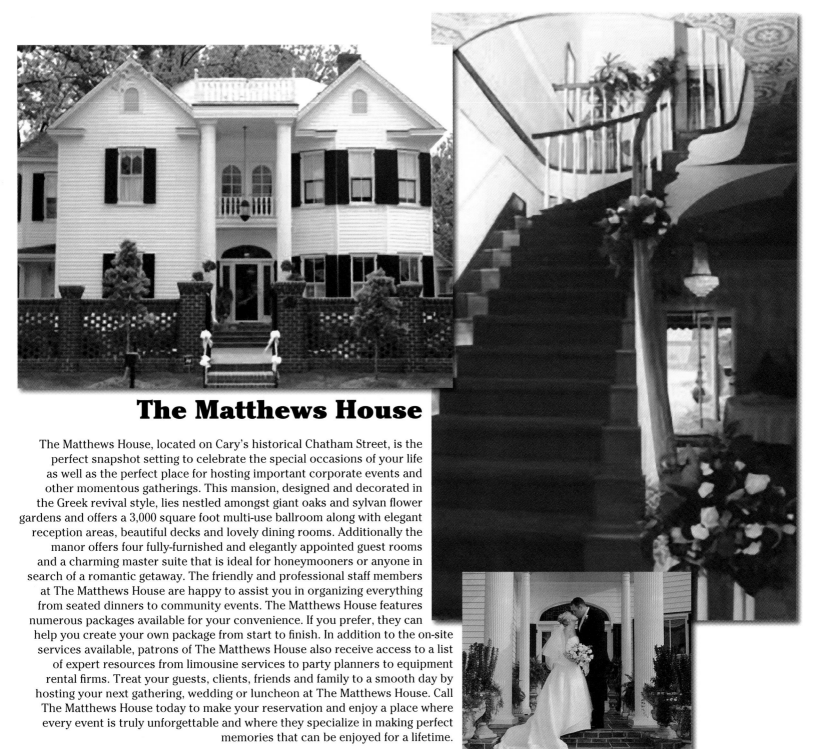

The Matthews House

The Matthews House, located on Cary's historical Chatham Street, is the perfect snapshot setting to celebrate the special occasions of your life as well as the perfect place for hosting important corporate events and other momentous gatherings. This mansion, designed and decorated in the Greek revival style, lies nestled amongst giant oaks and sylvan flower gardens and offers a 3,000 square foot multi-use ballroom along with elegant reception areas, beautiful decks and lovely dining rooms. Additionally the manor offers four fully-furnished and elegantly appointed guest rooms and a charming master suite that is ideal for honeymooners or anyone in search of a romantic getaway. The friendly and professional staff members at The Matthews House are happy to assist you in organizing everything from seated dinners to community events. The Matthews House features numerous packages available for your convenience. If you prefer, they can help you create your own package from start to finish. In addition to the on-site services available, patrons of The Matthews House also receive access to a list of expert resources from limousine services to party planners to equipment rental firms. Treat your guests, clients, friends and family to a smooth day by hosting your next gathering, wedding or luncheon at The Matthews House. Call The Matthews House today to make your reservation and enjoy a place where every event is truly unforgettable and where they specialize in making perfect memories that can be enjoyed for a lifetime.

317 W Chatham Street, Cary NC
(919) 467-1944
www.matthews-house.com

The Siena Hotel

Inspired by the beauty of Italy, The Siena Hotel will captivate you with its elegance. This AAA Four Diamond boutique hotel adds its distinctive European character to the Raleigh-Durham area. Listed as a reserve property on *Conde Nast Traveler's* Gold List for 2005, The Siena is modeled after a stylish Tuscan villa. The luxurious décor includes hand-selected European antiques and majestic columns against a backdrop of rich colors and fabrics. Each of the 80 spacious guestrooms and suites is individual in design, furnished with European armoires, marble-topped desks and beautiful artwork. All rooms offer marble bathrooms and a range of luxury items, such as European bath amenities, nightly turndown service and high-speed internet. Guests enjoy a wide range of activities, including complimentary membership to the nearby health club spa. The hotel's concierge can arrange tee times at a variety of North Carolina's top-rated golf courses. For total relaxation, guests can book an in-room appointment with the hotel's masseuse. The Siena's fine Italian restaurant, Il Palio, is a AAA Four Diamond selection. Executive Chef Jim Anile's modern Italian cuisine focuses on fresh, seasonal ingredients. In addition to innovative á la carte menus, special evening culinary delights include a Chef's tasting menu– five courses that showcase the day's special ingredients, chosen for your by Chef Anile. Il Palio's accolades include a Condé Nast recommendation and the *Wine Spectator* Award for Excellence. Attentive service and a friendly, relaxed atmosphere are hallmarks of the hotel, making The Siena the perfect Italian getaway

1505 E Franklin Street, Chapel Hill NC
(919) 929-4000 or (800) 223-7379
www.sienahotel.com

Morehead Manor Bed & Breakfast

Nestled in historic Morehead Hills, Morehead Manor Bed & Breakfast provides majestic comfort. Fine dining and quaint shopping are within walking distance. Nearby are local universities, area attractions and Research Triangle Park. The convenient location is only one of the perks enjoyed by Morehead Manor's guests. Homemade desserts and beverages are available in the evening. A full gourmet breakfast with delicious house-blended coffee greets guests each morning. The inn has several common areas for guest use, where music, tea, or a good book can be enjoyed at your leisure. Morehead Manor can be reserved for special events, such as weddings, corporate retreats, dinner parties and showers. Special individual and group packages are available. Four spacious guest rooms are wonderfully appointed, each with its own private bath. The Eagle's Inn room boasts a seven-head shower. The Tiger room is a brightly lit room with a king-sized bed, the Magnolia Suite includes a private sitting area, and the Jasmine room has a queen-sized bed. Pick your favorite room and enjoy the comfortable ambience. Whether you are looking for a relaxing getaway, a romantic weekend, or are just traveling through, you will appreciate Morehead Manor.

914 Vickers Avenue, Durham NC   (888) 437-6333   www.moreheadmanor.com

Triangle Area Attractions

Knight's Play Golf Center

Play in the sun or under the stars. Knight's Play Golf Center's par 3 course and its 60-station driving range are open, weather permitting, even at night. The course, owned by Richard Godwin, Nelson Hare and David Postlethwait, features 27 holes sure to challenge players of all levels. The course is fully paved for carts, but short enough to be an enjoyable walk. Knight's Play offers practical hands-on training with its PGA professional staff. Clinics range from pee wee (ages 7 to 10) to adults. Individual lessons are available. PGA pros can assist you in organizing your own private tournament at Knight's Play. It makes a fun outing and a great way to reward employees, encourage team building, kick off a new project or celebrate the completion of a goal. Consider a neighborhood tournament or an anniversary celebration. Head Golf Pro Kevin Jones has been with Knight's Play since its opening in 1998. He and the owners tout Knight's Play as being a great alternative golf course. On a par 3, you are able to play at a quicker pace, but the quality of the facility makes you feel as though you played a full-size course. The pace is relaxed, and the staff is friendly and committed to meeting your golfing needs.

2512 Ten Ten Road, Apex NC
(919) 303-GOLF (4653)
www.knightsplay.com

University Mall

Situated halfway between Washington and Atlanta in North Carolina's Piedmont region, Chapel Hill was incorporated in 1819. It is known as the home of the University of North Carolina, great basketball, excellent restaurants and the distinctive University Mall. Situated on South Estes Drive just off 15-501, the mall is full of shopping delights for all ages and interests. Here visitors can while away the hours in a comfortable, relaxed and friendly atmosphere, exactly what you'd expect in this charming town. Catch a show at the Deep Dish Theater or indulge in the gourmet offerings that abound in A Southern Season. Three art galleries on the premises provide imaginative, vivid artwork designed to thrill the senses. That must-have outfit is likely to be waiting at a shop like Metropolis, Dina Porter or O'Neill's Menswear. You can find the perfect gift for any occasion at one of the many locally owned specialty stores for which University Mall is known. The mall offers the largest selection of specialty shops at one address in Chapel Hill, affording its guests the kind of individualized, quality service not typically found in a mall. When you find yourself getting hungry, choose from one of Chapel Hill's great restaurants or stop by K&W Cafeteria. University Mall isn't just a shopping center, it's the quintessential Chapel Hill experience.

201 S Estes Drive, Chapel Hill NC   (919) 967-6934
www.universitymallnc.com

Triangle Area
Candies, Ice Cream, Bakeries & Coffee

Goodberry's Creamery

Back in the 1920s or 1930s, when people craved ice cream, they headed for the closest dairy and creamery. There it was made fresh, with real cream, fruit, nuts and care. It came to you semi-soft, straight from the churn. That kind of freshness is back at the several Goodberry's Frozen Custard locations in the Raleigh Triangle. Custard, did you say? Yes, frozen custard, the original French ice cream is made at Goodberry's. The process begins with fresh heavy cream, whole milk, natural cane sugar and eggs. Blended and cooked, the mixture next gets the flavor elements, including vanilla imported from Madagascar, home of the world's finest vanilla beans. The chocolate, dark and delicious, is imported from cocoa plantations in South America and Africa. Fruits used include berries of all kinds, cherries, peaches and bananas. Pecans and walnuts are just some of the nuts added to Goodberry's recipes. No one back seven or eight decades ago ever had it better than you'll find it at Goodberry's today. While at a Goodberry's, you can ask yourself this trivia question: Which American President left behind a recipe in his own handwriting for frozen custard, said to be the first known recipe for the dish? The answer: Thomas Jefferson. As you taste a Goodberry's, you're enjoying something that delighted one of our Founding Fathers. See their website or call for the many Goodberry's locations.

(919) 878-8870
www.goodberrys.com

Open Eye Café

Whether you are looking for an early morning wake-up or a late day pick-me-up, head over to Open Eye Café in Carrboro. This terrific coffee shop and espresso bar isn't your run-of-the-mill, grab-a-cup-of-Joe-and-go place. Due to its popularity, The Café recently expanded next door, allowing for more folks to enjoy it while maintaining the same comfortable feel. Open Eye Café is a place where friends gather, where communities come together and where really great coffee is made and served. Owners Scott Conary and Elizabeth Justus are both well known in the coffee world for their high standards. Justus has been a barista for more than eight years and has trained many award-winning employees. Conary is certified by the Specialty Coffee Association of America (SCAA) in espresso training and sensory evaluation and serves as a judge for national and world barista competitions. Open Eye Café has been awarded by the SCAA with the TOPS award for coffee excellence four times in the five-year history of the award. The Café carries an extensive selection of beverages, including espresso and coffee drinks, whole leaf tea, smoothies and shakes. It also carries tasty baked goods and savory food items. While enjoying your coffee and other treats, relax in the eclectic and comfortable atmosphere of this newly refurbished space. The Café features the work of local and traveling artists, and showcases national touring and local musicians throughout the week. With a mind toward its community, the Café contributes to many local, athletic and nonprofit organizations. Come see for yourself why the eclectic and vibrant Open Eye Café has been dubbed Carrboro's Living Room.

101 S Greensboro Street, Carrboro, NC
(919) 968-9410
www.openeyecafe.com

Coffee & Crepes

Who can forget a crepe in Paris? Soft, warm, fresh and light, yet oh so satisfying. When you step into Coffee & Crepes, you step into Europe, South America or Japan, where the paper thin, stuffed pancakes are abundant. The menu includes savory meal-sized crepes, such as mushroom Swiss or spinach ricotta served with a side of spring greens. Yes Europeans, they also serve Nutella, that famously delectable hazelnut chocolate and various fruit crepes with fresh whipped cream. In an exceptionally friendly, casual style, owners Terese and Andrés Pastrana are happy to modify any recipe to accommodate diet restrictions or preference. As a bonus, you'll enjoy the best coffee and espresso drinks in town. It is no wonder that the catering end of their business is in such demand. With so many wonderful fillings from which to choose, there is something for everyone at Coffee & Crepes.

315 Crossroads Boulevard, Cary NC
(919) 233-0288

Edible Art

In the 1760s, venturesome landowners operated taverns and ordinaries, early restaurants that served as meeting places and hubs of political activity to refresh travelers. Bobby and Lou Reynolds are continuing the visionary tradition of service and refreshment with their Edible Art Bakery and Dessert Café. They've offered the finest custom wedding and special occasion cakes to their delighted customers for more than 20 years. In June of 2000, the bakery grew by 3,000 square feet when it moved to the Royal Mall just across from Meredith College. The Dessert Café was added at this time, where desserts can be sampled by the slice with your favorite coffee, tea or espresso. Edible Art cakes are baked with the freshest, highest quality ingredients and a variety of flavor choices all designed individually for each customer. The on-site artisans create custom designs that range from fun and whimsical to breathtaking. Gum paste decoration is an option if ordered two weeks in advance, and special dietary needs can be accommodated. Delivery is available for all special occasion cakes. The fantastic variety makes it hard to choose just one, but you are invited to come in and try the sampler to find your own tasty top choice.

3801 Hillsborough Street, Raleigh NC   (919) 856-0604   www.edibleartbakery.com

Caffe Driade

Driade is Italian for the Greek word dryad, which is the spirit that lives in a tree, in essence, a wood nymph. In the case of Caffe Driade, an espresso bar, teahouse and wine bar, the name refers to the combination of magic and high quality that make this a superior place to unwind. The beautiful gardens and patios at Caffe Driade blend seamlessly into the surrounding woods for an atmosphere that is unique. Captivating art is displayed, and live music can be enjoyed by candlelight outside from May through October. The Specialty Coffee Association of America has awarded this establishment the coveted TOPS Award for coffee excellence four years in a row. The espresso, whole leaf tea and famous Driade shake are perfectly suited for the luscious baked goods made here. These artisan delicacies range from spinach and feta croissants to apple turnovers, as well as danish, biscotti and tortes. A select choice of premium cigars in the humidor will delight the aficionado, all handmade in Jamaica, Dominican Republic and Honduras. The wine and beer menu is carefully selected and features quality labels. Drop into Caffe Driade, comfortably nestled back from the street, and enjoy the epicurean delights that have been featured on the Food Network's show, *$40 Dollars a Day*. Caffe Driade is a gem of a find, where Europeans feel at home and locals bring their friends to impress them.

1215-A E Franklin Street, Chapel Hill NC
(919) 942-2333
www.caffedriade.com

Ashworth Drugs & Soda Fountain

Paul Ashworth is a pharmacist who knows the value of giving customers personal service. He is the owner of Ashworth Drugs & Soda Fountain, founded in Cary by his father Ralph. The Ashworths have been giving that personal attention to four generations of customers, many of whom use the store's charge and delivery service. The store is widely known for its hot dogs and, of course, its soda fountain. Wednesday is hot dog day. On any day, you will find ice cream sodas, sandwiches and more, which you can enjoy in Ashworth's outside seating. For your pharmacy needs and for tummy satisfaction, the Ashworth family has you covered at Ashworth Drugs & Soda Fountain.

105 W Chatham Street, Cary NC
(919) 467-1877
www.ashworthdrugs.com

Renaissance Chocolatier

Renaissance Chocolatier is a connoisseur's dream come true. Chocolatier Katherine Shaw has brought the South's finest chocolates to Cary's Waverly Place. Owner of Renaissance Chocolatier, she makes all the confections in her shop. By using only the finest base chocolate and absolutely no preservatives, artificial ingredients or wax, each taste of her chocolate has an exquisite freshness and delectable quality. She's so confident that no other chocolates come close to Renaissance Chocolatier's that she hosts a taste challenge in her store. She sets out a table with her Queen Elizabeth truffles and a separate table with a nationally or internationally famous chocolate. She then asks her customers to rank the chocolates according to five criteria: appearance, shell click, texture, taste and finish. Challengers are then encouraged to write their own additional comments. Renaissance Chocolatier has won each challenge by a long shot and it is no surprise to Katherine. "We believe our chocolates rank with the very finest in the country." Katherine credits her husband, William, a professor of Renaissance literature, with the shop's historic theme and its cleverly named products, from the flagship Queen Elizabeth line of truffles to the half milk chocolate/half dark chocolate Hamlet bar for those who can't make up their mind. When it comes to deciding where the finest chocolates are to be found, there is no vacillating. They're at Renaissance Chocolatier, without a doubt.

105D Colonades Way, Waverly Place, Cary NC
(919) 233-2921   www.renaissancechocolatier.com

Triangle Area Fashion

Traditional Terre

Traditional Terre is truly a notable place; it's both an up-to-the-minute boutique that's tuned in to the latest fashion trends, and a business deeply committed to its community and the people in it. Traditional Terre features clothing, accessories, jewelry and gifts in every style from classic to edgy. Terre Oosterwyk opened the 1,200-square-foot store during the 1999 Christmas season; since then, it has more than tripled in size. It's no wonder, when a the lines she carries include City Girl, Boho Chic, Lynn Ritchie, French Dressing, Co & Eddy, Live a Little, Berek, Belldini, Emily Ray, John Medeiros, and Timmy Wood. Every four to six weeks Terre hosts a special in-house event, such as the Emily Ray Trunk Show, author or artist signings and, of course, the annual holiday open house. All of these community events feature prize drawings and special products. Traditional Terre gives back to its community by making contributions to the American Heart Association, the Multiple Sclerosis Society, the American Diabetes Association, Arc, and the local home care and hospice agencies. When a customer buys one of Traditional Terre's special gold cards, all the money from the card sale is donated to Cure by Design. Anyone shopping at Traditional Terre will receive the best in personalized service and attention to their needs, which isn't surprising, considering the heart that runs this business.

107 Edinburgh South Drive, Suite 106, Cary NC
(919) 467-0022

Chapel Hill Sportswear

Chickadees

Chapel Hill has become a destination spot for North Carolinians in search of fine dining and shopping. It is also home to one of the state's premier children's stores, Chickadees. This fresh and charming children's boutique offers a plethora of fresh new designs and fashions that have been specially made with children's lifestyles in mind. Here you will find a treasure trove of fun playwear and timeless special occasion clothing that your little one will love to wear. Chickadees features Sarah Louise, Le Top and Kushies, as well as Zutano, Carriage Boutiques, Big Fish and more. This fabulous clothier, located at Meadowmont Village Circle, boasts a friendly and personable staff of professionals who are always happy to help you select the ideal outfit or wardrobe for your little one. In conjunction with its wide array of clothing, Chickadees carries an extensive selection of accessories and toys that are sure to delight. Your kids will be as happy to go shopping as you are. Enjoy an exceptional children's shopping excursion with a visit to Chickadees.

505 Meadowmont Village Circle, Chapel Hill NC
(919) 933-8247

Blue, blue, blue—everything is blue at Chapel Hill Sportswear, the largest off-campus store specializing in University of North Carolina clothing and gifts. The store has been on Franklin Street since 1989. It carries many well known brands, such as J. America and Gear for Sport, and offers clothing for fans of all sizes, from six months to adult. Chapel Hill Sportswear is the exclusive supplier for TarHeelBlue.com, the official online store of the UNC Athletic Department. Carolina fans everywhere can also order merchandise at the Chapel Hill Sportswear website. Members of the full-time staff are either Carolina graduates or long-time loyal fans. Chapel Hill Sportswear is proud to be a partner with the UNC Athletic Department in the Turn It Blue campaign. Profits from Turn It Blue T-shirts are donated to two local charities: the Stephen Gates Scholarship Foundation and the Interfaith Council. The store has donated thousands of T-shirts to celebrate the university and to make these charitable promotions a success. In the fall, the store publishes a great color catalog in time for holiday shopping. Call the store's toll-free number or check its website to order merchandise or a catalog.

133 E Franklin Street, Chapel Hill NC
(919) 929-0060 or (800) 585-0086
www.chapelhillsportswear.com

Scout & Molly's

At Scout & Molly's, you will feel like you just stepped into a closet full of your favorite designer clothing, complete with vintage furnishings. You can snag pieces by Trina Turk, Nanette Lepore, Diane Von Furstenburg, Joe's Jeans, BCBG, Three Dots and Kasil, among others. A girl with a dream opened the first Scout & Molly's location in April 2002. Lisa Disbrow and her husband, Jarrett, decided it was time to see the dream through. The store is named after their two Labrador retrievers, Scout and Molly, who can at times be seen lounging on one of the antique rugs. Scout & Molly's is the perfect place to find your style. You can find everything from a great pair of jeans to sophisticated suits and flirty cocktail dresses, not to mention the incredible selection of jewelry by local designers. Scout & Molly's has everything you need to update your wardrobe. The best part is that now you can shop at two locations. Two years ago, a love of their dogs and fashion brought Lisa and Jarrett together with Jessica and Mike Kenady. They met at the dog park, hit it off, and Lisa hired Jessica to manage her store while she had a baby. Their friendship grew, and a year later they decided to partner up to bring Scout & Molly's to Chapel Hill. Stop in at either store for a truly wonderful and friendly experience. Shop at Scout & Molly's of Raleigh and Scout & Molly's of Chapel Hill for a two-of-a-kind shopping experience.

Scout & Molly's of Raleigh: *4209-133 Lassiter Mill Road, Raleigh NC*   (919) 848-8732
Scout & Molly's of Chapel Hill: *105 Meadowmont Village Circle, Chapel Hill NC*   (919) 969-8886
www.scoutandmollys.com

Dina Porter

For those of you who wish to choose your entire wardrobe in one store, your wish has been granted. Dina Porter offers a choice selection of limited edition clothing to match every occasion, from casual and career to mother-of-the-bride and cocktail attire. The shop carries more than 100 lines, including the distinctive Eileen Fisher collection. Owner Susan Coker and her staff pride themselves on excellent customer service. To take advantage of this great service, Coker recommends you come when you have enough time to really enjoy what the store offers. This allows the staff to help you choose from the extensive collection of designer and handmade options available. Check out the new styles from Fat Hat, Elliot Lauren, Isda and Toofan. Career women who demand comfort will love the designs from Marla Duran, I Alex, J'Envie, Staples and Tank 18. If you're looking for a classic, stylish little number for the cocktail hour or an elegant mother-of-the-bride outfit, Dina Porter will have it. Many limited edition and one-of-a-kind ensembles are on display or can be ordered with your figure in mind. The staff's goal is to provide each customer with sophisticated, quality clothing that allows clients to move confidently, and comfortably, through any occasion. Sizes range from XS to 3X, and a full selection of limited edition accessories, including jewelry, handbags and scarves, will complement your purchases.

201 S Estes, University Mall, Chapel Hill NC (919) 929-4449 or (800) 813-6893 www.dinaporter.com

Flame Kissed Beads

Kaleigh Hessel's work may be small, and it graces wrists and necklines rather than gallery walls or plinths, but what she does is art nevertheless, simply on a remarkably smaller scale. Kaleigh creates fine art beads in rich and astonishing detail and custom jewelry that glows with an inner fire. Flame Kissed Beads is a combination art jewelry gallery, glass studio and bead shop. Flame Kissed Beads has a wonderful selection of flamework glass beads, Venetian and vintage glass beads, Swarovsky crystals, Bali silver beads and Myuki seed beads, to name just a few of the bead varieties Kaleigh features. Kaleigh has always been committed to championing emerging and local artists, and offers an exceptional collection of one-of-a-kind pieces of hand-crafted jewelry from top-notch bead artists on the regional and national level. The Gallery is home to Glenwood Glass, a working glass studio where Kaleigh creates her exquisite beads and jewelry pieces and teaches classes in different aspects of this delicate craft. Students learn how to make jewelry using a number of different techniques that include lampworking, fused dichroic glass and precious metal clay. Classes encourage participants to express their creativity with the emphasis always on student accomplishment. Come see why Kaleigh was enthralled the first time she worked a glass rod in a flame. You may discover the perfect gift or your own new passion at Flame Kissed Beads.

106 New Waverly Place, Suite 106B, Cary NC (919) 851-6412
www.flamekissedbeads.com

Black Mountain Gallery

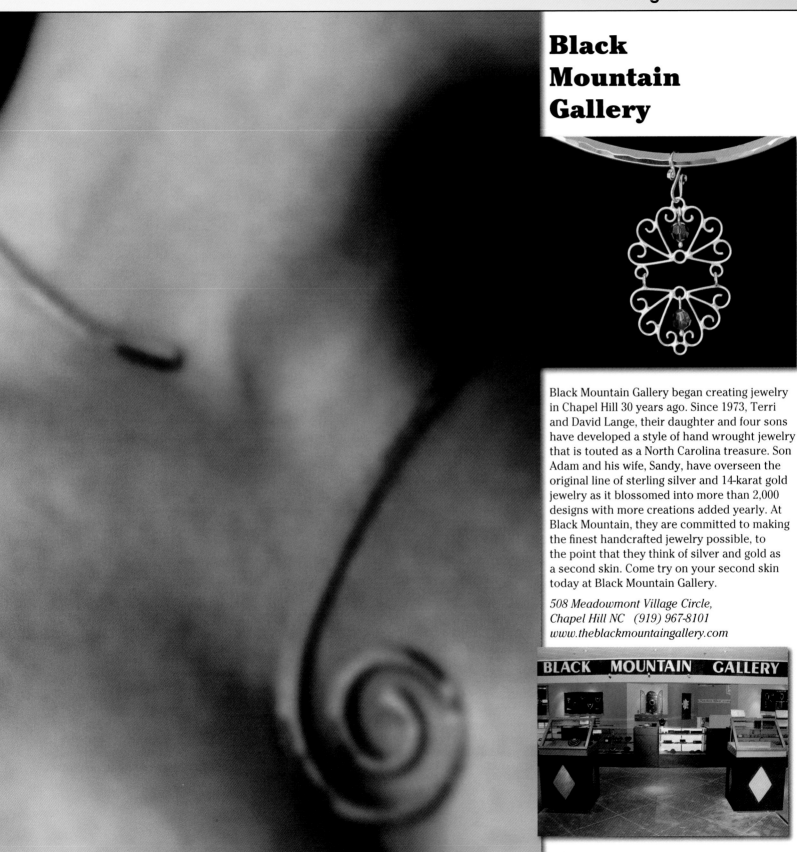

Black Mountain Gallery began creating jewelry in Chapel Hill 30 years ago. Since 1973, Terri and David Lange, their daughter and four sons have developed a style of hand wrought jewelry that is touted as a North Carolina treasure. Son Adam and his wife, Sandy, have overseen the original line of sterling silver and 14-karat gold jewelry as it blossomed into more than 2,000 designs with more creations added yearly. At Black Mountain, they are committed to making the finest handcrafted jewelry possible, to the point that they think of silver and gold as a second skin. Come try on your second skin today at Black Mountain Gallery.

508 Meadowmont Village Circle,
Chapel Hill NC   (919) 967-8101
www.theblackmountaingallery.com

Cravings, A Maternity Boutique

Cravings, A Maternity Boutique has all the special styles you've been searching for. This classy shop offers the latest trends in maternity fashions. From quality tailoring to moderate pricing, Cravings delivers scrumptious fabrics and delicious colors. Pregnancy is a special time and Cravings helps the mother-to-be celebrate with her own look. The foundation of Cravings' selection comes from established maternity lines such as Olian, Japanese Weekend and Duet Designs. Cravings routinely introduces new and emerging smaller labels that focus on specific wardrobe niches. They don't overlook the importance of detail at this hip little shop. Cravings offers a selection of maternity jeans, lingerie and nursing bras, as well as accessories like maternity Spanx, the Bella Band and Preggie Pops. They even have a play area for small children and comfy seating for dads. At Cravings, they believe your pregnancy is a time to feel as beautiful outside as you do inside. Come indulge your sense of style at Cravings. You couldn't wait to get pregnant. Now, you won't be able to wait to get dressed.

Falls Village Shopping Center
6675 Falls of Neuse Road, Suite 123, Raleigh NC
(919) 676-4446
www.cravingsmaternity.com

Triangle Area Galleries

Grace Li Wang Art Gallery

Grace Li Wang is an artist renowned for her ability to capture the radiance of nature in exuberant expressionist and impressionist works. She wants her art to energize and enrich the spirit in each of us. Her vibrant colors and graphic forms infuse a sense of radiant vitality in an imaginative and captivating world. Born in Taipei, Taiwan, Republic of China, in 1953, Grace Li Wang arrived in the United States in 1964. A graduate of the School of Design at North Carolina State University, she worked as an art and design manager for major corporations. She participates in numerous international, national and regional design conferences as a speaker, panelist and competitions jurist. Her years of experience and outstanding talent are evident in her gallery, Grace Li Wang Art Gallery in Raleigh, where she has been the director since the late 1990s. At her gallery, Grace's inspiring art is available in original canvases, giclees, prints or mixed-media works. Tapestries, throws and note cards featuring her art are sought after as gifts. Grace's work has been exhibited worldwide and collected by private art enthusiasts and public institutions. She is the recipient of numerous international art and design awards, including the Designers Choice awards from International Design Publications, the Distinguished Art and Design Graphics awards from the International Society for Technical Communications, and dozens of other awards. Please call for appointment.

2411 E Millbrook Road #116, Raleigh NC
(919) 412-6803   www.graceliwang.com

Stone Crow Pottery

The atmosphere at Joyce Bryan's studio, Stone Crow Pottery, invites you come and sit on the front porch of the log building located along the Haw River. Some of the logs are 120 years old and add ambience to the artistic environment. Joyce's pottery expresses her individual passion and the many possibilities for art created through clay. The first potter in the area, Joyce is known for her humorous pots, layered glazes and wizard handles. Recognized for the depth of her glazes and an extraordinary variety of textures and colors, her pots are creative and eclectic. Joyce has spent time in the Southwest, and that influence is evident in her work. Joyce's degree in art and her association with several area potters' associations have exposed her to promising new perspectives that are reflected in her work. Be sure to visit Stone Crow Pottery for old-fashioned charm and first-class pottery.

4269 US 15-501 North, Chapel Hill NC   (919) 542-4708   www.stone-crowpottery.com

Goldworks

Born of fire and age old tradition comes timeless jewelry forged in the Mokume-gane style. Mokume-gane, which means wood grain metal in Japanese, is a challenging and time-consuming process of laminating precious metals together. Originating in feudal Japan, this artistry

was put to use creating ornaments and fittings to complement Japanese fighting swords. Master jewelers have brought this exquisite skill back to life in the form of fashionable, functional and rings that are available to you through Goldworks, located in the University Mall in Chapel Hill. Various precious metals and methods of forging, carving and twisting create individuality, so no two pieces are alike. Four main artists design and make a majority of the store's jewelry. Each artist is able to maintain their own identity while offering consistent, quality pieces. Owners Wren and Ted Hendrickson have been making jewelry together for 30 years. Their combined experience and eye for detail lend themselves beautifully to the elegantly showcased merchandise. Not wanting to limit the store to just one art form, the Hendricksons also display a collection of hand-blown glass pieces and an extensive array of other American crafts. They pride themselves on the integrity and quality of the works they offer, and on creating custom pieces for their clients. Next time you are at University Mall don't forget to see these master Goldsmiths at work.

201 S Estes Drive, Chapel Hill NC (919) 932-1771 www.goldworks-nc.com

Minata Jewelers

Enchanting glass sculptures and engaging paintings draw the eye toward Minata Jewelers as you walk around the University Mall, an upscale shopping plaza in beautiful Chapel Hill. Upon entering, visitors are surprised and delighted by the display of incredible contemporary jewelry. Owner Linda Kornberg offers a venue to designers from around the world, such as Aldo Cipullo, who has works on display at the Museum of Modern Art, and Elsa Peretti, who has gone on to design exclusively for Tiffany's. "Being a designer myself I believe in the philosophy of functional art," Linda says. Her words ring true with displays of one exquisite piece of wearable or functional art after another. Linda displays the works of Stephen White, a local Chapel Hill artist who uses canvases of wood and glass along with more traditional surfaces. He creates one-of-a-kind oil paintings of a woman he first created more than 25 years ago. Minata also features a distinctive collection of Judaica, containing intriguing pieces like the brass and copper-fused menorah created by Gary Rosenthal. The stand-alone and often ingenious works of art that Minata features make perfect gifts for yourself or others, regardless of the occasion. More importantly, they are the classic heirlooms of tomorrow.

201 S Estes Drive, Chapel Hill NC
(919) 967-8964
www.minata.com

Tyndall Galleries

With University Mall's renaissance, Jane Shuping Tyndall moved the Tyndall Galleries to Chapel Hill in 2002 after 11 years at Brightleaf Square in Durham. Louis St. Lewis wrote in *Metro Magazine*, "Strutting into Jane Tyndall's new gallery space in Chapel Hill's University Mall makes you feel like you're almost in New York City. It is without a doubt a stunning space–high ceilings, great light and plenty of room." Tyndall Galleries represents accomplished contemporary American artists with connections to North Carolina. Figurative paintings by Beverly McIver, whose work was lauded in *Art in America* and recently acquired by the North Carolina Museum of Art, are presented alongside inspiring landscapes by Lynn Boggess and Jacob Cooley. You'll find vibrant abstract paintings by Linda Ruth Dickinson and Nancy Tuttle May, plus rich expressionistic works by Jane Filer. Sleek kinetic sculptures by George Beckman and Wayne Trapp's exquisite stone and metal creations will intrigue you. Award-winning photographer John Rosenthal, whose commentaries air on National Public Radio, is represented along with internationally known fiber artists Silvia Heyden and Susan Brandeis, and ceramicist Sally Bowen Prange. It's no surprise that Tyndall Galleries was voted Best Gallery in the Triangle by *Citysearch* and placed second only to the Ackland Art Museum at the University of North Carolina as Best Place to View Art in Orange County by readers of the *Chapel Hill Herald*. Make plans to visit this beautiful and inviting art gallery. You'll find yourself transformed.

201 S Estes Drive, University Mall, Chapel Hill NC (919) 942-2290 www.tyndallgalleries.com

Flame Kissed Beads

Kaleigh Hessel's work may be small, and it graces wrists and necklines rather than gallery walls or plinths, but what she does is art nevertheless, simply on a remarkably smaller scale. Kaleigh creates fine art beads in rich and astonishing detail and custom jewelry that glows with an inner fire. Flame Kissed Beads is a combination art jewelry gallery, glass studio and bead shop. Flame Kissed Beads has a wonderful selection of flamework glass beads, Venetian and vintage glass beads, Swarovsky crystals, Bali silver beads and Myuki seed beads, to name just a few of the bead varieties Kaleigh features. Kaleigh has always been committed to championing emerging and local artists, and offers an exceptional collection of one-of-a-kind pieces of hand-crafted jewelry from top-notch bead artists on the regional and national level. The Gallery is home to Glenwood Glass, a working glass studio where Kaleigh creates her exquisite beads and jewelry pieces and teaches classes in different aspects of this delicate craft. Students learn how to make jewelry using a number of different techniques that include lampworking, fused dichroic glass and precious metal clay. Classes encourage participants to express their creativity with the emphasis always on student accomplishment. Come see why Kaleigh was enthralled the first time she worked a glass rod in a flame. You may discover the perfect gift or your own new passion at Flame Kissed Beads.

106 New Waverly Place, Suite 106B, Cary NC (919) 851-6412 www.flamekissedbeads.com

Black Mountain Gallery

Black Mountain Gallery began creating jewelry in Chapel Hill 30 years ago. Since 1973, Terri and David Lange, their daughter and four sons have developed a style of hand wrought jewelry that is touted as a North Carolina treasure. Son Adam and his wife, Sandy, have overseen the original line of sterling silver and 14-karat gold jewelry as it blossomed into more than 2,000 designs with more creations added yearly. At Black Mountain, they are committed to making the finest handcrafted jewelry possible, to the point that they think of silver and gold as a second skin. Come try on your second skin today at Black Mountain Gallery.

508 Meadowmont Village Circle,
Chapel Hill NC   (919) 967-8101
www.theblackmountaingallery.com

Lee Hansley Gallery

The Modernist aesthetic, firmly anchored in the Bauhaus tradition, is alive and kicking in the Lee Hansley Gallery located in Raleigh's Glenwood South. The gallery's group and solo shows feature bold works by professional North Carolina artists. Lee Hansley, who is both founder and manager for the gallery, is a former curator at the Southeastern Center for Contemporary Art in Winston-Salem. His expertise is evident in the colorful and seamlessly staged exhibitions. A stable of 35 artists keeps the exhibitions fresh and exciting. Invitationals provide an outlet for non-gallery artists, and an annual historical show explores the work of a single artist or group of artists. Lee Hansley Gallery presents a diverse assemblage of art works, including painting, sculpture and mixed media. They represent a bevy of ceramicists and artists who work on paper. At least three fine art photographers display their creations in the gallery. In keeping with Hansley's commitment to the promotion of modernism, the showroom is used to mount frequent exhibitions of examples by older or deceased artists. The biennial show, Art I Have Loved, offers collectors consignment works for resale to

Howard Thomas: Red in Blue Contrapuntal, 1956

the public. Due to a recent transformation, the former Design Gallery's area is now dedicated exclusively to handmade objects, mainly ceramics and glass. Come in and enjoy the array of talent and variety presented by Lee Hansley Gallery, and while you're there, take advantage of their superb consultation, curatorial services and appraisals available for corporate and public hire.

225 Glenwood Avenue, Raleigh NC
(919) 828-7557
www.leehansleygallery.com

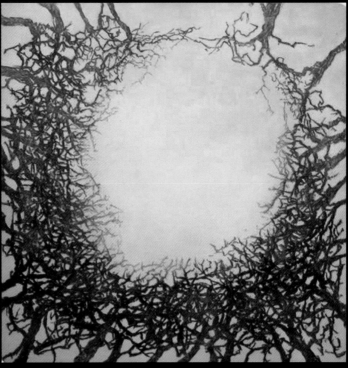

Janis Goodman: Rotating Vision, 2003

Artworks /The Studio

Artworks is a gallery and teaching studio. Owner Carol Weisberg Burgess offers classes to both children and adults. The students range in age from six to 90, and everything in between. They explore a variety of techniques through drawing, watercolor, pen and ink, pastels and acrylics. The artwork is accomplished in a fun, relaxed, and supportive atmosphere. Carol has been teaching for more than 25 years in many schools, as well as in art and community centers. When Carol is not teaching, she is working on her own paintings and drawings. Her specialty is water colors and oil paintings. Carol concentrates on form and movement to create her dancers in motion and other works. "The energy that makes us move, that makes us think, plan and look to the future, all of these thoughts are with me as I'm working." Enroll yourself or your child in a class at Artworks/The Studio and begin the journey of creativity.

1117 Country Ridge Drive, Raleigh, NC
(919) 878-5101

Moondance Gallery

A Top 100 Retailer of American Craft for seven out of the last nine years, Moondance is appreciated by craft lovers and artists alike. Moondance Gallery offers a unique collection of jewelry and gifts from artists and designers all over the United States. Founders Jeff and Janis Tillman opened their first Moondance Gallery in Durham in 1992. A second store followed four years later in Raleigh. After several years of operating in those locations, the Tillmans decided to move the business closer to home. It is now in its permanent location in Meadowmont Village in Chapel Hill. Moondance specializes in handcrafted jewelry, whimsical animal metal sculptures, North Carolina collegiate collectibles, and other fabulous gifts. The gallery represents an ever-growing collection of local artists. Moondance also offers a selection of many wonderful items online. If you are looking for something that isn't on the website, e-mail, call or fax and they'll work to find it for you.

603 Meadowmont Village Circle, Chapel Hill, NC
(919) 265-0020
www.moondancegallery.com

Triangle Area Gifts

Tarheel Book Store

The Tarheel Book Store, located on Franklin Street in the heart of downtown Chapel Hill, has all the latest gifts and apparel for Tarheel fans of all ages. Owner John Lindo has a brand-new, open and airy store full of extraordinary gifts and apparel. John has more than 20 years' experience running college bookstores on various college campuses, and it shows in the cleanliness and organization of the store. Visitors can browse the store for a huge selection of textbooks in a wide range of subjects. With more than 4,000 titles of new and used textbooks to choose from, Tarheel Book Store is known for having the items you seek. The store carries general reading books if you are not in the market for college textbooks. If you are looking for Tarheel gifts, this is the place to visit. Not only can you find clothing and gifts for everyone, but you will also find auto accessories, Carolinopoly (a board game derived from Monopoly) and gifts for your pet. Most merchandise is available for purchase online. See the wide selection of merchandise to support the Tarheels in the heart of Chapel Hill.

119 E Franklin Street, Chapel Hill NC
(919) 960-6021   www.tarheel.com

Ferdinand's Dog & Cat Boutique

It's not easy being an independent business owner these days. Ferdinand, the three-legged proprietor of Ferdinand's Dog and Cat Boutique, felt that his community would benefit from having a resource for all of the necessities and luxuries that the area's *domesticus familiaris* might need. Ferdinand, a pit bull mix, has designed a shop where canines, felines and humans alike can gather to find the highest quality supplies available on the market today. With the impeccable taste that he is known for, Ferdinand stocks a choice collection of designer accoutrements to fill his space, such as matching collar and leash sets in a vast array of colors and designs, all suited to match your personality, and a wide selection of T-shirts and toys. The boutique carries a delightful array of greeting cards, carriers, strollers, beds and dining accessories. Because Ferdinand is dedicated to promoting good physical health amongst his clients, he also carries high-quality food brands, such as California Natural, Wellness, Innova and Nu Dimensions. Ferdinand's Dog & Cat Boutique features a scrumptious spectrum of healthy treats and offers homemade dog biscuits from Gourmutt's Bakery. As with all children, Ferdinand knows that some home training is necessary, so he provides a good selection of training treats and books, along with Easy Walk harnesses for the canine that may pull too hard while on daily walks. Ferdinand is a big supporter of area rescue groups and frequently hosts adoptable felines from the Chatham Animal Rescue. Most Saturdays, adoptable canines visit the shop in search of companions. Ferdinand welcomes you and your friends to Ferdinand's Dog and Cat Boutique.

11312 US 15-501 N, Suite 102, Chapel Hill NC
(919) 928-0057   www.dogandcatboutique.com

Swagger—Gifts with Attitude

Mandy Becker graduated from Georgia Tech as an engineer, but eventually she followed her bliss and opened her own gift store. This longtime dream is now Swagger–Gifts with Attitude. Mandy, her mother, Jill Kratus, and their staff of gift-giving goddesses constantly search the world for specialty brands and products that are luxurious yet affordable. At Swagger, expect an exciting shopping experience, first-class customer service and tons of exquisite items that instill smiles. You can find jewelry, stationery, home accents, accessories and other one-of-a-kind items. Swagger prides itself on being able to personalize that special gift. Brand-new items are constantly arriving at the store, so the merchandise in Swagger is an every-changing kaleidoscope of cool stuff. Swagger frequently showcases local designers and hosts special events, such as the annual holiday open house/anniversary party in November. Mandy and Jill offer a personal shopping service. One phone call is all that is needed to give that perfect gift, wrapped in Swagger's signature zebra paper. Personal service is what makes Swagger a unique store.

2425 Kildaire Farm Road, Suite 503 Cary, NC
(919) 858-5884
www.swagger-gifts.com

Mary Phillips Designs

Let's face it ladies, sometimes there are just not enough hours in the day to say everything that needs to be said. Good thing Mary Phillips is on the job. Phillips, owner and designer of Mary Phillips Designs, creates fun and fabulous products that will jostle your funny bone and perk up your day. In chic boutiques and grand stores across the nation, along with select international locations, Mary displays her arsenal of inspiring, feminine quotes on a wide range of home and gift items. You can cut down on unnecessary bedtime questions with her "Because I'm the Mom that's why!" sleep shirt, or quickly get your point across with one of her black label tanks or T-shirts with sayings like "It's all about me." Mary carries notepads, mugs, cocktail napkins, drinking glasses and skillfully framed art. You can find Mary Phillips Designs at specialty shops, including Hallmark, Nordstrom, Papyrus, Parisian and Fred Segal. Internationally, you can find these fresh and sassy designs in Canada, the Grand Cayman Islands, Saint Thomas, Saudi Arabia and South Africa. Phillips and her company are active in philanthropic ventures. They design a line of pink ribbon items with a portion of those proceeds going to the Susan G. Komen Breast Cancer Foundation. Remember that "Good girls go to Heaven, bad girls go to Paris, Rome." Regardless of what type of girl you are, express yourself with Mary Phillips Designs.

4350 Lassiter at N Hills Avenue, Suite 310, Raleigh, NC
(800) 825-4575
www.maryphillipsdesigns.com

Salutations

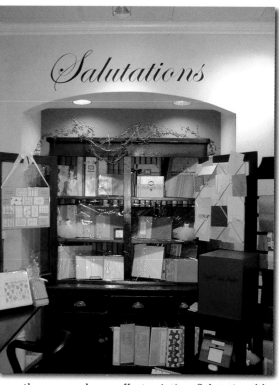

Everyone has their own style and way of doing things, which is why Salutations in Chapel Hill offers such a fabulous and diverse array of stationery and gift items. Located in the new Meadowmont Village, Salutations has an extensive inventory of stationery products, gifts and special occasion items, including hand-bound guest books, proof binders, photo albums, wedding journals and scrapbooks. Owner Holly Bretschneider and her staff are happy to assist you in choosing the perfect items to make your event a success. They carry a full and varied selection of wedding invitations, birth announcements, and party or shower invitations. Salutations can help you select personal stationery for your private or business needs, including boxed note sets and calling, business or correspondence cards. Several printing options are available, such as engraving, letterpress, thermography or offset printing. Salutations' fast in-store printing makes it even easier for you to correspond in style every time. You can even buy stamps personalized with your own photo. The Salutations boutique carries an extensive selection of Vera Bradley handbags, luggage and accessories, plus a myriad of distinctive gifts, such as monogrammed candles and unusual journals. Whether you want to announce an event or keep in touch with loved ones, Salutations can help.

106 Meadowmont Village Circle, Chapel Hill NC
(919) 918-1008 www.salutations.com

InkSpot

An unknown woman of the Antebellum period once remarked, "I shall never be proper, for I just don't have all the correct stationery." It's too bad for her she didn't have InkSpot, an inviting stationery and gift boutique in the Falls Village Shopping Center in Raleigh. This full-service, upscale store provides custom stationery in an elegant and comfortable setting. InkSpot offers beautifully designed correspondence materials and accessories that are perfect for any budget and taste. With a focus on providing customers with the ideal product for every occasion, they carry a wide range of invitations, announcements, boxed notes and thank you cards. InkSpot offers personalized social stationery, change of address announcements and calling cards. Owner Laura Neal Williams has been a regular columnist in *Heritage* magazine and uses this medium to provide excellent tips for brides, casual dinner hosts and perpetual party givers. InkSpot features a multitude of exciting lines, including Crane's, William Arthur and Carlson Craft. In the gift department, they pride themselves on unique gift options, including trendy purses, fun tableware and elegant candles and bath products. Whether you are searching for elegant personal stationery, witty invitations, or a fantastic hostess gift, head to InkSpot, where you will find something special for every occasion.

6675-115 Falls of Neuse Road, Raleigh NC (919) 844-9100 www.inkspotstationers.com

Scout & Molly's

At Scout & Molly's, you will feel like you just stepped into a closet full of your favorite designer clothing, complete with vintage furnishings. You can snag pieces by Trina Turk, Nanette Lepore, Diane Von Furstenburg, Joe's Jeans, BCBG, Three Dots and Kasil, among others. A girl with a dream opened the first Scout & Molly's location in April 2002. Lisa Disbrow and her husband, Jarrett, decided it was time to see the dream through. The store is named after their two Labrador retrievers, Scout and Molly, who can at times be seen lounging on one of the antique rugs. Scout & Molly's is the perfect place to find your style. You can find everything from a great pair of jeans to sophisticated suits and flirty cocktail dresses, not to mention the incredible selection of jewelry by local designers. Scout & Molly's has everything you need to update your wardrobe. The best part is that now you can shop at two locations. Two years ago, a love of their dogs and fashion brought Lisa and Jarrett together with Jessica and Mike Kenady. They met at the dog park, hit it off, and Lisa hired Jessica to manage her store while she had a baby. Their friendship grew, and a year later they decided to partner up to bring Scout & Molly's to Chapel Hill. Stop in at either store for a truly wonderful and friendly experience. Shop at Scout & Molly's of Raleigh and Scout & Molly's of Chapel Hill for a two-of-a-kind shopping experience.

Scout & Molly's of Raleigh: *4209-133 Lassiter Mill Road, Raleigh NC (919) 848-8732*
Scout & Molly's of Chapel Hill: *105 Meadowmont Village Circle, Chapel Hill NC (919) 969-8886*
www.scoutandmollys.com

Triangle Area Health & Beauty

UNC Health Care

North Carolina Memorial Hospital was built as part of the state's Good Health Plan adopted by the Legislature in 1947 to improve health care across the state. The Good Health Plan called for building new community clinics and hospitals, expanding the two-year medical education program at UNC into a four-year medical school, and building a large teaching hospital. Over the past 50 years, the organization has grown into the present UNC Health Care System. People from all 100 North Carolina counties come to the 708-bed UNC Hospitals for the kind of advanced treatment that, in some cases, they can get nowhere else in the state. For example, this is the only hospital in the state that performs all types of organ transplants for both adults and children. UNC surgeons perform four times as many children's open-heart procedures as anyone else in the state. The North Carolina Jaycee Burn Center is the state's only comprehensive burn facility. The N.C. Neurosciences Hospital includes psychiatry services, research labs and clinics. In 2002, UNC Hospitals opened two state-of-the-art facilities, the N.C. Women's Hospital and N.C. Children's Hospital, to serve families across the state. UNC Health Care is home to many nationally recognized programs. The UNC Lineberger Comprehensive Cancer Center is one of the few National Cancer Institute-designated centers in the country. Ground has been broken for the new $180 million N.C. Cancer Hospital, expected to open in late 2009. The Cardiology Division provides a full spectrum of services, while the Diabetes Care Center conducts studies on advanced treatments. Each of these entities is vital as UNC Health Care strives to deliver worldclass health care to North Carolinians.

101 Manning Drive, Chapel Hill NC   (919) 966-4131

Bath Junkie

Bath "stuff" designed by you is the idea behind Bath Junkie in Chapel Hill. Bath Junkie celebrates a new concept in bath and body enjoyment. Its mission is to provide high-quality bath products customized to your color and fragrance specifications. The innovative process involves four steps that are completed when you ask your friendly mixmaster to whip up the product you select. With more than 200 different fragrances to choose from, you can be as creative or as classic as you wish. What an exciting opportunity to find your own personal scent. Bath

Junkie's products are all natural, which means no mineral oils or drying alcohols are used. A few of the limitless possibilities are moisturizing detox rocks, salt scrubs, hair conditioners, hydrating mist and massage oil. You can even conjure up a special scent and color with Bath Junkie's shampoo for dogs. Accessories are plentiful and include natural loofah sponges, bath scrunchies, sisal fiber scrubbers, and microfiber robes and towels. In the evening, Bath Junkie closes the store and makes the facility available for private parties. Bath junkie is available for any type of party you can imagine. Any age group is appropriate, and you can bring as many people as can fit through the door to have a bubbling blast.

201 S Estes, University Mall, Chapel Hill, NC   (919) 960-6868   www.bathjunkie.com

Caju Apothecary & Salon

Nationally recognized Caju Apothecary & Salon features top products and stylists. Referred to by the media as "ultra-chic and modern," this destination is frequented by those in the know. The hip and airy boutique carries exclusive lines, such as Kerastase, Bumble & Bumble, Marvis Toothpaste, Lip Fusion and Dr. Hauschka. Caju Salon uses top-rated stylists from top metropolitan shops and it shows. Since opening its doors in 2003, Caju has proven its popularity. Owner Patricia Blizzard created the shop based on her idea that "you take a great location, add incredibly talented and up-to-date stylists, put it next door to an apothecary with amazing product lines and make the spot so beautiful that it's a pleasure to spend a few hours there." It's an unbeatable combination. Not only can you reliably receive gorgeous color, face-flattering cuts and head-turning blowouts, you can do it in style. Caju was named one of the nation's most beautiful salons in 2004. Booking at least two weeks in advance is recommended. Another local favorite is Caju's brow shaping program, with a who's who list regularly dropping by for an expertly performed tweak. Waxing and airbrush tanning leave you polished and glowing for parties, the beach or just running around town.

703 Meadowmont Circle, Chapel Hill NC
(919) 942-9000 www.cajusalon.com

Aria Skin & Laser Spa

Aria Skin & Laser Spa in Chapel Hill is a medical skin care clinic, a plastic surgeon's office and a luxurious day spa all under one roof. Aria offers traditional spa treatments, such as facials, chemical peels, microdermabrasion and massage, along with body treatments, mineral makeup, waxing and airbrush tanning. Additional services provided by Aria include laser hair removal for all skin colors, laser photo-rejuvenation, laser vein treatments, sclerotherapy, acne treatments, Botox®, Captique®, mesotherapy and bio-identical hormone replacement counseling. Each service is provided with the professional expertise and technology expected from a specialized doctor's office with the atmosphere of a rejuvenating spa. Owner Vernon Mulanix says, "lasting beauty begins with a healthy body" and to that end created Aria Skin and Laser Spa with the idea of focusing on creating beauty from the inside out. Many of the products used at Aria are organic or very close to organic, such as the Cosmedix® skincare line, which is medical grade and yet cruelty free with no preservatives, artificial fragrances or fillers. The spa also offers a complete line of organic creams, oils, lotions and soaps. Because of the spa's strong focus on skin care and protection, they carry the gloMinerals® makeup line, which has sun block built into it. Look and feel radiant with a visit to Aria Skin & Laser Spa.

11312 Hwy 15-501 N, Suite 106, Chapel Hill NC
(919) 968-7772 (YourSpa)
www.arialaser.com

Luxe Apothecary

In the days of old, the village apothecary was where locals gathered to have their recipes or (as we know them) prescriptions filled. Prepared concoctions of herbs and roots known to have medicinal value were packaged in vellum paper and small, clouded bottles with wax seals so customers could carry their wares home. While there, they would gossip with the proprietor and neighbors about their ailments and learn new remedies; this was also a good time to hear about goings on in the community. Today in Raleigh that tradition carries on, but with a modern spin. The Lassiter at North Hills shopping complex is the home of Luxe Apothecary, which offers a full spectrum of health and beauty products and accessories designed for every member of the family. Owner Fiquet Bailey and her small, well educated staff believe in taking their time and giving each customer the personalized attention they need. They place considerable emphasis on finding the perfect product to fit the diverse needs of their customers. Luxe, from the Latin luxus, means something luxurious, and that is what shoppers will find when they step across the threshold. Elegant displays hold choice product lines designed to relax and pamper you. The vellum and clouded glass are gone; in their place you will find modern tubes, contemporary pots and classically designed glass vessels. If you're not certain which products are best for you and would like extra consultation time, Fiquet and her staff are available after hours by appointment.

4421 Six Forks Road, Raleigh NC   (866) FOR-LUXE   www.luxeapothecary.com

Triangle Area
Home Décor, Flowers, Gardens & Markets

Consigning Design

Is your garage, spare room or attic filled with furniture and antiques that no one uses anymore? It's time for you to load them up and head to Consigning Design located at Waverly Place in Cary. Sandy West, owner of this ingenious shop, accepts once loved home décor items and furnishings and displays them in vignettes. With other complementary pieces, the displays present inviting arrangements that will attract buyers and allow them to glean an idea of how a piece will look in their home. Consignees are paid monthly for items sold the previous month and items are displayed for 90 days, allowing for both a likely sale of any given item and an oft-changing inventory that has loyal customers coming back regularly. The staff members at Consigning Design are friendly and helpful. This fantastic shop offers something for everyone and is just right for recycling your good-condition, but unwanted, furnishings and décor pieces. With Consigning Design, you never have to worry about the hassles, expenses and safety issues involved with having a garage sale or running an ad, nor will you lose money by giving or throwing them away. Sandy West, through Consigning Design, provides a great opportunity to do a bit of spring cleaning and earn some extra cash. With the wonderful selection of quality items available, you might find yourself re-investing your profits in new items for your home at Consigning Design.

Waverly Place, 201-D Colonades Way, Cary NC
(919) 233-7444
www.consigningdesign.com

Foster's Market

A lot has changed since Sara Foster opened her Foster's Market in 1990. Initially a specialty grocery store featuring locally roasted coffee and select wines, it also offered seasonal prepared food that could be taken home or enjoyed while dining amidst a funky collection of flea-market couture furniture. This original, non-traditional concept has worked for the past 16 years, during which time her clientele and quality product offerings have grown. Now, Foster's Market has expanded into multiple stores with two cookbooks, a private label line, catering and gifts, as well as online services and plenty of press. You know Sara's doing something right when she's been featured in media outlets as diverse as *From Martha's Kitchen* and *Southern Living*, to NBC's *Today Show* and QVC. You can still come in for delicious dinners from the daily changing menu of gourmet creations such as Cajun turkey meatloaf or grilled flank steak with maple chipotle sauce. After your satisfying meal, peruse the aisles for more great ideas to add to your ingredient lists. The private line has expanded to include a seven pepper jelly, BBQ sauce, applesauce, pancake mix, organic grits and house blend coffee. Sara even takes time out of her busy schedule to make appearances where she'll discuss her popular recipes and share ideas on how to prepare the perfect meal. Give your meal plan a nice refresher course with a trip to either Foster's Market locations. Your family and stomach will thank you.

2694 Durham-Chapel Hill Boulevard, Durham NC (919) 489-3944
750 Martin Luther King Road, Chapel Hill NC (919) 967-FOOD (3663) www.fostersmarket.com

Ivy Cottage Collections

What better place can there be to shop for home furnishings, décor and design ideas than in a place that feels like just like home? Welcome to Ivy Cottage Collections, a family-owned business that has been serving North Carolina's Triangle area for the last 10 years with two locations, one in Raleigh and one in Morrisville. This multifaceted shop provides patrons with a one-stop place for home furnishings, women's clothing and accessories, gifts and interior design services. In the home furniture section, look for mirrors, artwork, lamps, window treatments and rugs to add finishing touches to your home. Those in the market for furniture will be delighted with the upholstered and reproduction antique pine pieces. For help designing the kind of home that fits your lifestyle, set up a consultation for interior design services. The lovely, chic clothes and accoutrements that fill this shop will charm ladies of all ages. Fantastic purses, scarves, hats and other accessories lay in wait to entice you. Ivy Cottage Collections' gift selection offers something for everyone, including a choice array of candles, bath and body products, stationary, jewelry and kitchen accessories. Come home to Ivy Cottage Collections for the fine home furnishings, décor and personal accessories you need.

4151 Main Street, Suite 115, Raleigh NC
(919) 789-0404
2017 NW Cary Parkway, Morrisville NC
(919) 462-3434
www.ivycottagecollections.com

Fowler's Food and Wine

In 1925, John Fowler purchased a little one-room, full-service market that has since become a legacy of fine food and old-fashioned service. This delightful shop defies categorization as it provides a full spectrum of superior, imported goods and is staffed with personnel who could be considered experts in superior customer service. Fowler's offers incredible, completely personalized gift baskets which can include everything from Fowler's marvelous chocolates, imported from across the globe, to their North Carolina basket filled with native products from both local and state-wide companies. They have fabulous coffees, specialty candies from Europe, high-end grocery items and numerous imported wines. Their inventory makes Fowler's Food and Wine a truly original neighborhood market. In the deli, you can treat yourself to a delicious entrée during breakfast, lunch or dinner. Be sure not to miss out on their Sunday brunch, which has been named the best in Durham. Everything in the deli is prepared on-site using fresh, organic ingredients and prime, dry-aged meats. Fowler's can also cater your next dinner party or special event. Choose your selections from their extensive catering menu, then sit back and relax while Fowler's attends to your business breakfast, ladies' luncheon or special event dinner. When you're looking for food, drink or cookery, visit Fowler's Food and Wine.

112 S Dulce Street, Durham NC
(919) 683-2555   www.fowlersfoodandwine.com

Three Flamingos

Are you redecorating your home or office? Do you want to find that special color or print for your upholstery or bedding? Take a trip to Three Flamingos in Cary's MacGregor Village for a rich palette of fabrics to redecorate your home. With years of experience and friendly service, this family owned business offers complimentary in-store consultations, custom window treatments and interior decorating services. Merchandise available at Three Flamingos includes sumptuous decorator fabrics at great prices, custom furniture and cute home accessories. In addition to furnishings, you can also choose from a wide array of shutters and blinds. Discount prices are part of Three Flamingo's specialty, making it all the more tempting to go ahead with that redecorating project that's been put off for so long. When it's time to look at giving your home or office a facelift, you'll want to peruse Three Flamingo's inventory. New fabrics for covering that sofa or updated window treatments for the dining room can bring a fresh light and feel into your space. Start your redecorating project with a visit to Three Flamingos.

107 Edinburgh S, # 113, Cary NC
(919) 468-7002
www.threeflamingos.com

Quintessentials

The Lassiter at North Hills is commonly known as Raleigh's Madison Avenue. This chic and elegant shopping plaza is filled with stylish shops and lovely cafés. In Suite 104, you will find Quintessentials. This fabulous boutique has everything you need to make registering for your bridal gifts effortless and enjoyable. Owner Ann Divine Weaver and her staff are always on hand to provide exemplary customer service. The store itself is immaculate and filled with stunning displays of fine china, crystal and silver. The shop carries an extensive selection of patterns and designs from popular companies. In fine china, look for names like Anna Weatherley, Haviland and Royal Crown Derby. In everyday china, select from companies like Vietri, Gien and Mariposa. While Quintessentials is certainly the place to go for your bridal registry in the Raleigh area, it can also assist you with table settings for casual dinners, executive events and other special occasions. When every place setting has to be picture perfect, head to Quintessentials at The Lassiter and give your table the attention it deserves.

4421 Six Forks Road, Suite 104, Raleigh NC
(919) 785-0787

Jean's Berry Patch

Jean's Berry Patch is about sweet, sweet, high-quality strawberries. The strawberry patch season is from late April until the beginning of June. The Berry Patch doubles as a pumpkin patch in the fall, with pumpkin season from mid-September until Halloween. Jean and Ronald Copeland own the family business; the strawberry patch is named for Jean; Ragan and Holly's Pumpkin Patch is named for the couple's two grandchildren. In order to produce the sweetest strawberries ever, the Copelands grow the Chandler strawberry. It is meant to be eaten shortly after picking. Children are welcome, but please leave your pets at home. Even though the Patch has regular hours, call before you set out to go picking. Check the website for delicious recipes, that is if there are any left to cook after you finish nibbling on the way home. A few ideas are strawberry pizza, frozen strawberry salad, and the all-time favorite, strawberry shortcake. During the strawberry season, the Patch sells jams, jellies and freshly baked specialties. How about some strawberry bread made by Jean's mother or frozen strawberry pie? Goodness grows at Jean's Berry Patch.

3003 NC Highway 751, Apex NC
(919) 362-5800   www.jeansberrypatch.com

Hunt and Gather

Hunt and Gather in Raleigh is a fantastic treasure trove of home furnishings and décor items. Located just down the way from Five Point off Whitaker Mill Road, this popular home accent resource has everything you need to add interest, depth and pizzazz to every room of your house. The shop has several large and prominent pieces that draw Raleigh shoppers through the door, but once inside it's usually the smaller, original pieces that claim your attention. Owners James Britt and Cathy A. Matarese have gone out of their way to acquire an eclectic collection of mix-and-match styles that span a full spectrum of design with pieces from every era that are designed to cater to any mood. Hunt and Gather carries a delightful selection of sofas, chairs and ottomans alongside hand-carved cabinets that are optimal for everything from displaying your favorite collection to holding the family's entertainment center. The shop further carries wonderful art pieces, including original paintings, sculpture and Oriental rugs. Additionally, Hunt and Gather offers a fine array of accessories, such as wall-sconces, wrought-iron chandeliers and varied *objets d'art* that are designed to draw the eye and adds extra appeal to any room. For all of your home decorating projects, in-home consultations are available through Hunt and Gather. The friendly staff delights in answering questions and offering suggestions about any of the products in the shop. Find inexpensive and creative solutions to your decorating dilemmas at Hunt and Gather.

1910 Bernard Street, Raleigh NC
(919) 834-9989   www.huntandgathernc.com

The Eclectic Garden

The Eclectic Garden is truly a family affair. It is owned and operated by Raleigh natives Joyce Hawley and her two daughters Liz Hawley Ennis and Chrissy Hawley Pressley. These talented and resourceful women have combined their abilities to create Raleigh's most distinctive and unusual furniture and home accessories shop. Specializing in extraordinary painted and recycled furniture, The Eclectic Garden features items made by local artists and craftspeople, as well as a wide selection of eclectic, one-of-a-kind gifts and home accents. The Eclectic Garden offers design consultation services, custom furniture painting and an interesting selection of garden items. Joyce and her daughters began their business in 1988 at the North Carolina State Flea Market for one year, then relocated to a leased storefront on Hillsborough Street for another four years. They are now located in their own renovated property on Wake Forest Road. Here they are better able to display their unique collections of home art, painted and used furniture, and interesting home accessories. As a long time local vocalist, business woman, real estate renovator and painter, Joyce takes pride in providing a space to showcase the handmade items of fellow artists and furniture makers.

The Eclectic Garden is a place where the imagination is always in full bloom. You are invited to peruse this creative haven for yourself.

1932 Wake Forest Road Raleigh NC
(919) 821-0363
www.theeclecticgarden.com

The Sarah P. Duke Gardens

The Sarah P. Duke Gardens, the crown jewel of prestigious Duke University, welcomes more than 300,000 guests annually. These majestic gardens provide a place where anyone can come to reflect, learn, renew, and discover. Sarah P. Duke financed the original gardens, created through the dedication of Dr. Frederic M. Hanes, an early member of the Duke Medical School. Sadly, the original gardens were destroyed by torrential summer rains by the time Mrs. Duke passed away in 1936. Fortunately, Dr. Hanes was able to work with her daughter, Mary Duke Biddle, in constructing new gardens in her mother's honor on higher ground. American landscape pioneer Ellen Shipman was chosen to create the new gardens, and Duke Gardens are now considered to be one of her greatest works. Composed of four major areas offering five miles of allées, pathways and scenic walks, Duke Gardens presents diverse learning opportunities for those who wish to gain a greater appreciation of the natural world. The Gardens are free and open to the public year round, a living museum dedicated to horticulture and garden design. Duke Gardens hosts numerous events throughout the year, including special programs for children. Open yourself up to a world of beauty, education and renewal by spending time at The Sarah P. Duke Gardens.

426 Anderson Street, Duke University, Durham NC
(919) 684-3698
www.sarahpdukegardens.com

PORTO

Emily Barrett and Michael Perry developed a concept they call "the passage to civilized living." The premise started with the conviction that we are all part of a global community, and it is up to us to reach out to each other. The other side of the notion was to offer the means to create a personal living, working and playing space that completely complements and enhances an individual's lifestyle. Barrett and Perry fulfill the promise in PORTO, providing a vibrant space similar to a studio filled with extraordinary furnishings and fabrics, calm sounds and gentle fragrances. PORTO exudes incredible atmosphere, beauty and principle. The companies represented here are chosen for their integrity and skill, evidenced by commitment to their employees and products of high quality. If you are looking for furniture, lighting, home accessories or fine art, this is the place to go. PORTO's support of the art community is tangible in the shop. Clark Hipolito, the creative partner, embellishes the surroundings with spectacular murals. On the second Friday of every month, PORTO strives to unveil new and undiscovered artists, bringing the artist and collector together with its novel collection of fine art. For assistance in home design, you can depend on PORTO for ideas and products that will endure for a lifetime. PORTO is a shelter in the storm that can help to make your surroundings a reflection of yourself by introducing a new, reliable luxury into your life.

4151 Main at North Hills, Suite 120, Raleigh NC
(919) 341-2763
www.portohome.com

James Kennedy Antiques

James Kennedy Antiques has both an online store and a physical location in historic Brightleaf Square. Online shoppers will enjoy the professional, easy to navigate website. The eclectic mix of artwork is separated into categories; if the category has a large number of items, the items are organized into subcategories, as well. The shop features a wide range of items, including contemporary glass and pottery, fossils and minerals, and a map and chart gallery. The African arts inventory represents many tribes in an admirable collection of authentic works. Masks from the renowned Dogon (and other tribal masks when available) are prominently displayed. Bronzes and wood sculptures, textiles and beadwork are also represented. Oriental furniture and accessories comprise another fascinating category. Items from this section are diverse and recently included a detailed jade Han Dynasty horse head, a crude provincial Chinese wooden lunch box and an authentic Tibetan ceremonial drum with original red paint. A Chinese porcelain collection holds some surprising forms. The apothecary selections offer some medical supplies from the 1800s and early 1900s. The antique, estate and contemporary jewelry in this shop is not likely to be found anywhere else. From the scientific and nautical section, you might find a Newtonian telescope to scan the night sky or a fully renovated 15-foot Skowhegan trolling boat. These treasures and more await you at James Kennedy Antiques.

905 W Main Street, Durham NC
(919) 682-1040
www.JamesKennedyAntiques.com

A Southern Season

Where seeds are planted, great things will grow. When Michael Barefoot opened his tiny, 800-square-foot coffee roaster and gourmet shop in the college town of Chapel Hill, he wasn't thinking about corporate structure or mission statements. He was thinking that in such a small community he wouldn't have to advertise. His plan worked, and 30 years later that humble little shop has grown into a cornucopia of gourmet delights. In 2004, the National Association of the Specialty Food Trade named A Southern Season one of America's most outstanding retailers. Craig Claiborne (1921-2000) of *The New York Times* declared it, "Wall to wall and floor to ceiling...a visual and gustatory delight." Such high praise is not undeserved. The flagship store, located at the University Mall in Chapel Hill, is a veritable Disneyland for the true gourmand. Its 59,000-square-foot specialty market is divided into several independently managed departments. As patrons enter A Southern Season, they are still greeted by the aroma of freshly roasted and brewed coffee. After selecting a caffeinated sample, shoppers can begin their adventures. Where to start? Perhaps you can lose yourself in one of the many separate marketplaces or take lessons at CLASS, A Southern Season's state-of-the-art cooking school. If you would rather eat than shop, stop by Weathervane Restaurant adjacent to the retail store. Weathervane offers an expansive menu full of seasonal American cuisine featuring "secret" ingredients from the store. Whatever the season, A Southern Season is the place to feed your food fantasies.

University Mall, Chapel Hill NC   (919) 929-7133 or (800) 253-3663   www.southernseason.com

Dilly Dally

The creation of a magical baby nursery, teenage haven or alluring master bedroom is easy with help from Dilly Dally in Raleigh. Dilly Dally carries the kind of baby and family items that will take a room beyond the ordinary into luxury. Create a custom suite of your own simply by drawing from the selection of fine furnishings and linens available in the first-class showroom. Handmade and wrought iron cribs provide heirloom quality baby furniture that is as visually pleasing as it is functional. Beds from crib to king size can be found here, along with the coordinating linens to cover them. Uncommon accessories such as hand-painted lamps add a custom touch to complete the look. All of the amenities that make a room comfortable can be found at Dilly Dally with signature flair, including prints, step stools and area rugs. Sterling silver items add a touch of elegance, as well as making striking gifts. Dilly Dally carries a fantastic selection of far-from-common baby shower gifts. Oprah is a fan of the totes, which can be used as diaper bags or eye-catching handbags. The expert staff at Dilly Dally will be happy to assist you find what you are looking for, and help you in designing a spellbinding look of your own. In many cases, special orders can be accommodated for items not seen in the showroom.

6675 Falls of Neuse Road, Suite 127, Raleigh NC
(919) 235-2625, (888) DILLYHELP (345-5943)
www.babydilly.com

Triangle Area Restaurants

Jibarra

Much like snowflakes, no two Mexican restaurants are alike. Jibarra Modern Mexican is a true original, unlike anything you've ever experienced. This contemporary eatery combines a metro atmosphere, sophisticated ambience, and sensational Mexican dishes that are bold, innovative and delightfully complex. Jibarra's menu features dishes that you're not likely to find at other Triangle restaurants, such as lobster crepes or black squid pasta with molé sauce. Jibarra Modern Mexican is also home to The Tequila Lounge, where you can enjoy your favorite top-shelf liquor or sip on any one of the lounge's huge selection of premium tequilas. Savor the tequilas straight, or have one mixed to order with one of several fresh-squeezed juices. Jibarra Modern Mexican is known not only for their delicious entrees, but also for their fabulous service and attention to every detail. Perfect place settings enhance the décor and fresh sugar cane stalks or orchids put the finishing touches on your drinks. Between the expert and friendly service, chic surroundings, and truly sensational cuisine, Jibarra Modern Mexican is a dining treasure not to be missed.

7420 Six Forks Road, Raleigh NC
(919) 844-6330
www.jibarra.net

Prime Only Steak, Seafood, Wine Cellar & Bar

Casual elegance and substantial style come together at Prime Only Steak, Seafood, Wine Cellar & Bar. The finest Midwestern aged Angus beef is hand-cut and perfectly prepared. Seafood, chicken and pork are available to round out the meatier side of the menu. If pasta is your passion, Prime Only offers a Pasta of the Day. A library-style wine display complements the agreeable leather seating. Soft lighting and a soothing fountain provide the ambience of an exotic retreat. Full meals are served in the restaurant, while in the cigar-friendly wine cellar and bar, a piquant selection of lighter fare is available. Prime Only Restaurant, located in the popular Leesville Town Center, is available for corporate functions and special events. It is an ideal site for wedding receptions and rehearsal dinners. Whatever the occasion, Prime Only Restaurant is ready to exceed your expectations. Enter one of North Carolina's finest steakhouses and enjoy the attentive staff waiting to serve you.

13200 Strickland Road # 10, Raleigh NC
(919) 844-1216   www.primeonly.com

Il Palio Ristorante

Located within the elegant Siena Hotel, Il Palio Ristorante is the only AAA Four Diamond Italian restaurant in North Carolina. Known for its vibrant yet intimate atmosphere and innovative Italian cuisine, Il Palio has received national recognition from publications including *Southern Living* and *Cottage Living* magazines. The restaurant's décor combines the rich colors and fabrics of a sumptuous Italian villa with contemporary European touches. Known for his innovative style within the culinary world, executive chef Jim Anile brings a unique creativity to Il Palio—combining a deep knowledge of Italian cuisine with a wide range of international culinary techniques. The complete dining experience not only makes Il Palio a favorite with locals, but also places it squarely on the map as a destination restaurant. Chef Anile's modern Italian cuisine makes use of the freshest ingredients. He takes advantage of the abundance of high quality produce from local, independent farmers while also importing fine Italian food specialties, such as aged cheeses and proscuitto. Fresh pasta, bread and exquisite desserts are made in-house daily, and meats and fish are smoked in Il Palio's own smokehouse. In addition to innovative à la carte menus, special evening culinary delights include a chef's tasting menu—five courses that showcase the day's special ingredients, chosen by chef Anile with your personal tastes in mind. Other options include regional specialties, which highlight the diverse cuisine of Italy. The restaurant is named after *Il Palio delle contrade*, a horse race held twice a year in the city of Siena, Italy. Every participating horse and rider represents one of the 17 contrade, or city districts, each distinguished by its individual coat of arms. The race is accompanied by magnificent pageants, feasts and celebrations. There is live music nightly, wine tastings and other special events.

1505 E Franklin Street, Chapel Hill NC
(919) 918-2545   www.ilpalio.com

Spartacus Restaurant

Vassilios Makras opened his first cafeteria in North Carolina after his return from World War II. Later, the family moved to New York for a time, where his daughter Ralitsa and her husband Kyriakos Kalfas opened the first Spartacus Restaurant. Their ties to North Carolina brought them back in 1993, when they opened the Spartacus in Durham. Their return is cause for celebration. Offering exemplary service and the finest fresh Greek meals ever prepared, Spartacus has enjoyed local and national recognition. The food at Spartacus is offered not just for sustenance, but for the enrichment of the soul. The varied menu includes a fantastic *mousaka*, along with the best lamb and calamari in the Triangle. Look for a choice selection of vegetarian specialties and a large and varied selection of tender meat dishes and succulent fish recipes. For an exciting opener, try one of three varieties of the flaming *saganaki* appetizer. Pasta takes on a notable interpretation with offerings like lobster ravioli paired with shrimp in Chianti cream sauce. A gyro platter comes with mixed lamb and beef with vegetables, rice and *tzadziki* (a traditional yogurt and cucumber dip). The catering service is a Triangle favorite, featuring themed events and delivery. The level of comfort in Spartacus Restaurant makes it conducive to a special date for two, or a gathering of family or friends, and the lovingly prepared diversity of food will make you want to return on a regular basis to a restaurant where customers are family.

4139 Chapel Hill Boulevard, Durham NC   (919) 489-2848   www.spartacusrestaurant.com

Carolina Brewery

The Carolina Brewery has made a name for itself as Chapel Hill's first and finest brewery. It has long been recognized as a great place to meet up with friends for a beer, enjoy a great meal or host a first-class event. The Brewery's overwhelming success speaks to the initial research of Robert Poitras and Chris Rice, who developed the idea of the brewery while earning their undergraduate degrees in business. After spending a summer traveling in Europe and parts of the United States observing over 70 breweries, Poitras says, "We took the best parts of each brewery and put them together to build our own." Rice has since moved on, but Poitras continues to do his research and constantly applies it to the betterment of the Carolina Brewery. Breaking into regional and national markets has strengthened the Carolina Brewery name along with an abundance of awards and accolades throughout the years. To complement the traditional-style ales and lagers brewed on the premises, the Brewery serves contemporary American cuisine for lunch, dinner, late night snacks and weekend brunch. They offer full wine and liquor service, growlers and kegs to go, off-site catering and a private dining room for special events. An extra customer service is a free shuttle service to University of North Carolina football and basketball games. Brewmaster Jon Connolly and Poitras are constantly striving to create a unique experience for their customers. Stop by Carolina Brewery and see why they were voted best brewery in the Southeast.

460 W Franklin Street, Chapel Hill NC
(919) 942-1800
www.carolinabrewery.com

Fratello's

The hallmark of restaurants owned by brothers Salvator and Vincenzo Doria from Italy is that everything is made from scratch so that the food is authentic Italian. Fratello's is no exception, serving take-out deli and restaurant fare at its finest. The hand-trimmed veal, scrumptious seafood dishes and tasty desserts carefully crafted on the premises offer something for every palate. The family trademark, frutti di mare alfredo, and the chicken cacciatore were featured in *The News & Observer's* Specialty of the House. The ravioli bolognese is enjoyed by an eminently satisfied fan base. In addition, there are hot and cold submarine sandwiches, brick oven pizzas, and delectable house made sauces. Fratello's has an impressive and extensive wine list. The restaurant has an exclusive yet warm ambience with an upper level private balcony floor. The bar provides a comfortable combination of cozy yet elegant. The wine wall is conveniently located to give customers time to look over the various choices before making a final selection. Fratello's is open for lunch and dinner, does not close between meals, and offers corporate catering as well as service for private parties. A visit to Fratello's Italian Restaurant will introduce you to a magnificent example of the flavor of Italy.

107 Edinburgh Drive, Cary NC   (919) 467-2007

Wasabi

Those visiting Cary's sophisticated and fun MacGregor village have discovered a chic place to dine and socialize. They go to Wasabi, where a diverse menu filled with Thai dishes and sushi rolls was warranted delicious enough to earn a visit from the esteemed Iron Chef Mashaharu Morimoto. The stylish sushi joint gives late night diners, from the casual novice to the sushi fanatic, a cozy place to indulge their appetites. Inside, the colors are subtle and soothing with rich patterns and caramel colored wood to draw you in and give the space a gorgeous glow. The dining area gets an intimate feel from its division into separate rooms. The sushi selection is vast enough to please everyone. Beginners can sample such basics as the California (or vegetable) roll, while hardcore fans try new concoctions and combinations prepared especially for them by Wasabi's sushi chefs. Wasabi recommends beginners sample a bit of everything, starting with the luscious sweet *tom jha*, a Thai coconut soup with a hint of seafood. For a surprisingly light and flavorful taste, follow with crispy spring rolls packed with cabbage, celery and noodles. More adventurous patrons may wish to brave the fiery wasabi roll, which comes complete with its own powerful sauce, or the Mary roll, which arrives with a spicy mayo sauce ladled on top. Just be sure to take a moment in between bites to nibble on the ginger before the fire brigade receives a call. For choices, late hours and conviviality, visit Wasabi.

107 Edinburgh S, Suite 135, Cary NC
(919) 460-7980
www.wasabicary.com

Cinelli's

Delivery services have come a long way since transport by donkey, but Cinelli's takes the premise of your convenience one step further with an innovative system that delivers a respite from your voracious appetite to your front door. The authenticity of the recipes comes directly from an Italian ancestry. During WWII, the Cinelli's would deliver their delicious products by foot or donkey to GIs stationed throughout the region. When the current generation came to America it was time to try something a bit different. Taking a cue from good old American ingenuity, and in the interest of bringing the family history to a new community, it was decided that the restaurant would be brought to the customer by serving up freshly cooked meals anywhere within a 60-mile radius. Donkeys have long since been replaced by state of the art cars and trucks, each vehicle containing a 200-degree oven, as well as cold boxes, but resourcefulness and quality service have remained ageless. Cinelli's is steadfast in its quest to ignite innovation and create a unique dining experience.

1305 Kildaire Farm Road, Cary NC
(919) 461-3799
www.cinellis.com

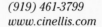

Waraji Japanese Restaurant

It was a fortunate day for Raleigh when chefs Masa and Kazu decided to build upon their success and expand their restaurant's offerings from sushi to a full menu of Japanese cuisine. After being named the best in the Triangle for their sushi for many years, and with more than 30 years of culinary experience between them, Masu and Kazu bring you an extensive menu at Waraji Japanese Restaurant. Look at the menu pages on their website and you will see that you have an extensive number of choices at Waraji. There are staples like teriyaki and tempura, as well as a wide range of other selections including sukiyaki. The chefs describe sukiyaki as, "a delicious dish of beef, vegetables and noodles, simmered together in a soy-based sauce. One of Japan's national culinary treasures." Come in and see what culinary pleasures Masa and Kazu create, and enjoy your meal in a beautiful Japanese garden atmosphere.

5910-147 Duraleigh Road, Raleigh NC   (919) 783-1883   www.warajirestaurant.com

Ciao Café & Wine Bar

Photo by Victor Fakkas

National publications have called the town of Cary a remarkable case study in suburban emergence. Cary, in the heart of the Triangle, is a wonder of transportation and technology in a thriving community that has managed to retain a hometown feeling. In the local Ciao Café & Wine Bar, head chef and owner Piero Potenza has a reputation for amazing personal service. Ciao is known for excellent food and is treasured by wine lovers in the Triangle. The café provides indoor and outdoor dining areas with an attractive patio and a romantic décor reminiscent of the old country. The menu is full of delights, offering up fine wine, coffee and teas, as well as salads and pungent, creamy real cheeses made the traditional way. They serve delicious desserts, as well as many types of outstanding Italian dishes. This is not a rushed place and the menu is designed for patrons to stay awhile. The Ciao Café & Wine Bar welcomes you to its retreat from a hectic day of shopping where you can choose to sit under the shade of a vibrant patio umbrella or in the warm and rustic indoor area. Some of their merchandise is available through their sister company Ciao Mercato.

201 W Chatham Street, Cary NC
(919) 469-3021
www.ciaocafeandwinebar.com

Second Empire Restaurant

Located in the elegantly restored Dodd-Hinsdale House, Second Empire Restaurant combines history, atmosphere and gourmet cuisine into an unforgettable dining experience. Owner-Manager Kim Reynolds and her family bestowed the name Second Empire on the restaurant in honor of the house's architectural style, built circa 1879. The house, which was commissioned by the mayor of Raleigh, is a superb example of the Second Empire style that originated in France under the reign of Emperor Napoleon III. After Ted and Peggy Reynolds and their children Kim and David acquired the property in 1995, they spent two years restoring it. Though the interior has been extensively modernized, many original features have been preserved, including the doors, windows, heart pine flooring and masonry walls. The rooms have been opened out to create a space capable of seating 188 guests in multiple configurations. Executive chef Daniel Schurr has created a menu that offers the finest in contemporary American cuisine. Daniel also oversees the wine list, which has won the *Wine Spectator*'s Award of Excellence seven times. For lighter dining, visit the Tavern, featuring superb appetizers and entrées in a casual environment. The pastry chef will be highly disappointed if you don't try one of the extraordinary creations, such as the Second Empire key lime pie. For elegant dining and all the trimmings, visit Second Empire.

330 Hillsborough Street, Raleigh NC
(919) 829-3663
www.second-empire.com

Sushi Blues Café

The Sushi Blues Café has been getting rave reviews for its great combination of Japanese food and American blues. *Citysearch* describes it as "sushi standards and hot improvs served in a hip hangout." Savor music greats like Billie Holiday and Ella Fitzgerald and enjoy live music while sampling the many delicacies, including numerous teriyaki choices, the shrimp and vegetable tempura and the BB King crab roll. You'll find a relaxing atmosphere throughout. Look for television sporting events, as well as live entertainment in the lounge. The Sushi Blues Café features an extensive selection of martinis, as well as imported and domestic beers. Opened in 1999, the café has quickly become one of Raleigh's favorite places. With more than 300 menu items, there is sure to be something for everyone. Come see for yourself why the Sushi Blues Café won the Best of *Citysearch* award two years in a row.

301 Glenwood Avenue #110, Raleigh NC   (919) 664-8061   www.sushibluescafe.com

Zest Café & Home Art

Here's an unusual combination—a café that's a feast for your eyes, your palate and your artistic sensibilities. Zest Café & Home Art is a breezy, light and casual restaurant with a reputation for the freshest and finest foods made daily using locally grown produce and products. The café has an ever-changing menu with traditional and contemporary American fare, wonderful vegetarian entrees, homemade soups, and signature dishes, such as the quesadilla with roasted chicken sweet potatoes and Monterey jack cheese in a crisp, whole wheat tortilla. Or sample something called a pizzesta, an inspired creation that features a crunchy crust topped with ingredients such as grilled shrimp, Spanish artichoke hearts and garlic goat cheese spread. Also delightful is the selection of fun, functional and whimsical gifts and home entertainment products. The marriage of crafts and cuisine has obviously proven to be a successful one for Marvin and Carla Swirsky who just celebrated the restaurant's 10th anniversary. You can dine inside, out on the patio or have them cater an party, meeting or gathering. You can find the perfect gift, sit down for a perfect meal, and while you eat, they'll gift wrap it for you at no charge. Their motto is: "till we eat again…" At Zest Café & Home Art, you will.

8831 Six Forks Road, Raleigh NC   (919) 848-4792

Cindy's House Café & Catering

Cindy and Andy Anderson, owners of Cindy's House Café & Catering, have found a creative way to share art with their community. Cindy, chef and co-owner, graduated from the Culinary Institute of America in Hyde Park, New York. She has always felt that cooking is her way of contributing art to the world. Her grandmother was a pioneer of modern dance, and her mother's artwork is featured in the café. However, Cindy doesn't just keep it all in the family. The sparkling orange and yellow walls showcase an ever-changing collection of consignment art, which gives the budding artists of the area a place to show their work and contribute to the community. She thrives in the eclectic and creative space that she and Andy have created. Cindy's House supports the fine arts league of Cary and hosts wine tastings, special dinners, poetry readings and live musical groups. Cindy's attention to quality and detail are evident in the meals she presents. One special favorite is her chicken Françoise with jumbo lump crab. Choice hors d'oeuvres include steamed mussels with basil and Oysters Rockefeller. Cindy's entrées are certainly works of art, but you'll have to taste them for yourself to believe it. Blackened scallop dumplings, garlic peppercorn roast filet mignon, and mustard and rosemary encrusted rack of lamb are just a few of her amazing dishes. Between the art on the walls and the artistic dishes Cindy serves up, there is something that will please everyone's palate at Cindy's House Café.

140 E Chatham Street, Cary NC   (919) 380-1193

Roma's Italian

Across from the train station, in the heart of Cary, sits a little deli and restaurant called Roma's Italian. It is family owned and operated with a friendly staff, fast service and great food. Roma's is unpretentious and serves simple, tried and true, fresh and exquisitely perfected traditional foods. Since 1996, Roma's Italian has served its authentic Italian homemade pizzas, macaroni salad, Boar's Head meats, fresh chicken salads, excellent green salads, sandwiches and fresh baked bread. Owner Lisa Hrehor has found a great formula for success, just make delicious food and provide excellent service with a smile. The result is a community gathering spot where food can be enjoyed without any distracting impediments. Regulars enjoy their tantalizing garlic mashed potatoes and the convenience of a full deli and pasta selection. Customers with a sweet tooth can choose from a variety of desserts, including New York black and white cookies. Roma's offers catering for special events and business occasions. Roma's Italian is locally popular, roomy and comfortable. So come in, relax and enjoy a great meal.

203 N Harrison Avenue, Cary NC
(919) 468-1111

Vespa Ristorante

Upon entering the Vespa Ristorante, the sight of the silver Vespa scooter parked within is the first sign that this will be more than just a restaurant. Chef and owner Marlo Gitto creates signature Tuscan cuisine while his European staff provides exemplary service. The interior of Vespa reflects the personal design and distinctive taste of Marlo. Warm wood floors and a striking marble bar complement the creamy walls, which are filled with colorful framed Italian posters and art. Potted plants and sprays of flowers adorn corners and tables alongside the sculptured busts and baskets of treasures. Since 1998, Vespa has created homemade mozzarella, pastas and sauces fresh daily. Appetizers such as the *scottata*, which is prosciutto and roasted peppers wrapped with fresh mozzarella, open the way for incomparable entrees such as the *spezzato paesana*: chicken, artichoke hearts and wild mushrooms flavored with garlic and rosemary and flamed with cognac. *Dolci* anyone? Continue your meal with an intriguing dessert, or one of a variety of specialty dessert liqueurs. With a wine list that enhances and complements the menu, Vespa hosts monthly wine dinners. The dinners are held to pair their outstanding wine selections with the perfect foods. Live jazz can be enjoyed when dining outdoors. A visit to Vespa in either the Cary or Chapel Hill location on Franklin will bring stars to your eyes. *Buon Appetito.*

200 S Academy Street, Cary NC   (919) 319-5656
www.vespasta.com

Cafe Zen Sushi & Asian Bistro

Café Zen Sushi & Asian Bistro serves large portions of fresh foods to the lucky diners who have discovered this eclectic bit of paradise. The café is located in the historic American Tobacco District, within minutes of Duke University and Research Triangle Park. Bike trails, restaurants, retail stores and the Durham Bulls baseball team keep this downtown neighborhood buzzing with activity. The area is punctuated with sparkling waterfalls, greenery and blooming clematis. Food offerings in the café range from traditional favorites, such as soft shell crab, to specialty foods, such as hamachi cama. Fiery foods are denoted with an asterisk on the menu, like the hibachi tofu or the seafood delight in Thai chili sauce. A full bar offers exotic drinks, and the sushi is top-notch. In addition to the food, the café is an attraction for people watchers everywhere. The café is mostly glass, enabling intriguing reflections and views from all angles. For the night crowd, Café Zen observes late weekend hours. Rich colors and a comfortable, artistic late night ambience bring patrons back regularly to Café Zen Sushi & Asian Bistro.

410 Blackwell Street, Suite 150, Durham NC
(919) 680-8888

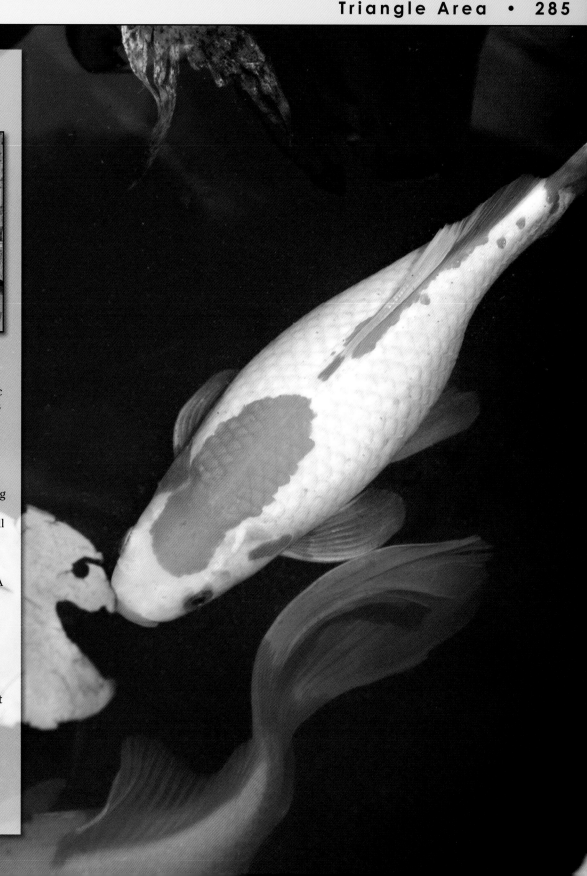

Bella Napoli Italian Restaurant

There is something innately satisfying about authentic Italian cuisine. The savory flavors blend together harmoniously. Creamy cheeses, rich, ripe tomatoes and homemade pastas all combine into a perfect marriage of texture and taste. Bella Napoli Italian Restaurant offers just such a dining opportunity with dishes carefully prepared by chef Giovanni Martusciello of Italy. Chef Martusciello provides patrons with entrées fit for a Medici family dinner. Favorites include Pasta Assaggio, bowtie pasta simmered with roasted peppers, eggplant and homemade mozzarella in a tomato cream sauce. Bella Napoli Italian Restaurant is one of 15 establishments owned and operated by Lucia Longo, husband Mario and their three children. The family emigrated from Naples. Lucia came to New York with her parents at age three, never suspecting that her destiny was to meet an Italian pizza man from Brooklyn, move to North Carolina and go into the restaurant business. Lucia gives Chef Martusciello and her team equal credit for making her restaurant such a success. She shares her love of food and entertaining with everyone who comes to Bella Napoli. The restaurant is smoke free and features a large outdoor patio area. The tiny sparkling lights and gentle, warm ambience is so authentic you will think you've traveled to Italy. Experience for yourself the feel and flavor of Italy with a visit to Bella Napoli Italian Restaurant.

210 W. Chatham Street, Cary NC   (919) 462-8001   www.bellanapoliitalianrestaurant.com

Carver's Creek Steakhouse

Let your hunger guide you to the best prime rib in the Triangle. Carver's Creek Steakhouse is waiting to welcome you to a feast fit for kings. The restaurant has been a Raleigh area favorite for the past 22 years, and with fantastic meals like theirs you will soon see why. The main dining room is open for both lunch and supper daily, offering a full menu sure to delight each member of the family. Enjoy perfectly prepared beer-battered shrimp, top sirloin or chicken primavera with linguini while delighting in the crackling fire. Handsome wood paneled walls gently reflect the glow of the flames, adding a distinctive warmth to the cozy atmosphere. A limited menu is available in the Carver's Creek Steakhouse Lounge, which offers a full bar and cigar friendly areas. Hungry-Hour appetizers are available in the lounge all day and include hearty and delicious selections, such as crab stuffed mushrooms and hot and spicy shrimp. Patrons can choose from a selection of domestic, imported and draught beers, as well as a full array of wines and champagnes. For those who reside in the Raleigh area, or for those who will be staying awhile, give Carver's Creek a call for help with your next backyard barbecue. Large groups, or those planning a gathering, can have their event catered by the Steakhouse; it offers a full menu to make your special dinner truly memorable. On your next visit to Raleigh make sure to visit Carver's Creek Steakhouse. Its comfortable atmosphere and friendly staff will have you coming back for more.

2711 Capital Boulevard, Raleigh NC
(919) 872-2300   www.carverscreek.com

Vic's Cafe

Located in the heart of Raleigh's art district amidst charming Old World cobblestone streets, Vic's Café serves some of the best and most authentic Italian fare in the area. Look for such traditional classics as *vitello alla maradone*, a dish made of medallions of veal sautéed with peppers, artichokes, and mushrooms in a white wine sauce, or *filletti ai funghi*, broiled filet mignon served in Barolo wine sauce with roasted potatoes and grilled mushrooms. Are your taste buds intrigued? If you're in the mood for something simple yet classic, try one of Vic's extraordinary pizzas. The White Pie pizza, pizza minus the sauce, echoes the simplicity and mastery found in the traditional Italian interpretation of pizza, with a few quality toppings that highlight the flavors of the individual ingredients while building on the complexities of their combination. Consider chopped garlic on an olive oil base, layered with fresh mozzarella and parmesan cheese, fresh tomatoes and onion. If your taste is more domestic, Vic's offers a wide variety of classically American toppings. As if all of this wasn't enough, Vic's has a personal wine shopper who makes regular trips to Italy to handpick his wine selection. Bring your friends and join Vic on the last Thursday of every month for his exclusive Italian wine dinner, a chance to indulge your culinary fantasies. Come sip fine Italian wines under the North Carolina stars in the beautiful outdoor seating area at Vic's Café.

331 Blake Street, Raleigh NC
(919) 829-7090

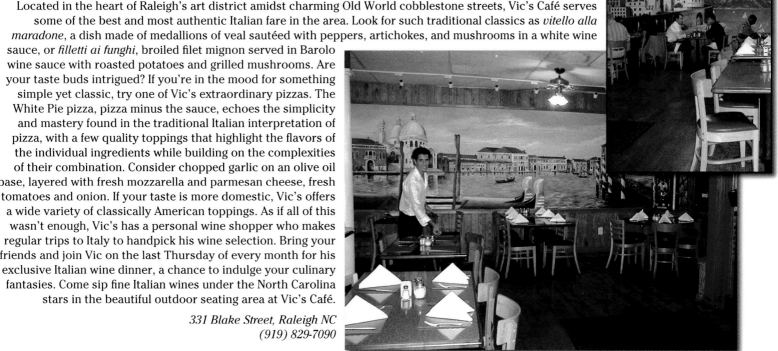

Zely and Ritz

Sarig and Nancy Agasi and Richard Holcomb are the owners of Zely and Ritz, Raleigh's favorite tapas restaurant and wine bar. They share a belief that the best food comes from local farmers who produce quality organic produce and meats. Richard's own recently acquired farm, Coon Rock, is their most important supplier. In addition to organic meats and vegetables, Coon Rock supplies Zely and Ritz with eggs and honey, and composts food refuse from the restaurant, completing the circle. Sarig is the master chef as well as a co-owner who specializes in combining fresh ingredients with Mediterranean and Middle Eastern spices in the most delicious way. Like Richard, Sarig comes from a farming background, having grown up in a kibbutz in Israel along the Mediterranean Sea. Nancy met Sarig during her second stay at a kibbutz and has a vast knowledge of wines which she puts to good use, selecting the perfect complements for Sarig's tapas. Together Sarig, Nancy and Richard have created one of the most highly acclaimed restaurants in Raleigh.

301 Glenwood Avenue, Suite 100, Raleigh NC   (919) 828-0018   www.zelyandritz.com

Manchester's Bar & Grill

In the Pinecrest Shopping Center of Raleigh, Manchester's Bar and Grill has been serving pizza and other classic American and Italian cuisine for over a decade. Manchester's draws a good crowd in the casual dining room and bar and has a separate room for private parties. The staff is friendly and it's the kind of place where everyone knows everyone else. As the local neighborhood bar, it's open and comfortable, not too dark or smoky, and a great meeting place. The grill specializes in Chicago-style pizza and a plethora of delicious toppings. Everything is made in-house.

Manchester's serves a variety of other foods, such as ribs, shrimp, burgers and steaks, but it is the spirit of the place that keeps customers coming back. The restaurant was named for Chuck Manchester, one of three partners who started the business. Current owners David and Cindy Steadman have kept the quality, service and affordable pricing intact. Their mission is to provide top-quality food in a comfortable atmosphere by an enthusiastic team of employees. Manchester's received the 1998 Spectator Award for the Best Neighborhood Bar and Grill. They also provide expert services for private parties and can cater corporate events. The Steadmans invite you to step in, pull up a chair, try the pizza and bask in the glow of camaraderie.

9101 Leesville Road, Suite 153, Raleigh NC   (919) 676-3310
www.mancestersgrill.com

Gianni & Gaitano's

Gianni & Gaitano's joins the resources of the Cinelli brothers to bring an extraordinary dining experience to Raleigh. The incredible selection of freshly prepared Italian cuisine is complemented by an award-winning wine list. You won't be able to resist telling your friends about the hand-painted décor, the gracious service, and the sumptuous food at both restaurants. Yes, it's two restaurants in one. At Gaitano's you will enjoy a family-style meal featuring chicken, fresh seafood and true Italian favorites like lasagna and manicotti. For an entirely different experience in the setting of a Tuscan Bistro, try Gianni's. Chef Cory Goodman will have you savoring every bite. Gianni's features osso bucco, filet mignon, rack of lamb and Chilean sea bass. Check the website for photos of their extraordinary catering service and special events. Children would not be left out of an Italian family restaurant, so there is a special kid's menu. Of their restaurants, the brothers say, "the rich family history of our restaurants stretches from Rome to New York to North Carolina under the Cinelli name and offers a true passion and dedication to quality that you can taste in every dish."

14460-171 New Falls of the Neuse Road, Raleigh NC
(919) 256-8100
www.gianniandgaitanos.com

MAMA DIP'S KITCHEN by Mildred Council. Copyright (c) 1999 by Mildred Council. Used by permission of the University of North Carolina Press. www.unpress.unc.edu

Mama Dip's

Southern home-style cooking, including fried chicken, mashed potatoes, chicken and dumplings, yams, and greens, is what Mama Dip's is famous for. It is a community favorite with loyal fans such as Michael Jordan. Owner Mildred Edna Cotton Council (Mama Dip) received her first cooking lessons from family members. In 1976, she opened her own restaurant with just $64. Mama Dip has been a guest on *Good Morning America* and featured in *Southern Living* and the *New York Times*. You may have also seen her appearance on the Food Network's *Cooking Live* with Sara Molton. She was the recipient of North Carolina's 2002 Small Business of the Year award. Dine in or take a dinner basket with you. The dinner basket comes complete with dessert and a checkered tablecloth. One taste of Mama Dip's cooking and you will crave it again and again. Take home your very own copy of *Mama Dip's Kitchen*, a book of 250 original recipes. You can also purchase a full line of Mama Dip's products at the restaurant's gift store. For one-of-a-kind Southern hospitality, come to Mama Dip's.

408 W Rosemary Street, Chapel Hill NC   (919) 942-5837   www.mamadips.com

Shaba Shabu

Charles Metee is a sushi chef. Charles wanted a Japanese restaurant, but his wife, Arada, whom he met in Bangkok, yearned for a Thai menu. The award-winning result was Shaba Shabu. Located in Raleigh, Shaba Shabu is really two restaurants in one, right down to the name. *Shaba* is the Thai word for hibiscus, a tropical flower, and *Shabu* is Japanese for swish, referring to a method of cooking tableside by preparing thinly sliced beef in a hot seaweed broth, adding spices and raw vegetables and swishing until the desired tenderness is achieved. The end result is dipped in a variety of sauces. Traditional Japanese cooking uses almost no spices, placing the emphasis on the pure flavors of the basic ingredients: fish, seaweed, vegetables, rice and soybeans. In contrast, the Thai meal uses many rich herbs and spices. Shaba Shabu is a harmonious blend of the spicy and subtle. The fare appeals to your eyes and nose as well as your taste buds. It is served in a warm, comforting atmosphere accented with authentic Thai details and furnishings. The popular lounge features Thai and Japanese appetizers, sakes, specialty drinks and extensive wines, along with traditional bar beverages and beers. The lounge features a 100-inch television screen and state-of-the-art sound system. The friendly staff invites you to sample a Thai or Japanese meal, where the artistic presentation is as fine as the food for a true culinary masterpiece.

3080 Wake Forest Road, Raleigh NC   (919) 501-7755   www.shabashabu.net

Rey's Restaurant

The famed French Quarter of New Orleans reached its peak in the 1830s, when it was the center of retail trade and banking. During that era of wealth and indulgence, the Quarter became the place to go for the best of everything. Certainly every epicurean in the city knew that to find the most flavorful,

delicious of dishes you went to the Quarter. Rey's Restaurant in Raleigh takes patrons back to the noble and elegant days of the Quarter with its magnificently prepared, quality dishes and excellent service. Owner Rey Arias founded his restaurant on the idea that if he never compromised on the quality of his food and provided a friendly, well trained staff in a comfortable, unstuffy atmosphere, then people would keep coming back…and they did. Rey's offers diners a classic menu brimming with dishes that will entice your palate. You can start with such appetizers as stuffed shrimp with garlic cream sauce or *pasta arribiata*. Entrées include *osso buco*, French Quarter chicken or pan seared black grouper. Rey's Restaurant also offers a nice selection of side dishes, desserts, wines and spirits. Rey's additionally features stunning artwork by painter Rhonda Meyers. Meyers, a longtime resident of New Orleans, used thousands of photographs of the famed city to create custom original works for the restaurant. The Voodoo Lounge features a portrait of famed Voodoo Queen Marie Laveau. You will find different, vividly done scenes from the city of New Orleans in each of the available meeting and dining rooms. Rey's is open for dinner only; you can make your reservation by telephone or online.

1130 Buck Jones Road, Raleigh NC   (919) 380-0122   www.reysrestaurant.com

The Lotus Leaf Café

The Lotus Leaf Café is an Asian restaurant specializing in Vietnamese cuisine with intriguing hints of French colonial flavors. Nestled in the Northwoods Market one mile from downtown Cary, this quaint bistro adds both culture and charm to a newly acclaimed city. Just one year after opening, *Citysearch* named the café best for Pan-Asian food, vegetarian food and outdoor dining.

Lotus Leaf promises a refreshing alternative to its guests, with such award-winning items as Vietnamese fresh summer rolls, asparagus and crabmeat soup, Saigon sizzling crêpe, grouper wrapped in banana leaf and grilled *aubergines* with shrimp and crabs. The truly delightful desserts include exotic lychee fruits in ginger-mango ice and ice cream with black rice liqueur. Specialty drinks flow in abundance with green tea bulbs featuring the dragon and Phoenix or individually brewed Weasel coffee with intriguing sit-top filters. Those who require even more authenticity may ask for an all-Saigon menu (no English) on the weekends. Diners can reserve tables on the wrought-iron patio. Come on weekends to enjoy live jazz and international music by some of the Triangle's favorite players. Wine sampling with Triangle wine expert Mike Crusenberry is a regular Friday event. Chef-owner Khai Do and wife Mai Mai place an emphasis on blending food and culture in their creative venture by having weekend chef's dishes, seasonal menus, art displays and periodic cultural events. Lotus Leaf Café is truly a happy find in Cary.

969 N Harrison Avenue, Cary NC   (919) 465-0750   www.LotusLeafCafe.com

Tir Na Nog Irish Pub

Food and Irish-style fun is what you can expect at Tir Na Nog Irish Pub & Restaurant. Partners Pete Pagano and Aiden Scally infused new energy into an Irish establishment that has been in Raleigh for a few years. The partners met while working in a restaurant in Belgium. They expanded the menu and added more microbrews. Bar manager Tom O'Brien is from Galway, and his bar features more than 50 kinds of whiskey. The new menu is a fusion of traditional Irish and European fare. Aiden, the chef, offers such specialties as beef and Guinness pie, and fish and chips, followed by desserts like deep-fried Bailey's ice cream. The entertainment at Tir Na Nog is decidedly Irish, with live music, a monthly ceili party, and Irish dance groups. With jazz, blues and rock, wonderful choices exist here for all music lovers. Check out the events calendar on the Tir Na Nog website for a full listing. The pub's setting is charming, with a big hardwood bar as the centerpiece. Come in to Tir Na Nog, named after a legendary enchanted land, and enjoy its bounties. Downtown's favorite Irish bar is better than ever.

218 S Blount Street, Raleigh NC (919) 833-7795
www.tirnanogirishpub.com

Four Square Restaurant

On Chapel Hill Road in Durham, you'll find the finest in casual elegance and dining at the Four Square Restaurant. This popular eatery epitomizes contemporary American cuisine, while offering excellent service in a delightful atmosphere. Listed on the National Historic Register, Four Square Restaurant makes its home inside the historic Bartlett Magnum house. The restaurant is the recipient of AAA's Four Diamond award and has been featured in top gourmet magazines, including *Bon Appetit* and *Southern Living*. Owner Elizabeth Woodhouse has created an elegant and tasteful dining getaway that offers patrons a fabulous menu, an extended and eclectic wine and beer list, along with a seasonal patio, cozy wine bar and private rooms for parties and functions. Four Square's talented executive chef Shane Ingram makes use of local delicacies to prepare savory and tasty dishes, such as roast wild sturgeon and duck confit, as well as an assortment of designer desserts that will make your mouth water, including an Irish whiskey cheesecake. Experience distinctive dining at its finest with the culinary delights that await you at Four Square Restaurant.

2701 Chapel Hill Road, Durham NC
(919) 401-9877

Babymoon Café

Located in the historic town of Morrisville, Joseph Leli's Babymoon Café offers an ever-evolving, innovative and consistently high-quality dining experience. Best known for its lunch offerings, the dinner menu has been embraced by Morrisville residents, as well. The café is a full-service Italian cuisine restaurant, serving pizzas and pastas, grilled seafood and chicken. Notable to the Babymoon menu are grilled portabella mushrooms and grilled chef salads. You can even order online at their website. The Café bakes their bread daily, and makes homemade mozzarella. They cater everything from brown bag lunches to black tie events. The catering menu includes salad boxes, sandwich platters, half-pans serving eight to 12 people and full-pans serving 12 to 20 people. Items such as the lobster ravioli sautéed in saffron cream sauce with crab and shrimp, or Chicken Papalina topped with proscuitto and fresh mozzarella in a mushroom wine sauce give a glimpse into the delights available in this culinary haven. A special Valentine's Day menu incorporates a delicious list of romantic choices to fulfill the two salad, one appetizer, two entrée and two dessert package. The impressive wine list includes numerous Italian wines, plus offerings from France, Washington and Australia. You will also find a Babymoon Café in Wake Forest.

100 Jerusalem Drive, Morrisville NC
(919) 465-9006

Brooklyn Sal's Famous Pizzeria

Brooklyn Sal's in Cary is owned by Salvatore and Vincenzo Doria, two brothers who came from Italy in 1965. They first lived in Brooklyn, where they ran Italian restaurants and pizzerias before moving to the Triad area of North Carolina. Vinny Doria is a partner with Dean Vincenzo in the ownership of Assaggio's in North Raleigh, and Sal and Vinny own Fratello's Trattoria & Market. Brooklyn Sal's Famous Pizzeria is located in the Brier Creek Shopping Center. The food is available for take-out, or you can eat in the pizzeria-style restaurant with its open kitchen, booths and tables. The clientele is a mix of all ages. Brooklyn Sal's makes amazing, authentic New York-style pizza, fashioning the light, thin and crisp dough from scratch. The result is a pizza that is not greasy, with a magnificent blend of cheeses and a tasty spread of sauce. All of the food is fresh and handmade. Besides the signature pizzas, they create calzones, stromboli and sandwiches made to order. Pizza can be purchased by the slice, and beer and wine are in reserve to accompany the meal. For a taste of New York-Italian right in the heart of Cary, take a seat in Brooklyn Sal's, and let the taste transport you.

107 Edinburgh Drive, Suite 107, Cary NC
(919) 405-1301

Mayflower Seafood Restaurant

Entering the Mayflower in Raleigh is akin to stepping aboard a historic wooden ship that's on a voyage to new savory discoveries. Mayflower Seafood Restaurant serves perfectly prepared provisions caught from the depths of the deep blue sea and awaiting the call of your appetite. Few can resist the oceanic flavors and nautical setting. Mayflower serves up a delectable variety of fish, lobster and other tasty denizens of the deep. Offering everything the most discerning seafood lover could desire, the restaurant expands its manifest to include something for everyone. If any member of the party harbors an inability to enjoy seafood, they will be particularly pleased to discover a multitude of tasty land-lubber alternatives. Survey breathtaking murals depicting vivid scenes inside the roomy restaurant space. Bask in the maritime ambience while anticipating a delectable dining experience. The Mayflower Seafood Restaurant will easily become your preferred place to drop anchor.

3301 Capital Boulevard, Raleigh NC
(919) 875-9007
www.mayflowerseafoodrestaurant.com

Top of the Hill

Conceived in 1994 to prevent a TGI Friday's restaurant from dominating downtown Chapel Hill, the mission of Top of the Hill Restaurant and Brewery is to embody and enlarge Chapel Hill's culture and heritage. Top of the Hill strives to be the community's favorite restaurant, brewery and bar, and also its most beloved and revered social establishment. Routinely featured in local media, as well as on ESPN and in *The Wall Street Journal*, Top of the Hill has won more than 25 Best in the Triangle awards, including Best Restaurant in Chapel Hill, Best Microbrew, Best Neighborhood Bar, Best Outdoor Dining and Best Place to See and Be Seen. Top of the Hill is located above the main intersection in town, making it literally the social crossroads of Chapel Hill, with a menu designed to appeal to every aspect of the community. Adjacent to the University of North Carolina, Top of the Hill's customer base is as varied and interesting as the University and the town itself. Faculty, students, parents, alumni, visitors, athletes and performers all find their way up to Top of the Hill for lunch, dinner or late-night fare. In 2005, Top of the Hill was the first microbrewery in the South to put its beer in a can. Ram's Head IPA and Leaderboard Trophy Lager can now be found at specialty food stores and golf courses throughout North and South Carolina. Stop in at Top of the Hill and discover the Southern part of heaven.

100 E Franklin Street, 3rd Floor, Chapel Hill NC   (919) 929-8676   www.TopoftheHillRestaurant.com

Nina's Ristorante

"I cook for my soul," says Nina Psarros, chef and co-owner of Nina's Ristorante. Nina's offers a winning combination of Tuscan and Sicilian cuisine. The dining room includes a romantic mural of the Italian countryside, floor-to-ceiling wine racks and textured walls that are a deep shade of pumpkin. The *News and Observer* calls the space "expansive and elegant, a tastefully restrained feast for the eyes." Take your time and enjoy the superb Italian wines at the wrap-around mahogany bar. To explore the ristorante's menu is to explore the food of Nina's childhood. Venture into an Italian experience with spicy *rigatoni amatriciana, cannelloni fiorentina, pollo imbottito*, homemade Italian sausage or a refreshing seafood selection. The passion that Nina feels for her food and cooking carries her time after time back to her native Italy to teach cooking classes at Proto, the culinary arts school in Luca. The beneficiaries of all that passion and dedicated learning are the dinner guests at Nina's. The staff strives to fulfill even the unexpressed wishes and needs of its guests, who are encouraged to make particular culinary requests. Nina's staff pledges the finest in personal service, food and drinks. Chris and Nina Psarros have given a great deal of thought to creating a memorable dining experience just for you.

8801 Leadmine Road, Raleigh NC   (919) 845-1122
www.ninasristorante.com

Est Est Est Trattoria

For more than 20 years, customers have loved the food and the ambience at Est Est Est Trattoria, a Northern Italian restaurant with a wonderful twist. In this casual, romantic setting you can choose from 15 kinds of pasta and 15 great sauces to create meals that are a delight. The pastas range from favorites like linguine and spinach fettuccine to more unusual treats like pumpkin fettuccine or sun-dried tomato. The sauces include everything from red and white clam sauces to vodka and putanesca. But as much fun as it is to create your own pasta combinations, you will be greatly tempted by the other dishes on the menu. Spinach ricotta penne and *pollo al limone* are just a couple of the excellent choices offered. The dishes are prepared by award-winning chef Nick Rossicci, and all the pastas, breads, fresh mozzarella and desserts are made in house. Full catering is available. The fresh menu and ambience guarantee a memorable dining experience.

19 W Hargett Street, Raleigh, NC
(919) 890-4500
www.estest.com

Pop's

In the tobacco warehouse district of Durham, in what is now known as Peabody Place, you'll find a wonderful Italian trattoria with the simple name of Pop's. The warehouse décor is sprinkled with a little artwork for good measure; you can expect to see brick walls, large pipes and large light fixtures hanging from the ceiling. Don't think that this industrial environment makes for an unpleasant ambience. It's just more room to enjoy the pasta and pizza being turned out by chef/owners Chris Stinnett and John Vandergrift, along with general manager/owner Matthew Beason and their staff. Start off with a Caesar salad or big bowl of mussels with toasted garlic, red chili flakes and roasted tomatoes. Order a pizza topped with shiitake mushrooms, sautéed spinach, or ricotta spread with white truffle oil. Fusilli, pork scaloppini and ravioli are all redone in delicious new ways, as well as salmon, striped bass and New York strip steak. No Italian meal would be complete without a little wine, so be sure to check out the impressive wine list. For a family meal with lots of appeal, make it a night at Pop's.

810 W Peabody Street, Durham NC
(919) 956-7677
www.pops-durham.com

Restaurant Starlu

There's plenty to enjoy at Restaurant Starlu, located by the fountain in southwest Durham. The elegantly hip décor of cherry, granite and stainless steel, with an open kitchen, copper bar and heated patio, is perfect for the eclectic mix of culinary creations on the menu. An upscale burger gets equal billing with chicken roasted to order, and the grouper that comes daily. Although funny names on the menu such as the Spanglish Special and a dessert called Coffee and Cigarettes make it seem as though Sam doesn't take life seriously, the opposite is true. The menu changes continually with an eye toward using the freshest local ingredients, organic when possible. The restaurant also helps others with a program Sam started called Bottles of Change. Each month the restaurant raises money for a different non-religious or non-political organization. To ensure that the restaurant always has the chance to treat customers as well as Sam thinks they deserve, dinner is served every night starting at five, along with lunch on weekdays and Sunday brunch. Your first visit will show you why they were rated as the best new restaurant in Durham for 2005, because the restaurant's motto is, "It's about the good stuff."

3211 Shannon Road, Suite 106,
Durham NC
(919) 489-1500
www.starlu.com

Jimmy V's Steakhouse

For a casual fine dining atmosphere, Jimmy V's Steakhouse is the place to go. Jimmy V's offers certified Angus beef cooked to juicy perfection, along with seafood, homemade desserts and an extensive wine list. Named for the former North Carolina State men's basketball coach, Jim Valvano, the restaurant keeps his legacy alive by linging the walls with the faces of those whose lives he touched. Jimmy V's is located in the back of MacGregor Village, which was a favorite local hangout for Valvano. If you are looking for a place to host a party, the boardroom can accommodate up to 90 guests for a sit-down dinner or 125 for a cocktail party. The boardroom features a full mahogany bar with three-quarter panel mahogany walls, providing the right atmosphere for any party or corporate function. The staff is eager to serve and willing to work with you to make your special occasion a success. Step inside this New York-style steakhouse for an evening of great food and friendly service. You're bound to have a memorable experience at Jimmy V's Steakhouse.

107-103 Edinburgh S Drive, Cary NC   (919) 380-8210   www.jimmyvssteakhouse.com

PHOTOGRAPHY BY ALAN GRADY

Mura

North Carolina has no shortage of fine restaurants. When you're looking for something with a bit of diversity, consider dining at Mura, located in Raleigh's North Hills district. The elegant and highly cosmopolitan atmosphere will be the first thing to catch your attention, but it is the international cuisine and excellent service that will leave you captivated. Diners are encouraged to come in early and relax at the bar before their meal to enjoy the sophisticated and glamorous décor. The dinner menu at Mura offers something for everyone, even those with the most discerning palates. You can choose from specialties such as aged filet mignon, boneless short ribs or grilled salmon. If those tempting dishes don't hit the spot, try Mura's fabulous bentos or the succulent Kobe Beef. If you prefer Asian cuisine, Mura features fantastic sushi, *Toro* (fatty tuna), *tora-yaki, and* a sashimi lunch that will

have you coming back again and again. Other Mura favorites include yellow tail and shrimp dishes, along with spectacular salads, such as avocado or octopus. Send your senses on a whirlwind adventure in fine dining with a visit to the delicious and popular Mura.

4421 Main, Raleigh NC
(919) 781-7887

The Angus Barn

The Angus Barn, a North Carolina landmark since 1960, is nationally known for exemplary service, certified Angus steaks aged in-house, homemade desserts and most of all, smiles. Thad and Alice Eure first opened the original Angus Barn with a dream and no prior restaurant experience. Their commitment to caring for their customers and listening to their employees made Angus Barn one of the most successful restaurants in the country. In 1964, the original restaurant burned to the ground. When it re-opened in 1965, the new restaurant was bigger and better, boasting a seating capacity of 550 and a gift shop. Due to the untimely death of both Thad and Alice, their daughter, Van, now operates the business and continues the family's legacy. "Our goal at The Angus Barn is to make each and every customer feel like the most important person in the world while dining here," says Van. "Although the food is top quality and homemade, what we do goes far beyond serving food and wine… we are mainly serving memories–memories of an evening or an event when you and your guests or family are treated as guests should truly be treated." Patrons receive complimentary cheese, homemade crackers and a huge array of relishes when they arrive, and an apple for good luck when they leave. The Chef's Table in the Kitchen is a unique dining experience where guests are served by chef Walter Royal, who was featured on *Iron Chef America* and who creates an unforgettable fare. For a unique and exquisite dining experience, guests may dine in The Wine Cellar, a private dining room which opened in 1991 where gourmet meals are served with white glove service. Whether you decide to dine in the elegant Wine Cellar or in the rustic casual restaurant, The Angus Barn is *the* destination when visiting North Carolina.

9401 Glenwood Avenue, Raleigh NC
(919)787-3505
www.angusbarn.com

Bella Monica

Bella Monica in Raleigh is a neighborhood Italian restaurant run by Julie and Corbett Monica. This true Neapolitan-style trattoria features recipes handed down from the Monicas' grandparents. Their authentic thin-crust pizzas, called FlatBreads, come in 16 flavors, from Amore and Bella to Vongole, with clams, garlic, pancetta and fresh mozzarella. Fresh, handmade foods are what Bella Monica is about. They use only imported San Marzano tomatoes for Nana's Gravy, their signature tomato sauce. Focaccia bread with herbs is made each morning, and the salads are crisp. Traditional recipes such as baked ziti and eggplant parmigiana share the menu with portobello and sun-dried tomato lasagne, garlic soup, and chicken with figs and chevre. Check out Bella Monica's website for a look at the full menu. From Antipasti and Favorites from Nana's Kitchen to the Menu dei Bambini, there is something for everyone. Save room for dessert, though, as the Monicas claim to have "the best cannoli you will ever taste." When you visit Bella Monica, you will be welcomed by a friendly and attentive staff. Holding true to Italian culture, the close kinship between the staff and clientele is apparent. Families, friends and businesspeople sit booth-to-booth in a chic color scheme with art-speckled walls. The wine bar features a reasonably priced, all-Italian wine list. On those balmy Carolina evenings, outdoor tables beckon. The Monicas invite you "to fill your stomachs and soothe your souls."

Olde Raleigh Village Shopping Center   3121 Edwards Mill Road, Raleigh NC
(919) 881-9778   www.BellaMonica.com

Nana's

Nana's is one of the premier restaurants in the Triangle. Nana's has recently been renovated to provide more seating and a kitchen that is state-of-the-art. Owner and chef Scott Howell has added Italian chandeliers and Dijon mustard colored walls, but the perfection of the food remains the same. Nana's is a combination of Mediterranean and American South cuisine. The famous risotto is still ideal with its creamy texture and subtle hint of sage. The menu continues to evolve with the market, so the risotto may be accented with sweet corn or lobster

mushrooms instead of English peas or smoked chicken. For the Southern side of your soul, the fried okra in cornmeal batter served with sweet German Johnson tomatoes and the salty tang of Celebrity Dairy goat cheese will have your taste buds jumping. Nana's wine list has won the coveted *Wine Spectator* Award of Excellence for seven years running. Pastry chef Kathy Edwards' repertoire of desserts includes crème brulee and grilled lemon pepper pound cake. The wait staff is well informed to help you choose the ideal wine selection for your food. Nana's is an exquisite place for relaxing and enjoying a great meal with inventive twists on tradition.

2514 University Drive, Durham NC   (919) 493-8545

Blue Martini

Blue Martini is the place to go for the best of Powerhouse Square, Raleigh's most popular spot for nightlife. It has everything for a memorable evening on the town—live music with blues and jazz until 2 am, a delicious variety of dishes, and a dazzling list of signature drinks, including a chocolate martini that blends Absolut Vanilla vodka, Godiva liqueur, Crème de Cacao and cream. Although the Upside Down Cake is actually a drink, you do have a great choice of desserts, among them a chocolate truffle cake with raspberry Frangelico sauce. Blue Martini offers a classy atmosphere for conducting business. With free high-speed Internet available, you could bring your laptop and get some work done while you enjoy grilled flatbread, a shrimp martini, or duck, scallion and shitake spring rolls with tamari sauce. With daily drink specials and a website for checking out the calendar of events and specials, Blue Martini will become your favorite nightspot and meeting place.

116 N West Street, #100, Raleigh NC
(919) 899-6464
www.bluemartiniraleigh.com

Amélia Café & Bakery

Brightleaf District in Downtown Durham is the cultural hub of this dynamic city. Brightleaf was the first commercial district in North Carolina to be put on the National Register of Historic Places. In the famous, revitalized duo of restored tobacco warehouses that became Brightleaf Square Shopping Center resides the Amélia Café & Bakery, and its neighbor, the award-winning Chamas Churrascaria Brazilian Steakhouse. The Amélia Café & Bakery serves Brazilian-Italian desserts, delicacies and cordials from around the world. Brazilian coffee, juices and Caseiro Gourmet cheese bread, (cheenies), are well represented. For any of your life events, a specialty cake can be made to order. The gourmet sandwiches and European pastries at the Amélia are everything an enthusiastic epicurean could hope for, because all of their signature treats are masterfully prepared and artfully presented. As for taste, the café website includes a passionate version of The Amelia Song translated into Portuguese and English, complete with chords. After one bite of an Amélia delicacy, you will feel like singing it out loud.

905 W Main Street, Suite 115, Durham NC
(919) 683-5600
www.ameliacafe.us

Chamas Churrascaria Brazilian Steakhouse

Welcome to the time-honored cuisine of southern Brazil. Chamas Churrascaria Brazilian Steakhouse brings to life the culture, traditions and flavor of Brazil in a convivial setting where loitering is not only accepted, but expected. Chamas is a Portuguese word that means flames, and churrascaria describes a meat-serving restaurant. *Rodizio* is the term used to describe the method of serving meats that has been a component of southern Brazilian fare since the early 1800s. Begin with a light salad, and then turn the card on your table to green to signal the start of your personal rodizio. You will be offered the juiciest, most tender beef, pork, lamb and chicken, carried in on skewers and carved tableside. There are more than enough meatless foods to satisfy the vegetarian or to complement the meat selections. The cheese boards display a variety of uncommon cheeses, and the meat sauces cover the range from chutney to pesto and back again. Staples include fried and sugared plantains and their beloved *pao de quejo*, a puffed cheese pastry. You are likely to be offered hearts of palm, marinated tomatoes, apple salad and other dizzying delights. During lunch and dinner, guests can enjoy either a buffet or the full rodizio. Bring your friends and family to Chamas Churrascaria, because this experience could last the whole evening.

Brightleaf Square, *905 W Main Street # 115, Durham NC (919) 682-1309   www.chamas.us*

Coastal Plain

Battleship North Carolina

Coastal Plain Accommodations

Fin 'N Feather Waterside Inn

If your idea of the perfect vacation consists of prime surfing, world-class fishing, fabulous dining and a wealth of recreational opportunities, head to Nags Head and the Fin 'N Feather Waterside Inn. This incredible Outer Banks motel is among the last of its kind. The Fin 'N Feather Waterside Inn offers guests comfortable and affordable rooms centrally located to all that the area has to offer. The Fin 'N Feather overlooks the Outer Banks and the picturesque Roanoke Sound. It offers several pet-friendly rooms, making this the ideal place for the whole family. Additionally, the Fin 'N Feather has a private boat launch and a 160-foot dock located just 25 feet from the motel. This complimentary feature allows you to avoid long lines at public docks, saves you time (as you only have to launch your rig once), and makes it as easy to get to your boat as it is to get to your car. The Fin 'N Feather Waterside Inn has been welcoming guests since 1963. Owner Dan Skelly is proud of the motel's long tradition of providing clean and family friendly accommodations to those coming to enjoy all that Nags Head and the Outer Banks have to offer. Experience Nags Head and return each night to peaceful comfort with a stay at the Fin 'N Feather Waterside Inn.

7740 S Virginia Dare Trail, Nags Head NC
(252) 441-5353 or (888) 441-5353
www.finnfeather.com

The Verandas

There is a Phoenix-like history behind the 1853 building that became The Verandas. A fire destroyed the structure in 1992, prompting a complete renovation, and out of the ashes arose a gloriously rebuilt sophisticated mansion. The charming inn that resulted owes its existence to owners Charles H. Pennington and Dennis Madsen. The Verandas is the site of many enchanting engagement parties, and the affordable luxury attracts many celebrities and discerning guests with an eye for quality. A four diamond award recipient and one of the top 10 travel destinations, the inn was voted Best in the South by *Traveler* magazine. In addition, their gourmet breakfasts are fit for royalty. The inn offers many gathering places, including four verandas, a garden terrace and a covered porch. The enclosed cupola at the top of the house can be reached by a spiral staircase, and it affords a breathtaking view that stretches out for miles. The Veranda's eight guest rooms each have private baths with rich marble floors and oversized bath tubs. A climate-controlled corner room is available, as well. Although the comfort of the inn makes guests want to stay there, the surroundings will pull you out. The inn is two blocks from Cape Fear River and the Riverwalk. It is walking distance to shops and fine restaurants, and a 15-minute drive from Wrightsville Beach. You are invited to return over and over to make The Verandas your vacation home.

202 Nun Street, Wilmington NC (910) 251-2212 www.verandas.com

Photos: Bill White/Whitelight Studios

Graystone Inn

Originally known as The Bridgers Mansion, Graystone Inn offers turn-of-the-century elegance and has been named one of America's Top 10 Most Romantic Inns by American Historic Inns, Inc. Elizabeth "Miss Betty" Haywood Bridgers, widow of Preston L. Bridgers, commissioned the magnificent home, which was built from 1905 to 1906. Architect Charles MacMillian designed the home, and general contractor Joseph Schad came from Germany to oversee the building. Preston was a local merchant as well as the son of two-time representative to the Confederate Congress Robert Rufus Bridgers. Robert was additionally the past president of the Atlantic Coast Line Railway and founder of the Wilmington-Weldon Railroad. After the death of Miss Betty in 1932, the home continued to serve as a private residence, and then went on to become

a boarding house and, later still, an American Legion Post. In 1998, the house was saved from complete dilapidation and underwent a nearly $1 million renovation. Today, the inn features nine stunning rooms with private baths, many of which have claw foot tubs. Rooms come with telephone, data port and cable television. Several of the rooms have cozy fireplaces. For your convenience, the inn offers an on-site fitness center and is within easy walking distance to numerous shops, restaurants and attractions. Graystone Inn has received a Four Diamond rating from AAA and is known as Wilmington's most luxurious inn. Graystone Inn has also been used in the filming of several movies, such as *Rambling Rose*, and in the television series *Matlock*. Pamper yourself and your special someone with a wonderful getaway at the gracious Graystone Inn.

100 S Third Street, Wilmington NC
(910) 763-2000 or (888) 763-4773
www.graystoneinn.com

C.W. Worth House

Step through the front door of C.W. Worth House and enter an oasis where time slows down and your only responsibility is to relax and enjoy yourself. This stunning Queen Anne home is detailed with whimsical shingles and stunning period furniture and décor. The seven guest rooms come with private baths and range from intimate to spacious, each with its own style and personality. Guests of the C.W. Worth House are treated each morning to a scrumptious breakfast, which includes private blend coffee, fresh fruit, juice, muffins and daily entrées, such as savory rosemary and goat cheese, bread pudding, artichoke mushroom quiche and banana-oat pancakes. After breakfast, you can lounge on the downstairs patio or upstairs veranda or go for a stroll through the lovely grounds. The tranquility of the gardens at C.W. Worth House allow the sound of the fishponds' waterfall to sooth your senses and help open you up to the splendor of the Southern flowers and fragrances that surround you. The C. W. Worth House was the first bed-and-breakfast to be established in Wilmington, founded in 1985 by present owners and innkeepers Margie and Doug Erickson and their resident cat Smokie. Charles W. Worth, a wholesale grocery merchant, originally commissioned the home in 1889. It was completed in 1893 and served as the Worth family home until 1930. The bed-and-breakfast is situated near the historical downtown area. It offers several packages ideal for family getaways and romantic rendezvous, so make your next vacation destination Wilmington and the C.W. Worth House.

412 S Third Street, Wilmington NC
(910) 762-8562 or (800) 340-8559
www.worthhouse.com

Coastal Plain Attractions

Battleship North Carolina

The Battleship North Carolina sits directly across from downtown Wilmington, serving as a reminder of the sacrifices made by seamen long ago. The ship earned its fame during World War II. Part of the line of British admiralty commissioned ships called Dreadnought first made in 1906, the battleship had an increased number of larger guns in her main battery, larger designed displacement, better armor and increased speed. After it was saved from the scrap heap in 1960, the ship was reborn as a memorial and museum. The Battleship North Carolina serves as the state of North Carolina's World War II memorial, as well as a museum of naval history that includes a gift shop. Inside the ship, you will find thousands of interesting items on display, ranging from World War II artifacts to items donated by former soldiers. Self-guided tours are clearly marked and may take up to a couple hours to complete. Most of the ship is wheelchair accessible, and fun activities are available for the young or young-at-heart members of your tour group. You can even have a picnic in Battleship Park overlooking the Cape Fear River and downtown Wilmington. School and scout groups are always welcome; feel free to contact the staff ahead of time for special arrangements. For a trip through naval history on an actual battleship and fun for the whole family, visit Battleship North Carolina.

Eagles Island, Wilmington NC
(910) 251-5797
www.battleshipnc.com

Coastal Plain Gifts

Bacchus Wine & Cheese

If you're looking for an exceptional wine and cheese venue on The Banks, head to Bacchus Wine & Cheese, where you can select from 750 different wines from across the globe, including fine wines from California and the Pacific Northwest, as well as vintages from France, Italy, Spain and Australia If you're searching for a bottle of something less traditional, you may prefer a wine from New Zealand, Chile, Argentina or South Africa. Each week Bacchus presents a wine tasting that features six different wines served alongside both hot and cold appetizers and accompanied by sumptuous desserts. Bacchus has over 35 imported and domestic cheeses, such as goat gouda and Manchego, which are served with a variety of noshes, including salsa, olives, pate and a selection of savory crackers. Additionally, Bacchus Wine & Cheese offers succulent entrées, including perfectly prepared filet mignon and rib eye steaks, pasta dishes and delicious artisan breads. If you've grown tired of giving the same old gift for special occasions, consider a gourmet gift basket from Bacchus instead. Each lovely basket is filled to the brim with delicious treats sure to please everyone on your gift-giving list. Bacchus can provide catering for your special events by providing appetizer platters, gourmet sandwich trays and all the desserts and fine wines to make your occasion successful. Eat, drink and be merry at the hottest wine bar on The Banks with a visit to Bacchus Wine & Cheese.

891 Albacore Street, Monteray Plaza, Corolla NC
(252) 453-4333
www.bacchuswineandcheese.com

The Cotton Exchange

Extraordinary treasures, old-fashioned customer service, and a glimpse into the history of Wilmington are all found at The Cotton Exchange. This collection of distinctive shops and restaurants elicits the feeling of the 19th century, when Wilmington was a prosperous river port. The most abundant export crop in the port was cotton, thus The Cotton Exchange's name. Original occupants of these buildings include the Cape Fear Flour and Pearl Hominy Mill, Sears Roebuck and Company, the LeGwyn Printing Company and a three-story mariner's saloon. The Cotton Exchange kept tradition alive when, in 1975, it was the first complex in North Carolina to utilize existing downtown structures, thus becoming a pioneer in local preservation efforts. Eight restored buildings comprise The Cotton Exchange, all connected by brick walkways and open-air courtyards. It's possible to spend the entire day browsing shops and admiring the beauty of the traditional architecture. The Cotton Exchange is the perfect place to find unique gifts for everyone. Local artists display seascapes and blown glass. Homemade candy and magic tricks abound. You will find trains, books, oils, jewels, and even grandfather clocks. With more than 30 exclusive shops and eateries, you are sure to discover what makes The Cotton Exchange such a popular destination when visiting historic downtown Wilmington.

321 N Front Street, Wilmington NC
(910) 343-9896
www.shopcottonexchange.com

Coastal Plain Museums

Bellamy Mansion Museum

Built by free and enslaved African Americans in 1859 as the city residence of prominent planter, physician and businessman Dr. John D Bellamy, the Bellamy Mansion Museum is a mixture of Greek Revival and Italianate styles. The Bellamy family moved into their new home on the eve of the Civil War, only to be displaced by a raging yellow fever epidemic and, later, by the conflict itself. When the family returned in 1865, they found their house occupied by Union forces. Soon afterward, Dr Bellamy reclaimed the property, and it remained the family residence until 1946. Visitors to the Mansion will see all four floors and the belvedere of the 22-room house. Tours emphasize the architecture, construction and restoration of the house, as well as the fascinating history of its former occupants. Two gallery spaces feature changing exhibits on architectural history, historic preservation and the design arts. Extensive archaeological and African American history research is underway in preparation for the restoration of the original slave quarters. Recently completed restorations include the formal gardens and the carriage house. The carriage house is a newly reconstructed building that houses the museum's visitors center, gift shop and offices. Bellamy Mansion Museum is one of North Carolina's premier architectural and historic treasures. Visit the mansion for an informative look at historic preservation in action.

503 Market Street, Wilmington NC   (910) 251-3700   www.bellamymansion.org

Photo by David Scaglione

Coastal Plain Restaurants

Bacu Grill

On your next visit to Nags Head, take a walk off the beaten path and head to Bacu Grill, where you can experience dining that is anything but ordinary. This fabulous restaurant is popular with the locals and offers a wide range of tasty Cuban dishes that will have your taste buds cheering. *Bacu* is a Cuban-American term for a taste or sight that reminds a person of home. Here, you can find a wonderful selection of traditional entrées, such as mojo roast pork and Cuban paella. Bacu Grill features wonderful sampler plates that include delicious appetizers of pepper fried oysters and Eastern Shore crab dip. Additional menu favorites include Bacu's quesadilla, made with a choice of pork, chicken, shrimp or tuna. On Sundays, stop in and enjoy the grill's famous brunch, which won the Best Brunch on the Beach award, and features delectable dishes, such as chicken and dumplings, cheese grits and spiced apples. Other brunch delicacies include several versions of eggs Benedict, including one with shaved prime rib and a chipotle hollandaise. Bacu Grill also offers a wonderful Wine and Cigar Cellar, as well as a cigar-friendly martini bar. The restaurant has an extensive dessert list along with specialized menus for children and late night diners. Indulge yourself at Bacu Grill in Outer Banks Mall with a made-to-order meal filled with flavor and inspired by fresh coastal fare.

5000 S Croatan Highway, Outer Banks Mall, Nags Head NC (252) 480-1892

Paddy's Hollow

The Cotton Exchange in Wilmington is an old warehouse that dates from the late 1800s. In the 1970s, local entrepreneurs Joe and Mel renovated the warehouse into a bustling hub of commercial activity. Steve and Kim Hagan opened Paddy's Hollow Restaurant and Pub at this rejuvenated site in 1982. The convivial pub atmosphere of Paddy's Hollow is enhanced by the exceptional food, served all day. There are 16 frothy beers on tap to accompany the menu choices. Paddy's favorite hot dishes, grilled sandwiches and flat breads vie for attention on a menu loaded with so many mouthwatering plates of food it is a wonder anyone can ever pick just one. A very English fish 'n' chips can be found, as well as eight different burgers. The steak and portabella mushroom skillet combines the tantalizing flavors of two usually separate worlds of food. A patio provides seasonal outdoor dining. Paddy's Hollow is named for a two-block lane of waterfront saloons popular during the days when cotton was king. At that time, paddle wheel riverboats were a common sight in the busy river town of Wilmington. Thanks to Paddy's Hollow, the lively atmosphere has returned to the waterfront. Head on over and have some fun.

Cotton Exchange, 10 Walnut Street, Wilmington NC
(910) 762-4354

Whitey's Restaurant

For more than half a century, Whitey's Restaurant has been serving up home-style cooking for hungry patrons. Specializing in breakfast, lunch and a scrumptious weekend breakfast buffet, Whitey's is more than a family restaurant, it's like coming home. When Whitey Prevatte first hitchhiked to Wilmington from his childhood farm in Bladen County, he had just five dollars in his pocket and the drive to succeed. He joined the army and then worked as a railroad dining car attendant. A train accident motivated him to take a chance and start his own restaurant. Since 1954, Whitey's has been a Wilmington legend. Even Hollywood has discovered Whitey's. An episode of *Matlock* used Whitey's, as did the movie *Weeds*. Even former Wilmington resident and NBA superstar Michael Jordan had a summer job working for Whitey's motel next door. Whitey's Restaurant is halfway between the downtown area and Wrightsville Beach on Business Highway 17, locally known as Market Street. Phyllis, Cora, Liz, Linda and especially Whitey will make sure you leave with a full stomach and lots of fond memories. Your next visit to Wilmington must include a stop at Whitey's for good food, great atmosphere and a taste of history.

4501 Market Street, Wilmington NC
(910) 799-1214

Elijah's & The Pilot House

The first restaurant to open in the restored Chandler's Wharf in Wilmington was The Pilot House, founded in 1978 by Mr. and Mrs. Thomas Wright, Jr. The building used to sit on Wooster Street, where it was built as a private residence in 1870. The Pilot House and its sister restaurant next door, Elijah's, overlook the Cape Fear River, a fact that inspired the

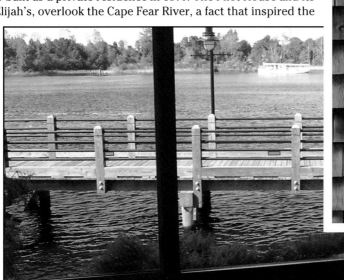

Pilot House tagline: where the only thing we overlook is the river. The Pilot House has seen several improvements over the years, including an expanded menu and kitchen facilities, plus a riverfront deck. Its varied menu includes such specialties as rack of lamb, grilled duck breast and filet mignon. You'll also find plentiful seafood entrées, featuring tuna, shrimp and catfish. The restaurant is well prepared to handle special events, with several dining areas, and has catered such high-profile events as *Dawson Creek's* final wrap-up party and Dick Cheney's dinner. Elijah's features a casual American grill and an oyster bar, where fresh oysters come with a variety of specialty sauces. Choose from an extensive fresh seafood menu and great salad entrées. These sister restaurants not only make fine dining destinations, they give the visitor an opportunity to capture a sense of the 19th and early 20th centuries when the Wilmington port did a bustling business in tar, pitch and turpentine, products made from long leaf pine once abundant in the area. The Pilot House and Elijah's invite you to enjoy fine dining in an historic setting.

2 Ann Street, Wilmington NC
The Pilot House: *(910) 343-0200*
www.pilothouserest.com
Elijah's: *(910) 343-1448*
www.elijahs.com

Penguin Isle Soundside Grill & Bar

Located on the Roanoke Sound, Penguin Isle Soundside Grill & Bar is one of the Outer Bank's premier dining destinations. Owner Mike Kelly and General Manager Tom Sloate have created an absolutely beautiful location to spend an evening with fine wine, delectable dinner selections and impeccable service. Their motto holds true, "Life, including Fine Dining, is not meant to be taken too seriously." Guests can enjoy a cocktail while lounging on one of the many decks as the sun sets over the water. Indoors, the large picture windows let the sun's afterglow paint the dining room

with a beautiful palette of colors that compliment the warm ambience. Begin your meal with a zesty appetizer, such as the corn-dusted tuna serrano chili bites. Then, continue on to a dinner menu that includes fresh Gulfstream fish, certified Angus beef, handmade pasta and duck. Penguin Isle specializes in very hot open-flame mesquite grilling, a process that seals in the natural juices and flavors. Accompany your meal with a selection from their assortment of more than 400 wines from around the world. The impressive list has garnered the *Wine Spectator* Award of Excellence for 18 years. Penguin Isle offers in-house catering facilities for weddings or special events from two to 250 guests. Dinner is served nightly from March to December, and seasonal wine dinners and tastings are offered in the spring and fall. With food as seductive as the setting, Penguin Isle Soundside Grill & Bar is a must visit while vacationing on the Outer Banks.

6708 S Croatan Highway, Nags Head NC
(252) 441-2637
www.penguinisle.com

1587 Restaurant

In 1587, English colonists braved the tumultuous Atlantic Ocean and found the solid ground of Roanoke Island a desirable place to settle. More than 400 years later, Donnie Just experienced the same sense of home and decided to drop anchor on his second restaurant in the Outer Banks, the aptly named 1587. Just and his first mate, executive chef Donny King, have created yet another unique eatery together inside the gorgeous Tranquil House Inn. As with any four-star restaurant, 1587 offers more than just a delectable menu. The interior aesthetics are accessorized by large bay windows with a view of the harbor. During the daylight, you can enjoy the ballet of sailboats and seabirds floating by. At night, the rising moon completes the twinkling show provided by hundreds of harbor lights. Though the menu varies a bit daily, the standards are anything but standard. For an appetizer, try an extraordinary selection like duck confit. Entrée highlights include specialties, such as rich chophouse steaks, a light mahi fillet and tender veal scaloppine. The restaurant serves salads à la carte and creates scrumptious soups daily. Vegetarian and children's menus are available upon request. Be sure to glance over the award-winning wine list for a choice complement to your meal. Next time you're in Manteo, coast on into 1587. It's an important number in Outer Banks' history and modern cuisine.

405 Queen Elizabeth Avenue, Manteo NC   (252) 473-1587   www.1587.com

Ocean Boulevard Bistro & Martini Bar

Back in 1949, residents of Kitty Hawk would drive to Beach Road in search of hammers, screws and jigsaws. These residents would be puzzled today as their beloved Virginia Dare Hardware store is no longer a home for aspiring Bob Vilas, but better suited for fans of Emeril Lagasse and Bobby Flay. In September of 1995, forks and knives replaced paintbrushes and shovels when the store was transformed into the upscale Ocean Boulevard Bistro & Martini Bar. Now the only screwdriver on the premises is a mixture of orange juice and vodka, although the house specialty is the signature Big O martini. Owner Donnie Just has retooled the décor with fire truck red bench seats and open-backed chairs that play nicely off the dark ceiling wood and brick walls. Ocean Boulevard's executive chef Donny King fixes up a nightly selection of gourmet cuisine influenced by international trends and the seasonal availability of freshly caught seafood. You can watch King and his staff create popular appetizers like rice flour-crusted oysters or desserts like white chocolate crème bruleé in the open kitchen. The end results are both visually stimulating and delicious. The wine list, which has won a *Wine Spectator* Award of Excellence, features more than 100 bottles from all over the world. Microbrew beer, coffee drinks and herbal teas are also available. Though the restaurant serves dinner seven nights a week, it's suggested you call during the off-season for hours and every night for reservations. Take your taste buds on a flight of fancy at Kitty Hawk's Ocean Boulevard Bistro & Martini Bar. Bring your appetite, but leave the tool belt at home.

Beach Road MP 2, Kitty Hawk NC
(252) 261-2546
www.ocean-boulevard.com

Index By Treasure

Index By City